CONSERVATIVE PARTY ATTITUDES
TO JEWS, 1900–1950

CASS SERIES: BRITISH POLITICS AND SOCIETY
ISSN: 1467-1441
Series Editor: Peter Catterall

Social change impacts not just upon voting behaviour and party identity but also the formulation of policy. But how do social changes and political developments interact? Which shapes which? Reflecting a belief that social and political structures cannot be understood either in isolation from each other or from the historical processes which form them, this series will examine the forces that have shaped British society. Cross-disciplinary approaches will be encouraged. In the process, the series will aim to make a contribution to existing fields, such as politics, sociology and media studies, as well as opening out new and hitherto neglected fields.

Peter Catterall (ed.), *The Making of Channel 4*

Brock Millman, *Managing Domestic Dissent in First World War Britain*

Peter Catterall, Wolfram Kaiser and Ulrike Walton-Jordan (eds), *Reforming the Constitution: Debates in Twentieth-Century Britain*

Brock Millman, *Pessimism and British War Policy, 1916–1918*

Adrian Smith and Dilwyn Porter (eds), *Amateurs and Professionals in Post-war British Sport*

Archie Hunter, *A Life of Sir John Eldon Gorst: Disraeli's Awkward Disciple*

Harry Defries, *Conservative Party Attitudes to Jews, 1900–1950*

CONSERVATIVE PARTY ATTITUDES TO JEWS

1900–1950

HARRY DEFRIES

FRANK CASS
LONDON • PORTLAND, OR

First published in 2001 in Great Britain by
FRANK CASS PUBLISHERS
Crown House, 47 Chase Side, Southgate
London N14 5BP

and in the United States of America by
FRANK CASS PUBLISHERS
c/o ISBS, 5824 N.E. Hassalo Street
Portland, Oregon, 97213-3644

Website: www.frankcass.com

British Library Cataloguing in Publication Data

Defries, Harry
  Conservative Party attitudes to Jews, 1900–1950. –
  (Cass series. British politics and society)
  1. Conservative Party – History 2 Jews – Great Britain –
  Public opinion 3. Public opinion – Great Britain 4. Great
  Britain – Politics and government – 20th century
  I. Title
  305.8'924'041'09041

      ISBN 13: 978-0-714-68206-8

Library of Congress Cataloging-in-Publication Data

Defries, Harry, 1951–2000
  Conservative Party attitudes to Jews, 1900–1950/Harry Defries.
    p. cm. – (Cass series – British politics and society, ISSN
  1467–1441)
    Includes bibliographical references and index.

    1. Jews – Public opinion. 2. Public opinion – Great Britain. 3.
  Conservative Party (Great Britain) 4. Great Britain – Politics and
  government – 20th century. 5. Jews – Great Britain – Public
  opinion. 6. Great Britain – Ethnic relations. I. Title. II. Series.
  DS102.95 .D45 2001
  323.1'1924041'09041–dc21

                                                        2001028856

Typeset in 11/12¹/₂ Palatino by FiSH Books, London WC1
Printed in Great Britain by MPG Books Ltd, Bodmin, Cornwall

Contents

Series Editor's Preface

In the first half of the twentieth century, a period in which, for most of the time, they were both electorally and politically dominant, the attitudes of British Conservatives towards Jews were tested in a number of ways. Particularly in constituencies with large amounts of Jewish settlement, there was the question of whether, and what, controls should be placed on the largely Jewish immigration from eastern Europe. Anxieties on this score were certainly not allayed after the Russian Revolutions of 1917, when many on the right were inclined to associate Bolshevism with the Jews. As Harry Defries shows here, both these domestic and external concerns played their parts in that other major event of 1917, the declaration by a Conservative Foreign Secretary, A. J. Balfour, in favour of a Jewish national home. The subsequent establishment of the Palestine Mandate was, however, to pose successive British governments with the fraught task of deciding how to interpret that declaration in practice. Not least was the vexed question of how to tackle the flight of Jews from Nazi Germany and whether, and to what extent, they should be allowed admission into both Britain and Palestine. Meanwhile, underlying all these issues was one that any party that, like the Conservatives, saw themselves as the party of the nation, and of social stability, might have been expected to address, that of assimilation.

These different issues, being posed in different ways at different points in time, militate against a simple typology. Conservative attitudes cannot be portrayed, at any point during this period, as monolithically anti- or philo-Semitic. Nor, indeed, do either these labels or others have much utility without some kind of context. Labels could be used as shields – *vide* the way in which those advocating immigration restrictions frequently protested that they were not anti-Semites. And they can mislead. Balfour, for instance, may have described himself during the post-1918 peace conferences as a 'Zionist', but this did not mean that he shared a common vision with Chaim Weizmann. Nor was it the same as being a philo-Semite.

Insofar as there are common threads in Conservative attitudes that can be discerned, one is the association of Jews with external threats: with Germany up to and including the First World War and with Russia thereafter. The other is the question of what role, if any, Jews might play within the British Empire. Defries shows the Edwardian linkages between Chamberlainite tariff reformers and anti-alienism. Some of Chamberlain's disciples were, however, during the First World War, to see a Jewish homeland as a way of bolstering the Empire in the Middle East, even if, by the late 1930s, in the light of the Arab Revolt, this was coming to be seen as increasingly unlikely.

The contradictions in Conservative attitudes towards Jews are reflected, for instance, in the views of Mark Sykes on these related themes; Jews were 'good' when constructively engaged in the building up of Palestine, but 'bad' when associated in some way with Bolshevism. Others could even portray Jews as 'good' when contributing to the building-up of the British economy, while at the same time worrying about the social and cultural threat they apparently posed. At bottom, the characterisation rested upon a construction of Jewishness which was widespread, if often only half-formed and even more frequently unstated, amongst Conservatives, as well as being manifested in very different ways across the party. For instance, Jews as modern, footloose capitalists might be useful, but could also be seen as outside, and predatory upon, a settled society coping with and scarred by industrial change. Accordingly, although 'Britishness' may be a cultural rather than racial construction, it could prove difficult fully to accommodate Conservative concepts of 'Jewishness' within it. Indeed, for some, the way they conceived of Jewishness was totally opposed to their conception of Britishness. However, as Defries points out, the importance of concepts like 'fair play' in the construction of Britishness nevertheless militated, for all but a handful of Conservatives, against overt anti-Semitism. Indeed, he argues that this conceptual framework helps instead to explain the apparent contradiction of the relatively accommodating attitude towards Jewish immigration from Germany adopted by the Conservative leadership in the 1930s, in contrast to the restrictionist agitation of the Edwardian years.

These are issues that have rarely been explored in histories of the Conservative Party. Similarly, the role of party in the elaboration of policy towards Palestine or immigration has been relatively neglected. Harry Defries has through this book made an important contribution to the understanding of all three subjects.

Regrettably, it is a contribution which will have to stand as, I hope, a suitable monument to Harry. This work was completed whilst he was struggling against the illness which eventually claimed him. Harry Defries died on 7 May 2000, leaving his widow, Penny Gostyn, to fine-tune the manuscript, a painful labour of love, for which I would like to pay her tribute. For myself, despite all the emails and correspondence that passed between us whilst Harry was working on this book, I am sorry that I only had the privilege of meeting him once, when we met and talked volubly for three hours about history and politics and religion in central London. It is a matter of bitter regret that I will not have the opportunity to converse with Harry in this way again. My only hope is that this book, which Harry worked on with such enthusiasm and dedication, will prove for him a worthy tribute.

Peter Catterall
Series Editor

Preface

The genesis of this book was a conversation which took place in the Loire Valley in 1991 when my wife, Penny Gostyn, suggested that I focused my interest in politics, modern British, and Jewish history by undertaking doctoral research. I am grateful to Professor Geoffrey Alderman, my original supervisor at Royal Holloway, University of London, who was prepared to supervise a part-time student who had not undertaken formal academic study, other than for professional qualifications, since graduating from the University of Sussex in the early 1970s. After Geoffrey Alderman left Royal Holloway to take up a position at the University of Middlesex I was most fortunate that Professor John Turner agreed to become my supervisor and I wish to record my thanks to him for his encouragement and advice. I am also grateful for the advice and encouragement of Professors John Ramsden and Colin Holmes, who were my PhD examiners. I am also appreciative of the advice and comments made by Dr Peter Catterall which have, hopefully, resulted in this work being more focused. Needless to say, I bear the sole responsibility for all the opinions and conclusions (and any errors) in this book.

I wish also to acknowledge the help I have received from all the archives and libraries in which I have worked while preparing this work. In particular I would like to thank the Institute of Historical Research at the University of London, the Jewish Studies Library at University College London, the University of London Library, the British Library and its Newspaper Library, the Bodleian Library, the Birmingham University Library, the Cambridge University Library, the Southampton University Library, the Churchill Archives at Churchill College Cambridge, the Greater London Record Office, the House of Lords Record Office, the Public Record Office at Kew, the Cheltenham Conservative Association, and the Central Zionist Archives in Jerusalem.

I would also wish to thank all those other members of staff at Royal Holloway who have had to deal with me both as a doctoral student and more recently as an honorary research associate. Finally, I wish to thank my wife, Penny, and my daughters, Rachel and Sarah, for tolerating my disposition to carry out historical research.

Harry Defries
Royal Holloway College, University of London
December 1999

Acknowledgements

I would like to take this opportunity to thank Professor John Turner for all his help in the final preparation of the manuscript for this book. Without his assistance, it would have been much more difficult for my husband to deal with the queries raised by Peter Catterall, the Series Editor. When Professor Turner heard that my husband was seriously ill, he asked if he might visit him. Little did he realise that he would spend that visit 'working' and that he would leave with 'homework' to be undertaken within a very unreasonable timeframe. I am deeply indebted to John Turner for his assistance at that difficult time. I also wish to recognise the contribution made by my step-daughters, Rachel and Sarah, who, although not history students, transformed themselves into history research students to assist in the final correction process.

Penny Gostyn

— 1 —

Introduction

The purpose of this study is to examine the attitudes towards Jews which were held by the Conservative Party, and the consequences which resulted from these attitudes, in the period 1900–48. By this means it is proposed to shed light on the way in which the Conservative Party viewed itself and British society in the first half of the twentieth century. The changes in the Party will be examined in the light of its outlook and actions throughout the period towards the Jewish community in Britain, Europe and Palestine. It is an examination of the perception, rather than the reality, of the Jewish community.

The study examines the important policy issues, primarily immigration into Britain and the Palestine Mandate, where the Conservatives interfaced with Jewry; it is not an attempt to explore those issues which may have been considered important to the Jewish community in general or the Anglo-Jewish community in particular, nor is it an examination of the relationship of the Conservative Party to the Anglo-Jewish elite. An examination of those issues would fall to those undertaking a study of Anglo-Jewry rather than the Conservative Party. Nor is this work an exploration of the Jews and the Conservative Party; that subject has been considered by Geoffrey Alderman, primarily in *The Jewish Community in British Politics*[1] and *London Jewry and London Politics 1889–1986*.[2] Similarly, this is not a study of the relationships of individual Jews with the Conservative Party, although it does consider the development of a number of episodes involving Jewish Conservative politicians, such as the opposition to Samuel Samuel in Putney and the role of Leslie Hore-Belisha as a member of Chamberlain's cabinet.[3] Thus a precise definition of 'who is a Jew' is not relevant for the purposes of this study.[4] It is considered that a definition of Jews as being persons of Hebrew descent or whose religion is Judaism was sufficient to identify them as a group to those involved in the period under review.

This is also not a study of party institutions,[5] but an examination of politicians, primarily Conservative parliamentarians. This study has deliberately focused on the parliamentary party. It will be suggested that the policies of the Party were largely decided by the parliamentary leadership. The backbench MPs would seek to influence those policymakers as would the Party officials and the voluntary Party; the effect of this influence diminishes the further one was removed from the seats of power. However, there are instances where contributions by local parties have made more than a local impact, such as the anti-Semitic references which appeared in the journal of the Ilford Conservative Association during 1926, which attracted the attention of the Board of Deputies of British Jews,[6] and the motion at the conference of the Junior Imperial League in 1931 to adhere to the Balfour Declaration.[7] The role of the Conservative national press, however, owing to its perceived influence and also to the interventions in political life during the period by their proprietors, will be reviewed, but this is not primarily an examination of the way in which the Conservative press established its policies or the role of its proprietors.

There is no distinction made between the Liberal Unionists and the Conservatives in that part of the study prior to their formal amalgamation in 1912 as it is suggested that there were no significant differences between those groups which affect this book.[8] This study also utilizes the popularly held name of the Party from time to time.

This work suggests that generally the factions which arose in the Party during the period under review did not have any direct or indirect influence on the attitudes towards the Jews. The exception is the Tariff Reform campaign[9] which had a significant impact and was perhaps a movement which had a fundamental impact upon the Party itself.[10] In addition, the divisions over India and the opposition to appeasement are both discussed in the context of Conservative policies towards Palestine.[11] The divergence in the Party between philo-Semites and anti-Semites did not result in the type of cleavage that was witnessed in other divisions in the Party, such as those outlined above. As will be examined throughout this study, there is evidence of anti-Semitism amongst those Conservatives who, objectively, may be regarded as pro-Jewish.

An anti-Semite is defined in the *Concise Oxford Dictionary* as a person 'hostile to or prejudiced against Jews'. The term 'anti-Semitism' was coined in 1879, from the Greek, by the German agitator Wilhelm Marr to designate the then current anti-Jewish campaigns in Europe.[12] It soon came into general use as a term denoting all forms of hostility manifested towards Jews throughout history. In any examination of the relationship between Jews and non-Jews, the reader, as well as the author, must be sensitive to the many different manifestations of what may be generally termed 'anti-Semitism'. The 'blackballing' of a Jewish aspiring club member because of his ethnic character cannot be placed equally alongside the actions of the Nazi state in deliberately attempting to kill all Jews within its control; yet both are examples of anti-Semitism. Thus an examination of Conservative attitudes to Jews and 'Jewish' policy issues requires a recognition of the relative positions on the spectrum of pro- and anti-Semitic views and actions which took place during the period under review. Whilst this work is not one which seeks to compare directly Conservative attitudes to Jews with those of other British political parties or those in continental Europe, it is hoped that this study does allow the reader to place the varying Conservative attitudes in context.

The modern term 'Zionism' also first appeared at the end of the nineteenth century, denoting the movement whose goal was the political return of the Jewish people to the Land of Israel.[13] Anti-Zionism, the opposition to the concept of the Jewish homeland and statehood, became almost synonymous with anti-Semitism in the 1970s in the writings of many left-wing intellectuals and politicians.[14] However, during the period of this study, anti-Semitism does not necessarily imply anti-Zionism, as is suggested in Chapter 3, although by the 1930s it will be demonstrated that anti-Zionists were employing anti-Semitic stereotyping.[15]

There are throughout this study repeated references to parliamentary and other public statements by Conservatives which set out their attitudes to the Jews. These are expressions of the rhetoric used by Conservative politicians. It is suggested that there was generally little difference between this public rhetoric and the private expressions of opinion. An example is the examination undertaken of the accusations by some Conservative politicians and some of the Conservative press that the Jews were engaged in an international conspiracy to dominate the world.[16] A further example is Lord Devonshire's private cabinet memorandum of February 1923, which reveals that he considered that anti-Zionism and anti-Semitism were linked by the anti-Jewish prejudice which had been intensified by the 'vague belief' in a world-wide Judaeo-Bolshevik conspiracy,[17] a view apparently also held by Neville Chamberlain in 1939, as noted below. The use of language in the first half of the twentieth century was different from that at the end of the century. It is suggested here that there was less 'coded' use of English then than is undertaken by contemporary politicians, who appear concerned increasingly with so-called 'political correctness'. Thus, the examination of the rhetoric in the earlier period is likely, at least in the case of this area of study, to be much closer to the true meaning which the speaker or writer wished to convey. Hence, it is legitimate for a historian to examine this public expression of opinion and give it due weight.

The period under examination begins at the commencement of a new century when the Conservative Party had won a general election and ends with the termination of Britain's mandate over Palestine. During this period of nearly half a century the Conservatives held office, alone or in coalition, for some two-thirds of the time; over 32 of those 48 years.

The Jewish community in Britain numbered probably about 160,000 in 1900[18] and 385,000 in 1945.[19] The total population during this period was about 41,460,000 in 1900 and 49,180,000 in 1945.[20] Anglo-Jewry thus formed about 0.39 per cent of the population at the beginning of the century. In 1945, although the Jewish community had disproportional growth compared to the general population, it formed only about 0.78 per cent of the inhabitants of the United Kingdom. Yet the perception of the size of the Jewish community in Britain was often very different from the reality. Northcliffe, the press lord, appeared to have an unrealistic appreciation of the number of Jews in the world. He is reported to have considered that in 1919 there were 1,500,000 Jews in London alone,[21] while in 1940 a group of Conservative MPs wrote to the prime minister requesting that the refugees present in Britain should not be naturalised as this would 'result in a permanent increase of our already over-large Jewish population'.[22]

It was not only the perceived size of the Jewish community which concerned Conservatives, but their perceived power. Leo Maxse, who had served as a vice-president of the National Union of Conservative and Unionist Associations and was the editor of the *National Review*, had run a vigorous campaign during 1912 on the Marconi affair and in the December dealt with the Indian Silver affair.[23] He wrote:

> Lest we be thought to write with prejudice on such matters –
> and we frankly confess to profoundly distrusting government
> by Isaacs, by Samuel, and by Montagu, not because they are
> Jews – for many Jews we have the greatest respect – but

because they are bringing discredit to this country, which is falling more and more into the hands, not of the best Jews, who make admirable citizens, but of that type of Jew who regards the whole duty of man as consisting in scoring some material advantage.[24]

The *National Review* was passionately concerned with the defence of the Empire and was anti-German. Maxse equated pro-Germanism with the Jewish community in Britain and essentially saw the Jews as acting as a fifth column for the German state. In March 1913 he devoted space to his own article on 'Disloyal Jews', maintaining that 'a certain number of disloyal Jews who infest both parties are equally active in playing Germany's game by intriguing against the Triple Entente'. Whilst protesting that he had no anti-Semitic prejudice, Maxse suggested that Britain would be 'infinitely richer in everything that is worth having if those other Jews, who are little better than German spies, are returned with their money bags to the various countries they came from'.[25]

The expression of negative views towards Jews were not confined to the extreme right of the Conservative Party. Even those who did not maintain that Jews were necessarily disloyal believed that they could not be true Englishmen. Arthur Balfour considered that Jews, 'however patriotic, able, and industrious, however much they threw themselves into the national life, still by their own action, remained a people apart and not merely held a religion differing from the vast majority of their fellow country-men, but only inter-married among themselves'.[26] Fifteen years later, another leader of the Conservative Party, Austen Chamberlain, wrote to his sister after the debate in the Commons in July 1920 following the Amritsar massacre in India and General Dyer's suspension from command:

> Our party has always disliked & distrusted [Montagu]. On this occasion all their English & racial feeling was stirred to passionate display – I think I have never seen the House so fiercely angry – & he threw fuel on the flames. A Jew, a foreigner, rounding on an Englishman & throwing him to the wolves – that was the feeling, & the event illustrates once again what I said of Dizzy. A Jew may be a loyal Englishman & passionately patriotic, but he is intellectually apart from us & will never be purely & simply English.[27]

It was apparently irrelevant to Chamberlain that Montagu's

family had immigrated to England in the late eighteenth century, that he was third-generation British, and that his father had sat in both Houses of Parliament. Montagu represented the Anglo-Jewish elite, which has been dubbed 'the Cousinhood', owing to the interconnected marriages which were consummated by this group.[28] This coterie represented the leadership of the Jewish community. They had mainly originated from western Europe, unlike those Jews from eastern Europe who came to Britain in the mass immigration which began in 1881. Whereas much of the pre-1881 community had become middle class, the later immigrants, at least for a generation or more, were working class.[29] Some of these working-class Jews were socialists or communists and, with similarly minded co-religionists elsewhere, were to provide further ammunition, if it were needed, for Conservative attacks on Jewry.[30] One such incident occurred in April 1938 when the Jewish Labour MP, Emanuel Shinwell, was told to '[g]o back to Poland' by the Conservative MP Commander Robert Bower.[31] Shinwell had been born in the East End of London and brought up in Glasgow.

It will be demonstrated here that consistent Conservative attitudes to the Jews were differently expressed in the period under examination, of which the preceding quotations are but examples. They arose because of the notion of 'Englishness' which formed part of the value system of Conservatives. It has been argued that the Conservatives have embraced no ideology or core principles, either because Toryism distrusts intellectual considerations or because the Party is extremely pragmatic and will abandon positions which no longer have popular appeal.[32] However, the cloak of anti-intellectualism does not, of necessity, mean that ideas are ignored. Nor does the adapting of ideas over a long period of changing social, economic, and moral patterns deny the principles upon which those ideas were founded. As Lord ('Rab') Butler wrote in 1977, the Conservative Party 'is not only the oldest in the State but it always responds to the national instincts of the people'.[33]

Lord Hugh Cecil considered that Conservatism unites three streams of opinion, which are 'the distrust of the unknown and the love of the familiar'; the defence of Church and King, 'the reverence for religion and authority'; and imperialism, 'a feeling for the greatness of the country and for that unity which makes its greatness'.[34] Thirty-five years later, Quintin Hogg wrote that the function of the Conservative Party 'is to protect, apply and revive what is best in the old. He therefore is a true Conservative who seeks to fit the old culture, the old humanism, the old Christian tradition of Europe to the world of radar and the atomic bomb, in such a way that our Christianity masters the bomb and not the bomb our Christianity.'[35] The rhetoric had changed but the sentiments were practically identical.

The notion of Englishness was articulated by Stanley Baldwin, many of whose speeches were subsequently published.[36] He argued that ideologies such as communism were alien to the English concept of freedom and that socialist propaganda 'that has for its basis class hatred, and which is being worked so hard today – none of that is indigenous to English soil'.[37] When delivering a speech in the month following the collapse of the 1926 General Strike, he said: 'I want to see our British Labour movement free from alien and foreign heresy. I want to see it pursued and developed on English lines, led by English men.'[38] Therefore, if Montagu could be considered a 'foreigner' it was not difficult for Conservatives to regard the vast majority of Jews whose families had arrived in Britain since 1881 as alien.

It would, however, be wrong to assume a simplistic analysis that due to their identification as disparate, the Jews were subject to anti-Semitic behaviour by the Conservative Party as a whole. This book illustrates that Conservative responses were varied and that Conservative ideas of Empire could be synthesised with Jewish national aspirations whilst mainstream Conservative views of English 'fair-play' would lead to a rejection of extreme anti-Semitism and granting of asylum to Jewish refugees from fascist persecution.

Yet in most studies in which there are, usually tangential, references to Conservative attitudes and behaviour to Jews, the former are habitually portrayed one-dimensionally as unsympathetic and anti-Semitic. In a study of the coalition government after the First World War, one historian alleged that the Liverpool Conservative leadership had, *inter alia*, opposed the 'couponed' Liberal candidate in the Fairfield division because he was a Jew. In fact, the Liberal was not Jewish. His uncouponed Unionist opponent, who was selected by Alderman Sir Archibald Salvidge and the Liverpool Conservative caucus, was a Jew – Jack Brunel Cohen who subsequently took the seat.[39]

The Conservative Party has been described in a book on British communism and Jews as accommodating itself during 1935–45 to the forces of fascism on the Continent. Whilst Chamberlain pursued a policy of appeasement until 1939, declaring war on Nazi Germany in the September of that year can hardly be considered an 'accommodation'. Furthermore, the rejection by the

Conservatives of the authoritarian model of right-wing continental parties and its repudiation of Mosley's approach to politics demonstrates the distance between it and fascism.[40]

Even a leading historian of twentieth-century Anglo-Jewry may misconstrue how the Conservative Party operated in relation to Jewish Conservatives by repeating a suggestion that, throughout the 1930s and 1940s, given that local constituency parties had more control over the selection of candidates (who had previously nominated themselves via personal finance), the demise of the Jewish Conservative MP was ensured.[41] As Stuart Ball has pointed out, however, before 1945 candidate selection tended to be taken by the inner caucus of leading officers. It was only after the adoption of the Maxwell-Fyfe reforms in 1948 that candidates' and MPs' financial contributions were capped, and the selection procedures became more formal and elaborate.[42]

In contradistinction, a recent revisionist history of Anglo-Jewry, maintains that 'British Conservatism was not anti-Semitic and never became anti-Semitic although, like the Liberal Party, it did contain its share of anti-Semites'.[43] It is argued here that this will also not be borne out by a thorough examination of the Conservative Party.

The history of the Conservative Party in the twentieth century was not well served by historians until the mid-1970s, with the exception of Robert Blake's *The Conservative Party from Peel to Churchill*, published in 1970 and reincarnated some 15 years later as *The Conservative Party from Peel to Thatcher*. In 1974, *The Conservative Leadership, 1832–1932*, edited by Donald Southgate, appeared. In 1977, *The Conservatives: A History from their Origins to 1965*, edited by Lord Butler, was published, and the following year saw the publication of John Ramsden's third volume of the Longman history of the Conservative Party, entitled *The Age of Balfour and Baldwin 1902–1940*. In 1979, T. F. Lindsay and Michael Harrington produced *The Conservative Party 1918–1979*. More recent surveys appeared during the 1990s. A major work, edited by Anthony Seldon and Stuart Ball, *Conservative Century: The Conservative Party since 1900*, was published in 1994. The following year saw publication of Stuart Ball's, *The Conservative Party and British Politics 1902–1951*, A. J. Davies's *We, the Nation: The Conservative Party and the Pursuit of Power*, and John Ramsden's *The Age of Churchill and Eden*. In 1996, Anthony Seldon edited *How Tory Governments Fall: The Tory Party in Power since 1783* and John Charmley produced *A History of Conservative Politics 1900–1996*. A work arising out of a conference at the University of Wales which took a wider perspective was edited by Martin Francis and Ina Zweiniger-Bargielowska and entitled *The Conservatives and British Society, 1880–1990*.[44] In 1998, John Ramsden produced a history of the Conservative Party since 1830, entitled *An Appetite for Power*. That year also saw the publication of a history of the Party by Alan Clark, entitled *The Tories: Conservatives and the Nation State 1922–1997*.

However, only in *Conservative Century* and *We, the Nation* are there references to Jews and the Party. In *Conservative Century*, Richard Cockett, in 'The Party, Publicity, and the Media', deals with the anti-Semitism of Sir Joseph Ball in *Truth*, which he had secretly acquired for the Party.[45] Peter Catterall, in 'The Party and Religion', appears to rely heavily on Alderman for those comments regarding Jews which reflect Anglo-Jewry's views of the Conservative Party rather than the Conservatives' attitudes towards the Jews.[46] Davies produces snippets of information in two and a half pages of text from the time of Benjamin Disraeli to Margaret Thatcher illustrating anti-Semitism in the Party;[47] this survey, by the limitation of its length, must be considered superficial.

Monographs dealing with specific periods, such as Frans Coetzee's *For Party or Country: Nationalism and the Dilemmas of Popular Conservatism in Edwardian England*[48] or Neville Thompson's *The Anti-Appeasers: Conservative Opposition to Appeasement in the 1930s*,[49] also make scant mention or fail to refer to Jews. Richard Cockett, however, deals with anti-Semitism in general, and the attacks on Leslie Hore-Belisha in particular, in his work *Twilight of Truth – Chamberlain, Appeasement and the Manipulation of the Press*.[50]

The lacuna in these works is a little surprising because, although Jewish issues were generally peripheral to British political life, there were moments when Jews featured somewhat prominently. The mass immigration which took place prior to the First World War, the potential immigration during the 1920s and the refugees resulting from Nazi persecution in the 1930s were major issues affecting not only the Jewish community. Fear of communism following the Russian Revolution in 1917 also had important implications for the Anglo-Jewish community. The other major issue was Britain's involvement with the Jewish National Home in Palestine. The Balfour Declaration of 1917 and the acceptance of the Mandate for Palestine resulted in an ongoing involvement by the Party in the issue of Zionism until the creation of the State of Israel in 1948. However, in the period after 1948 there are few policy issues which directly affected the Jewish community; immigration had effectively ceased and the Palestine Mandate had been relinquished.

One of the most emotive issues that has formed part of the political agenda in twentieth-century British society is the subject of race and immigration. It is an issue where the Conservative Party has been identified as having moved its policies increasingly towards greater restriction and exclusion of immigrants. To date studies of immigration control have not focused upon the development of Unionist and Conservative philosophy in this area, which has its roots in the late Victorian and Edwardian period. The examination in this book focuses exclusively on Jewish immigration, which formed the largest and most ethnically identifiable group in the period under consideration.[51] Chapter 2 of this book deals with Jewish immigration from 1900 until the fall of the Baldwin government in 1929. There have been a number of works dealing with both the nature of Jewish immigration and the detailed history of the Aliens Act 1905.[52] The examination in this work does not seek to reiterate the narratives with which these studies have been concerned but rather considers the political context in which the demands for legislation were made. It does, however, examine the restrictionist pressure from within the Conservative ranks after the passage of the Aliens Act 1905 until the 'Coupon Election' of December 1918. The evolution of anti-alienism during the First World War reveals intense hostility towards the Jews, who were increasingly identified as a danger to the stability of the state. The post-war period is examined with its focus on the tenure of Sir William Joynson-Hicks as home secretary from 1924 until 1929.

The developments within the Conservative and Unionist Party in the period 1900–29 are examined, and in particular the impact of tariff reform in relation to anti-alienism. It is suggested that the radicalisation of Unionism produced a more combative political party which was ideologically more inclined towards anti-Jewish attitudes.

The use of what was essentially anti-Jewish rhetoric and policies is examined in their electoral context, particularly in relation to the East End of London, where the overwhelming number of Jewish immigrants were to be found. It is argued that these anti-Jewish policies had some electoral benefits in those constituencies, particularly in the earlier part of the period. However, the study shows that anti-alienism was not restricted solely to Conservative campaign tactics in East London but was used nationally from time to time.

It will be suggested that the view of the Jews as 'a people apart', and therefore outside of the Conservative conception of what constituted British society, increased and deepened over the course of the first three decades of this century. It is also, therefore, suggested that political anti-Semitism cannot be dismissed as the domain of the extreme right fascist fringe in this country. Yet an examination of the Conservative attitudes to the Jews in the 1930s, which is dealt with in Chapter 7 and outlined below, reveals the differing nature of Conservative views from those of the extreme right.

In November 1917 the war cabinet authorised the foreign secretary, A. J. Balfour, to issue a Declaration to Lord Rothschild of the English Zionist Federation which made a commitment to the establishment of a Jewish national home in the Ottoman territory of Palestine. The Declaration, which was subsequently to be restated in the Mandate to Britain of Palestine, was perhaps one of the most controversial undertakings made by Britain in the twentieth century, the consequences of which, over 80 years later, are still the cause of tension and bloodshed in the Middle East. Chapter 3 examines the reasons and motivations which resulted in the letter of 2 November 1917 and its immediate aftermath.

It is suggested that the examination of scholars hitherto has not been sufficiently focused on the actual decision-makers who were responsible for the Declaration. Those few men were Unionist politicians, and in order to understand their motivation it is necessary to begin not in 1917 or 1914 but in the first years of the century, when Balfour was not Britain's foreign secretary but the prime minister, and consequently there is an examination of Conservative views from the turn of the century when the issue of alien Jewish immigration was a major concern to many in the Party.

Chapter 4 considers the identification of Jews as a people hostile and inherently 'un-English' in the context of the attitudes which emerged during the First World War and its aftermath. The loyalty of British Jews came increasingly into question, particularly by the Conservative press. It will be shown that the success of the Bolshevik *coup d'état* in November 1917 caused renewed attacks on the Jews, who were seen by some elements as being primarily responsible for this state of affairs. This led, particularly following the publication in English of *The Protocols of the Elders of Zion*, to accusations by some sections of the Party that the Jews had substantial and clandestine power. Some accepted the canard of the world Jewish conspiracy by which Jewish capitalists and Jewish communists would come to dominate world affairs. The acceptance of the proposition of 'Jewish power' had influenced Conservative thinking in relation to Zionism and was to remain in the Party at least until the end of the period of this study.[53]

Chapter 6 surveys Palestine from the establishment of a civil administration in 1920, which, it is argued, was the catalyst for the commencement of a campaign that was by 1923 to have obtained the backing of a substantial number of Conservatives to reverse the policy to support the Jewish national home in Palestine. There is an examination of this opposition and the effect it had in modifying British policy towards the Palestine Mandate by the reinterpretation of the Balfour Declaration. It will be shown that opposition to Zionism was to a large extent conducted by means of anti-Semitism, both in the Conservative press and in Parliament.

Chapter 7 looks into the changes which occurred in Conservative policy towards Jewish immigration to Britain in the period from the rise in Germany of the Nazi Party to the outbreak of the Second World War. During this time anti-Semitism increased in many European countries and Britain experienced blatant political anti-Jewish prejudice from the British Union of Fascists and other fascist organisations. Britain continued to have high unemployment in various parts of the country which was exploited by those who opposed the admission of aliens.

It will be argued that, despite the strong feeling of anti-Semitic prejudice which pervaded the Conservative Party, there were vociferous proponents of the policy to admit into Britain Jewish refugees fleeing from Nazi terror. It will be demonstrated that a change in government policy began to emerge in early 1938 but that it was surreptitiously pursued to avoid criticism from the opponents of Jewish immigration. It will be postulated that this change in policy, which allowed a relatively substantial number of Jews (and others) to find refuge in the British Isles, was made not because of a reduction in the anti-Jewish outlook of the Party, but because the treatment of the Jews by the Nazis, in particular, was considered to be inhumane, uncivilised and 'un-English', and therefore required a positive response.

Chapter 8 scrutinises the changing Conservative policy towards the Jews in Palestine in the period from 1930 until 1939. The Labour Party's Passfield White Paper, which reversed the Conservative policy of support for the Jewish national home, was vigorously attacked by the Conservative front bench but nonetheless received support from some anti-Zionist Conservative backbenchers. Although that policy was abandoned it was to be the precursor of the policy position which was ultimately adopted by the Conservative-dominated government in 1939.

The roles of the Conservative supporters and opponents of the Jewish national home in the 1930s are examined against the background of increasing anti-Semitism in continental Europe and Arab violence in Palestine. It will be shown that the anti-Zionists used anti-Semitic stereotyping in their description of Jews and that the Conservative-led government, notwithstanding the consistent support for Zionism among many Conservative MPs, as illustrated by speeches and other interventions, would increasingly adopt policies which attempted to appease the Arabs at the expense of the Jews.

Chapter 9 considers Conservative attitudes to the Jews during the Second World War. After the outbreak of hostilities many European Jews, as 'citizens' of Axis countries, were treated as enemy aliens. Large numbers of Jews were interned along with German Nazis, notwithstanding their clear and obvious hostility to the regime.[54] Those Jews escaping from Europe increasingly sought refuge in Palestine and came up against British immigration policy which, despite Churchill's premiership, remained that which had been introduced in 1939 by Chamberlain's government. The Conservative Party increasingly ceased to function as a co-ordinated political machine during the wartime period and the study will therefore focus on the role of Conservative ministers exercising their duties in accordance with established Conservative policies. Furthermore a detailed account of British government policy and the Jews of Europe during the Second World War has been produced by Bernard Wasserstein.[55] In view of this study and the comments made above regarding the nature of the Churchill coalition, the chapter deals only selectively with events during the wartime period.

Following the victory in Europe, party politics returned to its pre-war pattern and after the General Election in July 1945 the Conservative Party went into opposition for the first time since 1931. Chapter 10 examines the period from July 1945 to May 1948, when the Palestine Mandate came to an end. The Labour Party had publicly supported Zionism during the war, but Attlee's government adopted a hostile attitude towards Zionist aspirations for a state and unrestricted immigration into Palestine. It will be shown that the Conservative responses to Labour's conduct were mixed but increasingly the Conservative Party exhibited antipathy to Jewish issues. There was also a movement towards a coalescence of policy positions in respect of the immigration of Jewish displaced persons into Palestine and the future of the Jewish national home. It will be argued that the anti-Semitic rhetoric that had been exhibited in earlier parts of the period under examination were again utilised but without there being many voices in contradiction.

Chapter 11, in conclusion, argues that this book demonstrates that the Conservative Party exhibited prejudice against Jews throughout the period under review. This prejudice was often very strong and can be seen as blatant anti-Semitism. Yet, at the same time, there were those in the Conservative Party, often with influence and power, who actively assisted the Jews. Thus, whilst Conservative attitudes placed Jews as a people apart, they were not universally considered people to be rejected and opposed.

This study argues that there was a link between the two main issues under examination, namely Jewish immigration and the Jewish national home. The consequences of those decisions made by Conservatives in the period under review have had dramatic consequences in the subsequent 50 years. The absence of peace in the Middle East and threats to the possible stability of the world can find their genesis in the consequences of the attitudes of the Conservative Party towards the Jews in the first half of the twentieth century.

2

The Conservatives and Alien Jewish Immigration, 1900–18

Mid-Victorian Britain had welcomed political refugees and economic migrants from Europe, but the numbers who came were relatively small. The number of alien residents increased by some 70,000 over the 30-year period to 1881 to total some 118,000. However, there had been far greater numbers of Irish migrants settling in England, and there was movement by rural migrants to the large conurbations. The alien immigrant was, therefore, less distinctive amid this more general internal movement within the British Isles. Economic growth was also a factor which shielded the immigrant from hostility. This economic expansion had, however, turned to a depression from the 1870s, which was prolonged and caused much hardship, particularly in rural areas. The failure of agricultural prosperity led to even greater numbers of former farm labourers and others from the rural communities migrating to the cities.[1]

The period from 1881 saw a qualitative and quantitative change in the nature of alien immigration into Britain. It was following the pogroms of 1881–82 in Tsarist Russia, the anti-Semitism of the Romanian government and the continuing economic hardships that faced Jews in Galicia and elsewhere in eastern Europe that mass immigration into Britain occurred. It was not only Jews who came to Britain's shores, and not all of those who did were to remain as permanent residents. However, the largest number of immigrants who settled in England over the following 25 years were Jews who came mainly from eastern Europe.

The Jews settled primarily in inner city areas. There were relatively large concentrations in cities such as Manchester and Leeds and they were also to be found in increased numbers in other provincial towns like Sheffield and Leicester where manufacturing industry was seen as providing opportunities for employment generally. However, Jewish settlement was concentrated most notably in the East End of London. It has been estimated that the Anglo-Jewish population increased from approximately 65,000 in 1880 to almost 300,000 by 1914, of which approximately 200,000 were located in London.[2]

There was, therefore, a substantial increase in the number of immigrants, now primarily Jews from eastern Europe, who were seen as competing with the existing population and native migrants for housing and work in an economy which was in recession.

Opposition to immigration manifested itself in the trade union movement, which was fearful that the jobs of its members would be threatened by the immigrants. Aliens, it was alleged, would work for lower wages and for longer hours and, furthermore, their presence forced up rents in the working-class areas in which they lived.

Unionist politicians began to consider the issue of alien restriction in the early 1880s. The momentum was to gather pace in the following decade. Lord Salisbury, whilst in a brief period of opposition, introduced an Aliens Bill in July 1894 which passed its second reading before falling. Although it has been argued that Salisbury was more concerned with anarchists than Jews, his Bill did contain a clause to exclude pauper aliens.[3] However, whilst still in office Salisbury's government announced in May 1892 that it was preparing an Aliens Bill. The matter was not pursued as the Liberals took office that August, having obtained a 'home rule majority' of 40 at the general election which the prime minister had called in July.[4] At the next general election in July 1895, alien restriction was confirmed as Unionist party policy. Salisbury's government committed itself to introducing legislation in the Royal Address in 1896. However, no parliamentary time was allocated by the government for an Aliens Bill.

THE 1900 GENERAL ELECTION

In the autumn of 1900 the Unionist government fought the general election principally on the issue of the South African War. The war had reached the stage by October 1900 at which organised Boer resistance to the British invasion had ended, although fighting was to continue as guerrilla warfare until May 1902. Opposition to the war was mounted by radical Liberals and Labour, many of whom saw the conflict as having been instigated by a mainly Jewish capitalist conspiracy. J. A. Hobson, the *Manchester Guardian*'s correspondent in Johannesburg, was of immense influence in developing and expounding this view.

He maintained that the Jews manipulated the Uitlander agitation as they had half the land and nine-tenths of the wealth in the Transvaal, which was the subject of the Uitlanders' claims. His book on the war in South Africa was published in 1902 and argued that the war was fought in the interests of a 'small group of international financiers, chiefly German in origin and Jewish in race'.[5] At the Trades Union Congress in September 1900 there were numerous references to taxpayers' money being used in South Africa in the interests of 'a number of cosmopolitan Jews, most of whom had no patriotism and no country'.[6] Unionist candidates could not openly accept these arguments, which were an early manifestation of the 'world Jewish conspiracy' theory. However, it is conceivable that privately, and especially as the war dragged on with mounting costs in British casualties, financial expenditure and diplomatic isolation, this view of Jews may have been harboured by Unionists.

There were, of course, other issues with which the electorate was faced. One of these issues was alien immigration which had particular significance in the East End of London, and it occupied a significant part of the campaigns conducted in the parliamentary divisions in Tower Hamlets. Sir Thomas Dewar, in St Georges, pledged to support strongly any measure which was brought forward to restrict any further 'pauper alien' immigration. William Evans-Gordon in Stepney stated that he was prepared to 'propose or support' the restriction of alien immigration.[7]

The government's majority had fallen from 152 in 1895 to 128 prior to the election. It rose marginally at the general election to 134. In East London the Unionists were to retain Stepney, with Major William Evans-Gordon returned; St Georges with Sir Thomas Dewar; Bow and Bromley with Walter Murray Guthrie; Mile End with Spencer Charrington; Bethnal Green North-East with Sir Mancherjee Bhownaggree; and Limehouse with Harry Samuel. The Unionists won Bethnal Green South-West with Samuel Forde Ridley and Hoxton with Claude Hay. Anti-alienism helped the Unionists to maintain and increase their parliamentary strength in an area which may otherwise have been vulnerable to Liberal gains. It is notable that in this election the Unionists only increased their parliamentary representation by three seats, two of the three net gains being obtained in East London.

THE GROWTH OF ANTI-ALIENISM AND THE ALIENS BILL, 1904

With the return of the Unionist government it was, therefore, not unexpected that agitation for the introduction of legislation should increase both inside and outside Westminster. Sir Howard Vincent, who was the Unionist member for Sheffield Central, continued his campaign for restriction which had commenced in 1887. Yet it was the East London Unionists, and Evans-Gordon in particular, who were to spearhead the issue. Evans-Gordon quickly dominated the British Brothers' League, which was founded in December 1900.[8] This was a mass movement which, although not exclusively Conservative, was controlled by Unionist politicians and their supporters.

On 31 July 1901 the Parliamentary Pauper Immigration Committee was formed with Vincent heading its leadership. It contained up to 50 members including all the MPs for the East End constituencies with the exception of Stuart Samuel. The committee, therefore, included Liberal members and one Jewish Unionist, Harry Samuel. In January 1902 Evans-Gordon, seconded by Forde Ridley, proposed an amendment to the Royal Address because of the failure of the government to give an undertaking to introduce restrictive legislation.[9] The motion was withdrawn when the government proposed setting up an enquiry. Gerald Balfour, the president of the Board of Trade and the nephew of the prime minister, confirmed that the government's opinion had not changed that 'great evils have followed in the train of unrestricted alien immigration'.[10]

In February 1902 Vincent and Evans-Gordon repeatedly pressed for the establishment of the Royal Commission, which was set up the following month. It was composed predominantly of restrictionists, such as Evans-Gordon and the Liberal member for Wolverhampton, Henry Norman,[11] and of the seven members only Sir Kenelm Digby, the permanent under-secretary at the Home Office, and Lord Rothschild opposed restriction. The Royal Commission reported in August 1903 and not surprisingly advocated restrictionist legislation be introduced. However, the time taken in its deliberations had angered some Unionists such as Vincent and James Lowther, the member for Kent Thanet, who continued to press for the introduction of legislation in Parliament.[12]

The King's Speech on 19 February 1904 heralded the proposed and, by some, long-awaited legislation when a measure for the purpose of 'dealing with the evils consequent in the immigration of criminal and destitute Aliens' was outlined. The Aliens Bill was introduced by the home secretary, Aretas Akers-Douglas, at the end of March 1904. He stated that aliens caused overcrowding and strain with the native population which was a serious menace to law and order. He maintained also that the type of alien settling in Britain had been rejected by the United States and would not make the best citizens. The Bill proposed to empower immigration officers to exclude criminals, prostitutes, the diseased, the destitute, and those of 'bad character'. The Bill was also to include areas which were to be prohibited to aliens.[13]

The Bill's second reading took place on 25 April. The measure was supported by speeches from Unionist MPs who sat for East End constituencies and also from Sydney Buxton, the Liberal Member for Poplar, together with the Liberal member of the Royal Commission, Henry Norman. Walter Long, the president of the Local Government Board, maintained that 'men of British origin were turned out of their homes at the shortest notice by alien landlords to put in alien occupants'.[14] The Unionists' majority on second reading was 124.

Somewhat curiously, the government then proposed to send the Bill to the grand committee on law. This committee had been set up in 1882 to deal with non-contentious issues. The Bill hardly fell into this category. The Liberals, who had opposed the reference to the committee, were able effectively to prevent progress by tabling numerous amendments which resulted in consideration of the Bill being reduced to half a line a day.[15] Sydney Buxton considered that the Unionist government were never serious with respect to the proposed legislation, stating that, in his view, 'it was only a shop window Bill and it was never intended to be passed'.[16] Winston Churchill, who was in the process of transferring his allegiance from the Conservatives to the Liberals, offered a different reason for the Bill's failure. He considered that wealthy Jewish supporters of the government had led it to choose to drop the Bill.[17]

It has been suggested more recently that Balfour either intentionally allowed the Bill to fail in order to avoid clashes between the different factions within the Unionist Party or that his preoccupation with the tariff reform issue caused him momentarily to lose his grasp of parliamentary tactics.[18] Neither of these two hypotheses is a very satisfactory explanation. The government was to announce the reintroduction of an Aliens Bill in February 1905. This renewal of the Unionist commitment demonstrated that anti-alien legislation was part of government policy. Furthermore, the tariff reform issue had not reached any critical juncture by June 1904. Indeed, at the end of that month Joseph Chamberlain had begun to evolve a policy which he believed would enable him to work with Balfour again.[19]

It is possible that the practical difficulties in the proposed legislation, with its draconian application, persuaded the government to reconsider the detail. Also Churchill's comments may well have had some foundation in truth. The Rothschild family were an important potential source of Party funds. The leadership of the Jewish community had themselves favoured a tempering of immigration. It is possible that Balfour, by allowing the 1904 Bill to die, could reintroduce a modified version which, whilst satisfying Unionist policy, would not alienate his Jewish Unionist supporters. He would have been able to see the purported difficulty into which the 1904 Bill had put at least one Jewish Unionist MP, Benjamin Cohen, who represented Islington East. Cohen had said that he supported the Bill with reluctance and only because he wished to see criminals and other dissolute classes kept out of Britain.[20]

EAST LONDON BY-ELECTION, 1905

In January 1905 a by-election took place in Mile End following the death of the sitting Unionist member, Spencer Charrington, who had represented the constituency for many years and whose family's brewing business was a major employer in the East End. The Unionist candidate was the Hon. Harry Lawson, who was, as he freely stated, half-Jewish. His Liberal opponent was a practising Jew, Bertram Straus. In 1900 the Unionists had achieved almost double the Liberal vote with a majority of 1,160. However, the 1905 campaign showed the change in Unionist fortunes.

Straus ran a conventional Liberal campaign in favour of free trade but also appealed to the Jewish vote[21] in opposing anti-alien legislation. Straus believed that he had the support of 85–90 per cent of the Jewish vote.[22] However, by the end of the campaign Straus was advocating limited alien restriction. Lawson managed to retain the seat for the Unionist interest with a majority of 78. It is possible that his stance in favour of restriction may have helped in holding the seat. Whilst the Liberal vote increased by 60.9 per cent over the 1900 general election result, the Unionist vote only fell by 12.4 per cent. The Unionists had lost ten by-elections between January 1904 and January 1905. Holding Mile End may, therefore, have reinforced the government's determination to reintroduce an Aliens Bill in the next session.

THE ALIENS ACT, 1905

The second Aliens Bill was introduced on 18 April 1905. It was a modified version of its predecessor. There were no longer the clauses relating to 'good character', registration with police, or prohibited areas. Immigration officers were now to decide on entry in conjunction with medical inspectors and there now would be a right of appeal against a decision of an Immigration Board. Entry of aliens was to be restricted to eight designated ports. Admission was not to be denied if immigrants could prove political persecution.[23] The Unionist measure this time received only muted opposition from the Liberal benches. The Liberal leadership had decided not to oppose formally the second reading of the Bill, which was passed on 2 May by 211 votes to 59. This change of attitude may well have been because of the entreaties of Liberal MPs and candidates from the East End constituencies who, with the exception of Stuart Samuel, petitioned the Liberal leadership not to oppose the second reading; a fact that Evans-Gordon delighted in relating to the House.[24] Liberal amendments to the Bill were, not surprisingly, defeated in committee. Yet concern had not only been expressed by opponents of the Bill but by such supporters of the government as the influential backbencher and cousin of the prime minister, Lord Hugh Cecil, who was concerned to ensure the right of asylum for the oppressed was not lost.[25] Consequently, Akers-Douglas did modify the Bill by introducing another ground for admission in the event that aliens had been persecuted for religious beliefs.[26] The Bill passed its third reading in the Commons on 19 July by 214 votes in favour to 136 against, a majority of 78. The Unionist parliamentary majority at this time was 70 seats. On 3 August 1905 the Bill had finished its passage through the Lords and on 11 August received the Royal Assent.

THE FAILURE OF NATIONAL SELF-CONFIDENCE

During the debate on the second reading of the 1904 Aliens Bill, James Bryce, the Liberal member for Aberdeen South and a previous president of the Board of Trade, who had represented Stepney in the Commons from 1880 to 1885, said that 'Stepney was not England, and they [the Unionist government] could not legislate for all England for the sake of one borough'.[27] But was that not the course of action that the Unionists took? Immigration was not, of course, confined to one part of the East End of London. However, the substantial increase in the alien population was to be found there.[28] Yet, in relation to the overall population of Britain at this time, the alien immigrant community as a whole represented only a very small fraction.

In 1901, the census figure for the total United Kingdom

population was 41,459,000. The alien population was probably in the region of 350,000. It has been estimated that the total number of immigrants who settled in the United Kingdom between 1871 and 1911 was 400,000, compared with 6,000,000 British emigrants. It was certainly true that a much larger number of migrants landed in Britain but these overwhelmingly were in transit to the United States. Jewish immigration has been estimated to have totalled in the region of 135,000 during this period and the total Jewish community of the United Kingdom in 1905 was probably some 250,000, of whom some two-thirds lived in London.[29]

There had been a growing fear in late-Victorian England that Britain's place in the world was under threat. This view was much more pronounced in the Edwardian period. Britain and its Empire were seen as being in a state of potential degeneration. Other powers were seen as making progress, particularly in the economic sphere, whilst Britain had fallen behind in the leadership of world trade. The physical size of the British Isles was considered to be an inhibiting factor in world leadership when compared with the United States, Russia or Germany. These countries had rapidly rising populations, which would, therefore, further enhance their relative strength.[30]

Although the late Victorians and Edwardians had only limited statistical data available to them, the general trends in population growth and economic indices were discernible. The population of the British Isles rose from 37.4 million in 1890 to about 41.1 million in 1900. During the same period Russia's population rose from 116.8 million to 135.6 million and that of the United States from 62.6 million to 75.9 million. Germany saw a population growth from 49.2 million to 56 million, while that of Austria-Hungary rose from 39.9 million to 46.7 million. The relative populations by 1910 were: Britain – 44.9 million, Russia – 159.3 million, United States – 97.3 million, Germany – 66.9 million, Austria-Hungary – 52.1 million.[31] Britain was, therefore, faced with the other Great Powers which had increasingly larger populations.

Britain's place as the 'workshop of the world' had also undergone serious challenge during this period. The share of world manufacturing output saw the United Kingdom's percentage peak at 22.9 per cent in 1880 with the United States having 14.7 per cent, Germany with 8.5 per cent, France with 7.8 per cent, Russia at 7.6 per cent and Austria-Hungary at 4.4 per cent. The position in 1900 had relegated Britain to second place with 18.5 per cent whilst the United States had risen to 23.6 per cent. Germany had increased its share to 13.2 per cent and Russia to 8.8 per cent. France had decreased to 6.8 per cent while Austria-Hungary marginally increased its share to 4.7 per cent. Britain's relative decline was to continue in the Edwardian period and by 1913 its share was only 13.6 per cent compared with the United States with 32 per cent and Germany, having overtaken Britain, with 14.8 per cent.[32]

Concern was also widely expressed as to what contemporaries termed the degeneracy of the English race. The experience of recruitment for the army in the Boer War revealed the unsatisfactory physical condition of the British working-class male. General Sir Frederick Maurice revealed in January 1902 that 60 per cent were unfit for military service.[33] The government felt obliged to set up an interdepartmental committee to examine the allegations. It reported in August 1904, concluding that the position of the urban poor had worsened since mid-Victorian times.

A young Tory pamphleteer named Elliot Mills wrote a satire entitled *The Decline and Fall of the British Empire*, which was published in 1905. He outlined what he considered to be the eight causes of British decline as: (1) urbanisation with its effect on health and faith; (2) forsaking seafaring; (3) growth of refinement and luxury; (4) decline in literary and dramatic taste; (5) decline in the physique and health of English people; (6) decline in both intellectual and religious life; (7) excessive taxation and municipal extravagance; and (8) the inability of the British to defend themselves and the Empire.

The pamphlet was favourably reviewed in *The Times*, the *Evening Standard*, and the *Spectator*. General Baden-Powell, in a speech early in 1906, recommended it to his audience in order that the reader could see what should be 'his share in saving his country from the possibility of disaster'.[34] Some 12,000 copies of the pamphlet were sold in six months.

LITERARY MOTIFS

There was another type of popular literature which flourished at this time and also exploited the anxieties of late-Victorian and Edwardian England. This was the literature of invasion. The common theme was the international isolation of a Britain which had no continental alliances, and the fear that radical politicians would weaken England's ability to defend itself. The external threat was not initially restricted to German invasion but in the years after 1900 Germany increasingly was identified as the enemy. The most enduring of these stories is Erskine Childers' *The Riddle of the Sands,* written in 1902, in which Germany's invasion plans are discovered by two English yachtsmen.

Jews were increasingly identified as the allies of Germany. The journalist and leading figure in the Anglo-Jewish Association, Lucien Wolf, was a prolific writer who was widely published in leading newspapers and journals; he was considered by many to be a mouthpiece of the German government.[35]

Jews had been portrayed in English literature as stereotypes. It has been argued that late-Victorian and Edwardian writers characterised them as either 'good Jews', who acted in the interests of Britain and the Empire, or 'bad Jews', who attempted to subvert British interests.[36] John Buchan, who was a Conservative politician as well as a novelist, represented both Jewish stereotypes in his works.[37] In *A Lodge in the Wilderness,* which was published in 1906, he wrote: 'if we must have magnates, I would rather Jews had the money. It doesn't degrade them and they have the infallible good taste of the East at the back of their heads.'[38] However, by 1915, Buchan would describe Jews as members of a world Jewish conspiracy which was bent on the destruction of Christian civilisation. In his extremely popular *The Thirty-Nine Steps* he had the following proposition expounded by the neighbour of Richard Hannay, the hero of the novel, at its outset:

> Away behind all the Governments and the armies there was a big subterranean movement going on, engineered by a very dangerous people... The capitalists would rake in the shekels, and make fortunes by buying up the wreckage. Capital, he said, had no conscience and no fatherland. Besides, the Jew was behind it, and the Jew hated Russia worse than hell... Yes, sir, he is the man who is ruling the world just now.[39]

RACE AND CULTURE

Even if Jews were not seen as necessarily being a part of an international conspiracy to undermine the British Empire, they were considered to have a debilitating effect on the British character. Joseph Chamberlain remarked to the Italian foreign minister that he only despised one race, which was the Jews, whom he considered to be all physical cowards.[40] This was a theme which would re-emerge after Britain entered the First World War. Jews were also accused of creating slum living conditions and furthering vice and crime.[41]

For some, national salvation would depend ultimately upon the kind of race that was bred. In November 1899 Chamberlain had advanced the possibility of a triple alliance between Germany, Britain and the United States which he described as 'the Teutonic race and the two branches of the Anglo-Saxon race' as in his view there was little difference in the character of the two and such an alliance would be natural.[42] The term 'race' was used fairly loosely at this time and often was meant to refer to 'culture'.[43] However, the view existed that the white man was superior to the dark- or yellow-skinned man and that, whilst the privileges, rights, responsibilities and duties fell on all whites, it was an obligation particularly on the Anglo-Saxons.

TARIFF REFORM

The political responses to these *fin-de-siècle* anxieties took a number of forms. These have been described generically by the phrase 'national efficiency'. This has been defined by G. R. Searle as 'an attempt to discredit the habits, beliefs and institutions that put the British at a handicap in their competition with foreigners and to commend instead a social organisation that more closely followed the German model'.[44]

The politics of national efficiency split along essentially party political lines. The Liberal Imperialists were able to separate their desire for maintaining the imperial tradition and the desire to improve the conditions of society at home, particularly in respect of the working classes. The Unionist solution was to combine what appeared to be imperial and domestic policy through the programme of tariff reform.[45] Ostensibly the campaign launched by Chamberlain was primarily to strengthen the cohesion of the Empire by the method of granting reciprocal trade preference. This would, therefore, create trade barriers with the remainder of the world. This policy, it was argued, would increase employment as the domestic manufacturing market would be protected from 'dumping' of goods by the United States and Germany. Furthermore, revenue obtained by the imposition of tariffs could provide funding for social welfare schemes.

Chamberlain, on 6 October 1903, opened his campaign at St Andrew's Hall in Glasgow by setting out the two objects. Firstly, he wished to maintain and increase the national strength and prosperity of the United Kingdom and, secondly, to 'consolidate the British race'. He was not prepared to regard the downfall or decay of industrial Britain with complacency or resignation. 'I do not believe', he said, 'in the setting of the British star, but then I do not believe in the folly of the British people.'[46] Chamberlain directed his appeal to the working classes on the basis of self-interest. The unfettered market economy, by allowing cheap imports, would threaten employment and direct taxation to fund social legislation would reduce living standards.

The tariff-reform campaign launched in 1903 was not an original shift in Conservative political thinking. It had had its precursor in the Imperial Federation League and the Fair Trade League of the 1880s. This movement had captured considerable support at that time. At the National Union of Conservative Associations' conference in November 1887 a motion which called for reform of policy in respect of both foreign imports and 'the influx of indigent foreigners' was carried by 1,000 votes to 12.[47] The motion had been introduced by Sir Howard Vincent. However, Salisbury was in no position to act upon this resolution, even though he personally may have desired it. At that time it would have seriously undermined the relationship between the Conservatives and the Liberal Unionists and, consequently, the stability of the Unionist government.[48]

The tariff reformers strove to capture the support of the Unionist Party. The meeting of the National Union in Sheffield on 1 and 2 October 1903 was predominantly in favour of the views expressed by Chamberlain.[49] The Liberal Unionist Association was captured in early 1904 which led to the withdrawal of the free-fooders from the organisation. On 8 July 1904 a banquet to celebrate Chamberlain's sixty-eighth birthday was attended by 177 MPs who expressed their support for preference. The National Union conference held at Southampton on 28 and 29 October 1904 passed a resolution in favour of tariff reform, as did the conference held the following year in November 1905.[50] However, it was not the National Union that controlled Conservative policy. The Party leadership under Balfour resisted the extremes of the protectionists' policies whilst also distancing themselves from the free traders. Balfour's middle line, contained in a pamphlet entitled 'Notes on Insular Free Trade', advocated creating an environment to enable 'fiscal negotiation' to take place which would threaten to impose retaliatory tariffs. He had written to the king in September 1903 that, although 'Colonial Preference is eminently desirable in the interests both of British commerce and Imperial unity, it has not yet come within the sphere of practical politics'.[51] This view was actively supported only by a minority of the parliamentary party, but it was the Unionist free traders who were an even smaller minority, numbering perhaps no more than

40 members. Thus Unionist Party policy from 1903 proposed 'fiscal reform', if not 'tariff reform'. In the general election of January 1906, 98 per cent of Unionist election addresses featured fiscal reform as a major issue.[52]

TARIFF REFORM AND ALIEN RESTRICTION

The dynamics behind tariff reform, or even the modified fiscal reform, policies were present in the policy of alien restriction. It is not, therefore, surprising to find that restrictionists were also opposed to the maintenance of free trade. There was little ideological difference between free trade in goods and free trade in populations. As noted above it was the leading restrictionist, Sir Howard Vincent, who had proposed the motion to impose trade tariffs at the National Union conference in 1887. The domestic agenda of the tariff reformers was to appeal to the working class vote. The parliamentary restrictionists often were concerned with working-class conditions and many were themselves members representing working-class, or partially working-class, constituencies.[53]

In his election address for the 1900 general election Evans-Gordon stated that he was prepared to propose or support the restriction of immigration of pauper aliens in the interests of 'our own workers' (and also the existing alien wage earners). This commitment was found in the section of the address headed 'The Better and Cheaper Housing of the Working Classes'.[54] Evans-Gordon would maintain this theme throughout the period until legislation was passed. In July 1904, at a meeting in his constituency, he said that those who supported an Aliens Bill were 'fighting to prevent the wholesale expropriation of their own homes and to prevent their being employed by foreigners'.[55] William Hayes Fisher, who had been a whip and financial secretary to the Treasury, sat in the Unionist interest for Fulham, which Henry Pelling described as a mixed-class constituency.[56] In his speech in support of the Aliens Bill 1904, he described himself as a social reformer and imperialist.[57] Chamberlain, in his speech supporting the second reading of the 1905 Aliens Bill, said: 'the whole of our action is based on the belief that the time has come to protect the working man in his employment'.[58] This was not, of course, the whole reason, even if it did represent an important part of the philosophy behind Unionist restrictionist policy. The perceived threat to the 'Anglo-Saxon race' was as much an issue, even if it tended to be hidden beneath the surface.

Overt anti-Semitism was not considered 'acceptable' in main-stream British politics. Therefore there was, through the many years of debate regarding restriction, only limited reference to Jews as such. Although restriction was aimed primarily at Jewish immigration to Britain, the terminology used generally described them as 'aliens', which did not identify any particular ethnic group. Leading restrictionists would often maintain that they were not anti-Semitic.[59] There were also references made by them to Jewish bodies such as the Jewish Board of Guardians which had increasingly discouraged Eastern European Jews from settling in Britain.[60] It was the perceived threat to English culture which was overtly expressed. Forde Ridley had lamented the desecration of the Christian sabbath. The aliens, he said, had made Sunday a business day and compelled others (presumably by this he was referring to English Christians) to open their businesses in self-defence.[61]

Balfour's speech in the Commons in July 1905, to which reference has already been made, expanded on this alleged danger:

> it would not be to the advantage of the civilisation of the country that there should be an immense body of persons who, however patriotic, able, and industrious, however much they threw themselves into the national life, still by their own action, remained a people apart and not merely held a religion differing from the vast majority of their fellow country-men, but only inter-married among themselves.

Balfour stated that although the state of things had not yet become a 'national danger', some 'undoubtable evils' had fallen upon parts of the country from what was primarily Jewish alien immigration. He feared that there would be, in the future, a danger that Britain could therefore follow the 'evil example set by some other countries' of political anti-Semitism.[62] The Jews were, according to the prime minister's contention, responsible for the creation of political anti-Semitism and more particularly of undermining British society by virtue of their maintenance of ethnic identification.

THE 1906 GENERAL ELECTION

The issue of tariff reform had split the Unionists in Parliament, leading free-fooders to vote with the Liberals.[63] It had, in the words of one historian, 'split the Conservative Party from top to bottom, creating a disastrous appearance of vacillation and dissension'.

The grass roots campaign of the tariff reformers had led by January 1906 to their control of some 300 Unionist constituency associations.[64] At the beginning of December 1905 Balfour and his ministers resigned. Henry Campbell-Bannerman formed a Liberal administration and called an election which took place between 12 January and 9 February 1906.

Although it was the general issue of free trade versus tariff reform which dominated the election, about 100 Unionist candidates referred in their election addresses to the Aliens Act, defending the Unionist government's action in enacting this piece of legislation. This was a greater number than those candidates who made reference to the issues of constitutional reforms, housing, workers' compensation, reform of trade-union law, or the successful war in South Africa.[65]

The aliens issue was an important matter in the campaign in East London. Forde Ridley received loud applause at his adoption meeting when he announced that 24 aliens had already been refused admission. Bhownaggree, at a public meeting in his constituency, received cheers from his audience when he spoke about the Aliens Act.[66] At one of Lawson's public meetings he said that the Jewish community had suffered a great injustice 'because it was made responsible for the mis-doings of a certain number of unworthy members, most of them the scum of foreign populations'.[67] David Hope Kyd, the Unionist candidate in Whitechapel, at his adoption meeting stated that he wished to see the Aliens Act strengthened while at the same time advocating adoption of a 'territorial' solution for the Jews by diverting aliens to Africa.[68]

The election was to change dramatically the balance of political representation at Westminster. At the general election of 1900 the Unionists returned 402 members to face an opposition comprising 184 Liberals, two Labour members, and 82 Irish Nationalists. By the date of the dissolution the Unionists had been reduced in number to 369 whilst the Liberal benches now contained 215 members, with four Labour members and the 82 Irish Nationalists completing the opposition. The outcome of the 1906 general election resulted in the return of 400 Liberals, 30 Labour members and 83 Irish Nationalists, to be opposed by only 157 Unionists. Whilst the election was a disaster for the Unionist Party it was a partial victory for the tariff reformers whom contemporaries considered numbered 109 of the parliamentary party, with only 16 free traders and the balance Balfourites.[69]

Both the leading proponents of restriction who fought for the

Aliens Act, Vincent in Sheffield Central and Evans-Gordon in Stepney, were returned to Parliament. However, with the exception of Claude Hay in Hoxton, the other East London Unionist proponents of restriction, or the candidates who fought in their place, were defeated. Yet the Unionists performed relatively well in East London despite the loss of seats. It is considered here that the Unionists, even where they fielded candidates of Jewish origin, were unlikely to have received much of the Jewish vote. Furthermore, the Unionists were also likely to have suffered from the consolidation of Irish support for the Liberals.[70] In all of the East End constituencies of Tower Hamlets, Bethnal Green and Shoreditch the number of registered electors had diminished from the levels in 1900. Yet, with the exception of Stepney and Poplar (seats which did not change hands), the number of electors voting actually increased in real terms.

Claude Hay in Hoxton and the Hon. R. Guinness in Haggerston were the only East End Unionists to increase their actual vote in the 1906 election from those achieved in 1900.[71] The largest falls in the percentage of the Unionist vote between elections occurred in the two Bethnal Green constituencies, which were both captured by the Liberals. The smallest fall was in the Liberal seat of Whitechapel. The national average percentage vote for each opposed Unionist candidate was 44.1 per cent. In the 13 London working-class constituencies[72] outside of the East End only three had a vote equal to or greater than the national average. However, of the 11 East End working-class constituencies, six Unionist candidates achieved a percentage vote higher than the average. Therefore, over half the East End constituencies, compared with less than a quarter of the other London working-class constituencies, outperformed the average vote. In the seat at Mile End, which he had narrowly retained for the Unionists at the by-election in January 1905, Lawson actually increased his vote by 31 (1.5 per cent). However, Straus was able to increase his vote by 235 (11.5 per cent), thus overturning a Unionist majority of 78 and establishing a Liberal majority of 126.

It is the view of the author that whilst tariff reform was probably the major factor contributing to the Unionist defeat in 1906, anti-alienism resulted in the retention of some measure of working-class support for the Unionists. It could, therefore, be argued that the restriction of alien Jewish immigration had popular support and electoral advantage. The Unionists returned to Parliament in 1906 would increasingly display a more strident approach to party politics and continued antagonism towards Jewish immigration.

The Unionists did not have the opportunity of administering the Aliens Act 1905 as it came into force on 1 January 1906. Herbert Gladstone, the Liberal home secretary, was to operate the Act more leniently than the Unionist anti-alienists wished. The Act, for example, allowed him to designate a ship carrying 20 aliens, as opposed to only 12, to be subject to inspection. Furthermore, the aftermath of the 1905 Russian Revolution resulted in the home secretary stipulating that immigration officers, when considering claims by immigrants that they had been subject to religious or political persecution, should give them the benefit of the doubt.[73]

Evans-Gordon complained on more than one occasion in the House in March 1906 that the Aliens Act was being administered too leniently by the Liberals which, he considered, 'amounted, in fact, to a repeal of the main provisions of an Act of Parliament'.[74] Vincent, like Evans-Gordon, demanded stricter implementation of the Act and in November Vincent accused the Board of Deputies of British Jews of trying to get the government to weaken still further the administration of the Act.[75]

The Unionist agitation was not restricted to the actions of Evans-Gordon and Vincent in the House. Unionist Party activists were also concerned at what was seen as the Liberal failure to operate the Act properly. On 10 July 1906 Unionist representatives from 50 metropolitan parliamentary divisions waited upon their Party's chief whip, Sir Alexander Acland-Hood, to protest against the administration of the Act.[76] The number of constituencies that these delegates represented illustrates the widespread level of support from within the rank and file of the Unionist Party for anti-Jewish restriction. Yet the Unionists prevented another restrictionist Bill from becoming law. James O'Grady, the Labour member for Leeds East, had introduced a Bill in the Commons that would have further restricted immigration during a trade dispute. Although the measure had passed the Commons without a division it was rejected in the House of Lords in May.[77] One possible reason for the rejection of this measure by the Lords would have been a reluctance by Unionists to allow their opponents to enact restrictionist legislation which might have led to further eroding of their own support in working-class constituencies.

The previous March, Walter Rothschild[78] had attacked both the Liberal administration and the Aliens Act by reporting to a public meeting in Chesham that aliens who had been refused entry had been shot on their return to Russia.[79] The worsening conditions of Jews in Russia resulted in a pogrom in Bialystok between 1 and 3 June 1906, which claimed 70 Jewish dead and 90 gravely injured.

In the debate on the massacres in the House of Commons it was Evans-Gordon who asked whether the Government would break off diplomatic relations with Russia.[80] He had also written to *The Times* deploring the massacres. However, he had not changed his views on immigration but advocated that the resultant migrants be guided 'into the right channels' and urged support for the Jewish Territorial Organisation which was seeking a Jewish homeland.[81] Support for a territorial solution for the Jews, be it in Palestine or elsewhere, was to find favour with many Unionists who opposed Jewish immigration into Britain.[82] Zionists would exploit this view, particularly during the First World War in their campaign for the Jewish national home; this is examined in Chapter 3.

BY-ELECTIONS IN EAST LONDON

The Unionists were to continue to criticise the Liberal government's administration of the Act. However, Evans-Gordon relinquished his seat in the Commons in May 1907.[83] When he resigned owing to ill health the prominent tariff reformer, F. Leverton Harris, who was a member of the Tariff Reform Commission, was adopted as the Unionist candidate. The issue of anti-alienism was a major element of the Unionist by-election campaign. At his adoption meeting Harris spoke of the 'great danger and injustice of the great alien influx' and that he would follow his predecessor to 'press the alien question in the same manner'. These remarks produced loud cheers from his audience. In his advertisements in the local press Harris proclaimed he was in favour of tariff reform, colonial preference, a strong navy and army, plenty of work for British working men and 'no undesirable aliens'.[84]

Harris's campaign tactics were successful and he held the seat, increasing the Unionist percentage of the vote from 57.3 per cent (in January 1906) to 63.0 per cent and improved their majority from 637 to 949. In 1907, there were 14 contested by-elections. The Unionists won six, including one gain at Brigg in Lincolnshire.[85] Only one other Unionist-held seat, the Kirkdale division of Liverpool, could be described as urban working class. In this latter seat the Unionist majority over Labour in September 1907 increased by only 78 votes which produced a Unionist share of the vote of 54.6 per cent compared with 54.2 per cent in 1906. The Stepney campaign can therefore be seen as another successful utilisation of restrictionism to win votes for Unionism.

There was a further by-election in the East End of London the following year as a result of the death of Sir William Cremer, the

Liberal member for Haggerston. The Hon. Rupert Guinness again fought the seat in the Unionist interest against both Liberal and Socialist opponents. In his election address Guinness gave a prominent place to tariff reform and was 'anxious to give earnest consideration to all questions which affect the comfort and well being of our people at home such as ... the suppression of sweating'. At an election meeting held on 28 July Guinness abandoned coded references to aliens by stating that he believed that local industry, which was primarily the manufacture of furniture, was injured not only by free importation of foreign goods but also by the competition of aliens who 'worked cheaply in the division'. He continued that 'the late Government did much to stop the importation of the alien, and tariff reform was the remedy for the importation of the foreign-made goods'.[86]

Guinness was returned with a majority over the Liberal candidate of 1,143 and a majority over the combined Liberal and Socialist vote of 157. The Unionists took 51.4 per cent of the votes cast compared with 46.1 per cent in 1906. In 1908 there were 19 contested by-elections, of which the Unionists won 11, seven of these being gains. Four of these seats were urban. Manchester North West[87] and Newcastle-upon-Tyne were mixed middle- and working-class constituencies. However, like Haggerston, Camberwell Peckham was another working-class constituency. The Unionists increased their share of the vote in March 1908 to 60.1 per cent compared with 37.6 per cent in 1906. This result was better than the victory at Haggerston four months later. However, when compared with the general election of 1900, the Haggerston result produced double the increase in the percentage share of the vote of that achieved in Peckham. Thus, the Unionists' continued use of anti-alienism in the East End appeared to have electoral advantage.

Unionist demands for increased restriction continued, although the emphasis shifted towards encouraging new legislation to deal with particular groups of aliens. Claude Hay, who sat for the Shoreditch constituency of Hoxton, proposed in February 1909 an amendment to the Royal Address for the introduction of measures to expel alien anarchists.[88]

However, anti-alienism was not confined to Unionist MPs representing working-class constituencies. Arthur Fell represented Great Yarmouth in the Conservative interest and, like most of his colleagues, was a tariff reformer. He had stated in April 1907 that employment in the East End of London, particularly among cabinet-makers, was only given to aliens. He called for the introduction of measures 'to prevent this interference with the rights of English labour to work in England'.[89] Sir Frederick Banbury, who represented the City of London, accused the Liberals in March 1908 of administering the Aliens Act in such a way 'as to change it entirely from what Parliament intended it to be'.[90]

The Liberals were not, in fact, ignoring or circumventing the Act as some Unionists maintained, nor did the Liberals attempt to repeal the Act despite a request to this effect in April 1907 from Major John Seely, a former Unionist free trader, who had crossed the floor of the House in 1904.[91] Indeed, it has been argued that the defeat of Churchill at the by-election in Manchester North West in April 1908 was caused, at least in part, by Jewish voters being disgruntled with the Liberal government's administration of the Aliens Act.[92] In June 1909, Akers-Douglas opined that the Act had 'to a great measure succeeded'.[93] The number of aliens admitted as religious or political refugees fell from the figure of 505 in 1906 to 43 the following year, and declined to a figure of 5 in 1910.[94] The overall number of Jewish immigrants who settled in Britain between 1906 and 1914 was probably between 4,000 or 5,000 per annum, which was about two-thirds of the annual average for the period 1891–1904 and half that of the peak year of 1905.[95]

THE GENERAL ELECTIONS OF 1910

It is possible that Liberal acquiescence to the principle and implementation of the Aliens Act was the reason why anti-alienism was not an election issue in either of the general elections which were held in 1910. The more general tariff reform slogan of 'British work for British hands' was used by Unionists in election notices in both elections and no doubt conveyed to some electors the spirit of anti-alienism.[96] These elections did not, however, result in any net gains for the Unionists in the East End. Nationally, the Unionists increased their parliamentary representation from 168 members on dissolution in December 1909 to 273 after the January general election. In the East End the Unionists regained Mile End and Bow but lost the two Shoreditch constituencies of Haggerston and Hoxton. Bow had been won owing to the intervention of George Lansbury as the Labour candidate, thus splitting the progressive vote. In the constituencies of the East End, only in Mile End, Stepney and Hoxton did the Unionist percentage of the vote exceed the national average. However, in eight other London working-class constituencies this national average was exceeded.[97]

In December 1910 the position of the Unionists in the East End deteriorated further with the loss of Stepney to the Liberals and

Bow to Labour. Nationally, the Unionists lost only one seat overall, having 272 members returned. The Hon. Harry Lawson in Mile End was now the sole Unionist MP in the East End of London but in 1900 the Unionists had been returned for eight of the 11 constituencies. It is possible that the absence of anti-alienism as part of the election policies of East End Unionist candidates may have contributed to their electoral failure.

PROPOSED LEGISLATION

Even if the electoral campaigns in 1910 had not focused on the alien issue, Unionist restrictionists were returned for constituencies which were not directly affected by the presence of large numbers of Jewish aliens. In February 1911 Edward Goulding, the Unionist member for Worcester and a 'whole-hogger' tariff reformer, introduced an amending Bill to the Aliens Act.[98] The proposals would have required all aliens to register with the police, public health officials were to report aliens to the police for overcrowding and the home secretary was to be given the right to expel any alien convicted of a crime, even if no court had made a recommendation to this effect. Furthermore no alien was to be allowed to own unlicensed pistols and justices of the peace could issue search warrants if the police suspected an alien of possessing a weapon. The Bill was supported by F. E. Smith, who as Lord Birkenhead would become Lord Chancellor, A. S. T. Griffith-Boscawen, who was to sit in the Coalition and Conservative Cabinets from 1921, and Viscount Wolmer, a junior minister from 1922 and secretary of state for economic warfare in 1942.

During his speech during the debate on the second reading of his Bill, Goulding stated that he had a profound respect for the Jewish race whom he considered had contributed very largely to the prosperity and wealth of the country. He went on to say that those proposing to stop the growth of 'undesirable alien immigration' were not only doing 'a great work to prevent the rise of anti-Semitic agitation here' but simultaneously were securing the protection of those of the Jewish community 'who live here in our midst at the present moment'. This echoed the remarks made by Balfour in 1905 in the debate on the Aliens Act. The Jews were a people apart who would bring anti-Semitism upon themselves.[99] The second reading of the Bill was passed with 118 votes in favour to 84 against.

Winston Churchill, the home secretary, introduced a measure of his own, the Aliens (Prevention of Crime) Bill.[100] This proposal sought to prevent foreign criminal activity by creating penalties for carrying unlicensed pistols. It also proposed sureties for aliens with criminal records who were admitted to Britain. Furthermore, it included procedures for the home secretary to question judges who did not decide to expel convicted aliens whom they sentenced.

Both measures were undoubtedly motivated in part by the siege of Sidney Street in Stepney the previous January in which anarchist gunmen fought armed police and troops under the personal supervision of Churchill. However, both Bills were to fall in the grand committee, but their introduction indicated the continuing desire by many to increase the restrictions beyond those which had been imposed by the Aliens Act of 1905.[101]

THE FIRST WORLD WAR

Those who wished to see further legislation enacted were to obtain their desire in August 1914 when the Aliens Restriction Bill passed through all its stages in Parliament in a day. The home secretary, Reginald McKenna, in introducing the Bill, said that one of its main objects was to remove or restrict the movements of 'undesirable aliens, especially with a view to the removal or detention of spies'.[102] The Act empowered the government to restrict or prevent aliens from landing in or leaving Britain. It allowed the deportation, registration, detention and arrest of aliens. Prohibited areas could be designated and travel restricted. An order in council could further be made for 'any other matters which may appear necessary or expedient with a view to the safety of the realm'.[103] The Act was passed as an emergency war measure when hysteria regarding spies had already come to the fore. The invasion literature of two decades received its reward by the passage of this legislation.

The Unionists became increasingly dissatisfied with the Liberal government's administration of the Act, particularly in respect of the internment of enemy aliens.[104] From August 1914 until May 1915 the government had adopted a selective internment policy but following the sinking of the *Lusitania* on 7 May 1915, Asquith announced the intention to intern all male enemy aliens. William Joynson-Hicks, who had, in March 1915,[105] already urged that the control of aliens should be placed in the hands of a minister responsible to Parliament, stated that he considered that 'enemy aliens would only be allowed out [of detention] in exceptional circumstances'.[106] Joynson-Hicks was to move an amendment to reduce the supply vote in June 1916 as a further protest against what he saw as the reluctance of the home secretary, Herbert Samuel, to intern greater numbers of enemy aliens.[107] In early 1916 the Unionist backbenchers established a war committee whose principal figures were Sir Frederick Banbury, Ronald McNeill and Sir Edward Carson. By March 1916 it numbered about 150 Unionist MPs. This body was out of sympathy with the support by the Party leadership of Asquith's premiership and wished to see the war pursued more vigorously.[108] In October 1916 the War Committee met to consider the status of aliens. It appointed a sub-committee, whose membership included Joynson-Hicks and McNeill, to recommend legislative changes that it considered would eliminate enemy influence in the conduct of the affairs of Britain and in its public service. The sub-committee reported to the Unionist War Committee in January 1917.

The sub-committee considered that naturalisation was too easily obtained. They considered that in order to be a 'natural born' British subject, that person's father should have been, at the time of birth, a British subject. The sub-committee considered that the conditions for naturalisation should be strengthened by requiring: (1) seven years residence; (2) sponsorship by at least four natural born British subjects who would attest to the alien's character; (3) full disclosure of the history and business of the applicant; (4) renouncement of allegiance to the country of previous nationality; (5) public notice of intention to apply for naturalisation; and (6) a delay of at least one year from an application to the grant of citizenship.

In addition, limitations were to be placed upon naturalised subjects who were not to be allowed to become MPs, members of the House of Lords or privy councillors. They were further to be denied civil office where the salary would exceed £160 per annum. Those holding commissions, if 'of hostile origin', were to cease to do so. They were also to be forbidden to acquire property in 'prohibited areas' and were not to be allowed to change their name without a licence from the home secretary, who would also have the power to revoke naturalisation certificates.[109] This was a serious attack on what was primarily the alien Jewish community, many of whom had family members serving in the armed forces. Had legislation followed on these proposals many British subjects might have lost their citizenship. This was a clear attempt to make 'second-class' citizens of naturalised aliens.[110]

No immediate action followed from the proposals of the Unionist war committee. However, legislation was to be enacted the next year when the Nationality Act 1918 amended the British Nationality and Status of Aliens Act 1914, which made it possible for the home secretary to revoke citizenship from former enemy aliens and deport them, and the Aliens Restrictions Act followed in 1919.

The Unionists had been actively advocating military conscription since before the Asquith Coalition. In January 1916, the Military Service Act was passed conscripting unmarried men and childless widowers between the ages of 18 and 41. A second Conscription Act, in April 1916, applied to married men on the same terms as had the first to the unmarried. In April 1918 the Manpower Act raised the age to 50 and extended conscription to the Irish who had hitherto been exempt.[111] Aliens were exempt from conscription and this caused resentment when Russian Jews of military age failed to enlist in the British army or returned to fight in Russia. Samuel, who was the minister responsible from January to December 1916, sought to encourage and then coerce recruitment.[112] The Military Service (Convention with Allies) Act was passed in July 1917 which gave the choice to Russians of military age to either serve in the British Army or return to Russia. The pressure to pass this legislation had come primarily from local politicians in the East End of London. The Municipal Reformers (Unionists) controlled the boroughs of Shoreditch, Stepney and Poplar whilst the Progressives (Liberals) only controlled Bethnal Green. A conference was held in February 1917 by the East End boroughs to consider the position of the alien community. A resolution urged the government to 'remedy the evil' of aliens increasing their commercial strength by taking over businesses that had had to be sacrificed by men called to serve in the forces.[113] The agitation did not end with the passing of the Convention Act. In June 1918 Stepney Borough Council adopted a resolution that called for the internment, repatriation or forced labour of enemy aliens and required that no aliens, including 'friendly' aliens, 'should be permitted to open or acquire the business of our own people, relinquished owing to the national crisis'.[114] This type of pronouncement was seen by many in the Jewish community as being directed against the Jewish population.[115]

The parliamentary opposition to the government's alien policy was conducted mainly by Unionist backbenchers. In an attempt to defuse this criticism, Lloyd George appointed a committee of MPs to investigate the enemy alien question and report to the prime minister. The committee comprised six members, of whom four were Unionists, including Joynson-Hicks who had by now established for himself a leading role in the campaign against aliens. The committee reported on 8 July 1918, recommending the internment of all male enemy aliens aged 18 or over (with only exceptional grounds for exemption), the deportation of alien females, and a review of the naturalisation of enemy aliens.

The following day the executive committee of the National Union of Conservative and Unionist Associations decided to press upon the government the 'necessity for immediate action to deal effectively with the danger to this country arising from the presence of alien enemies in our midst'.[116] Two days later the government conceded to its critics and announced new policies, which included a review of those aliens who had been exempted from internment, a review of naturalisation certificates granted since the outbreak of war, the prohibition from employment in the civil service for anyone who was not either the child of a natural born subject of the United Kingdom or an Allied country, and identity books for all aliens.[117]

Public demonstrations against the failure of the government to intern all enemy aliens were organised by Mrs Norah Dacre Fox of the Women's Freedom League. A meeting held at the Albert Hall at the end of July 1918 was attended by about 8,000 people at which a resolution was unanimously passed in favour of the immediate internment of 'all persons of enemy blood, whether naturalised or not, without distinction of sex or position'. Among the speakers at the meeting were two Unionist MPs, George Harland Bowden and Walter Faber, and one former Unionist MP, Lord Beresford.[118] The Unionist press had depicted Jews and particularly Jewish aliens as being cowards, pacifists, socialists and pro-German.[119] In March 1918 the *Morning Post* stated that 'those who know him know that the Russian Jew will remain what he has ever been since hostilities began, an enemy alien at heart'.[120] In July *The Times*, in its leader column, made what was probably an even more damaging attack on the Jewish community:

> Our alien problem is by no means limited to enemy aliens. Neither the obvious, nor even the camouflaged German is likely, as a rule, to be the most efficient spy, while we suspect that the natural outcry against 'job-stealing' – as expressed for instance, at the very recent meeting of London Mayors – is very largely directed against the great Russian Jew population of the East End. Our own counter-espionage organisation … would probably say that the bulk of their real difficulties have come from this elusive element … In the meantime the public

will do well to remember that their legitimate grievances against alien 'job-stealers' can never be satisfied solely by the internment of Germans and Austrians. This is only part of the problem.[121]

The Unionist Party, particularly through its influential backbench committees and the Conservative press, had expounded hostility during the wartime period not only to 'enemy' aliens but also to those of foreign backgrounds whether 'friendly' aliens or British subjects. The ending of the war in November 1918 was not to see the end of anti-alien agitation but would herald a campaign to strengthen the wartime measures in the post-war period.

3

The Unionists and Zionism, 1900–18

Although there was little open debate about the making of the Balfour Declaration there has been much academic debate since. In 1957 Barbara Tuchman suggested that 'the English Bible was the most important single factor' that led to the issuing of the Declaration.[1] Stein, however, in *The Balfour Declaration*, considered that Balfour's approach to the whole question of British relations with the Zionists 'was coloured by a genuine desire to give the Jews their rightful place in the world'.[2] The conclusion reached by Mayir Verité was that the motivation was essentially one of fulfilling British imperial interests. 'Had there been no Zionists in those days', he wrote, 'the British would have had to invent them.'[3] Isaiah Friedman, writing in *The Question of Palestine* in 1973, offered a similar conclusion, as did Ronald Sanders in his 1984 narrative, *The High Walls of Jerusalem*.

David Vital in *Zionism: The Crucial Phase* also considered that the Balfour Declaration was an act designed primarily to achieve advantages for the British in the short term. He maintained that for the Zionists it represented a promise of great things to come although this 'was incidental to its main and immediate purpose'. The advantages which were expected in the short term proved disappointing as the 'international power of the Jewish race' turned out to have been vastly overrated.[4] In an article entitled 'The Balfour Declaration: A Case of Mistaken Identity', Mark Levene suggested that the Declaration was the product of a perception of world Jewry having extensive influence and power. 'By extension of my argument', he wrote, 'the origins of the Balfour Declaration are to be located less in the wartime policies and strategies of Britain in the Middle East and more in the murky waters of modern anti-Semitism.' He proposed that there was the fear that 'a collective, potentially conspiratorial Jewry knew something which the rest of the world did not know and could manipulate it accordingly for its own ends'.[5]

As previously observed, it is the view of this study that scholars have not been sufficiently focused on the actual decision-makers responsible for the Declaration; those few men were primarily Unionist politicians. It is believed that in order to understand their motivation it is necessary to examine Unionists' attitudes to the Zionist movement from the beginning of the century.

THE UNIONIST CONCEPTION OF THE JEW

In 1903 a book was published entitled *The Alien Immigrant*. Its author was the Unionist Member of Parliament for the East End of London constituency of Stepney. Evans-Gordon had also served on the Royal Commission on Alien Immigration which had been established the previous year. Evans-Gordon, as has been examined in Chapter 2, had become one of the leading exponents of restrictionism since he had been elected to Parliament in 1900. Evans-Gordon's book was almost exclusively concerned with Jewish immigration. He considered that Jewish immigrants were unique in that they were unassimilable. The 'Hebrew' colony 'unlike any other alien colony in the land, forms a solid and permanently distinct block – a race apart, as it were, in an enduring island of extraneous thought and custom'.[6] Furthermore, he articulated the view that if the Jews were allowed a free hand they would 'eventually monopolise all that is worth having in the countries they inhabit'.[7]

Evans-Gordon's book relates his experiences when he visited Russia, Russian Poland and Austrian Poland to examine the condition of eastern European Jewry. Whilst he was not unsympathetic to the suffering the Jews endured, he did not consider that they were especially discriminated against by the Tsarist authorities which, he considered, imposed cruel conditions on Catholic Poles, Finns and others.[8] He considered that the Kishinev pogrom could have been the result of both the revival by the authorities of the 'unpardonable lie' about ritual murder together with the 'usurious practices', which was 'a greater curse to the Hebrew community than to those whom they victimise'.[9]

Whilst he believed that the impoverished conditions of many Jews in Galicia was because of their own inability effectively to organise the economic life of the community, the exodus from Romania was caused by the anti-Semitism of the Romanian government.[10] Indeed, Evans-Gordon considered that the disastrous economic conditions in Romania could have been lessened if the government of that country had availed itself of Jewish financial counsel.

Evans-Gordon wrote that he considered that a large percentage of the Jewish immigrants in Britain were 'useful settlers, industrious, thrifty, and sober'. He considered that the very qualities that keep them distinct were excellent, but 'they are, necessarily, a race apart'. He believed that by pride in their traditions, ideals, the mission of their race, they were 'Jews before all things: their first loyalty is to Israel'. He concluded that the Jews were a nation without a territory and considered that a Jewish nation on Jewish territory could deal with the 'parasitical and the predatory' types of Jews who became prominent 'where-so-ever Jews are congregated in numbers'.[11] He ended this polemic by quoting Israel Zangwill's plea for Jews to solve their own problems. 'That is', concluded Evans-Gordon, 'a most concise statement of my case.'[12]

JOSEPH CHAMBERLAIN AND ZIONISM

One of the proposed solutions to the problems faced by Jewry found expression in Zionism, the desire of the Jews to return to Palestine. In 1897 Theodore Herzl called the first Zionist Congress, which met in Basel and the programme it adopted called for the Zionist movement to secure for the Jewish people a publicly recognised, legally secured home in Palestine.

The desire of the Zionist movement for assistance from the Powers to achieve its aims led to Herzl's contemplation of a settlement, if not actually in Palestine, then geographically close to it, such as in Cyprus or in the British-controlled Egyptian territory on the Ottoman border with Palestine at El Arish in the Sinai. Egypt was administered by the British under the direction not of the Colonial Office but the Foreign Office. Nevertheless, Herzl initially obtained an interview, through the offices of Lord Rothschild, with Chamberlain, then colonial secretary, in October 1902.

Although Chamberlain dismissed the suggestion of a Jewish settlement in Cyprus because of the existing inter-racial mix of Greeks and Turks, he had sympathy for the idea of Zionism. Herzl's diary records that Chamberlain was particularly minded to assist Jewish settlement in a part of the British Empire which had no white population. While denying British anti-Semitism, Chamberlain indicated that intensified Jewish immigration would lead to restrictive legislation and 'that was evidently a hint to me, the gypsy-chieftain, to warn off my hordes'.[13]

Chamberlain agreed to arrange a meeting for Herzl with the foreign secretary, Lord Lansdowne. According to his biographer, Herzl was accorded another friendly reception at the Foreign Office.[14] Herzl wrote to Chamberlain in January 1903 that a preliminary commission of investigation was to be sent to the Sinai Peninsula.[15] However, the El Arish scheme was to fail as the Egyptian government objected to the proposal on political grounds as well as having technical objections such as the difficulty with water supply to the area.

Chamberlain, who had visited Africa in late 1902, suggested to Herzl, when he met him again in April 1903, that he might wish to consider 'Uganda' for a Jewish settlement. The territory to which Chamberlain referred was the uplands of the British East African Protectorate, which became the colony of Kenya. Although rejecting this idea whilst the prospect of El Arish was still alive, Herzl was to take up the suggestion in July 1903. A draft scheme was prepared for the Zionists by the firm of solicitors, Lloyd George, Roberts & Co.,[16] and was submitted to the Foreign Office. Lansdowne noted on the original draft that 'I fear it is throughout an *imperium in imperio*'.[17] As a result of government disquiet with the original form, a modified text was agreed which would provide a wide measure of municipal autonomy under a Jewish 'super mayor'. The response, therefore, which was made to the Zionists in time for the sixth Zionist Congress, although guarded, did contain the assurance that 'Lord Landsdowne will be prepared to entertain favourably proposals for the establishment of a Jewish colony or settlement on conditions which will enable the members to observe their National customs'.[18] The East Africa scheme, however, did not proceed owing to opposition from both the British settlers in Kenya and many of the Zionists in Basel.[19]

The formal rejection of the scheme by the Zionists occurred in July 1905, a year after Herzl's death. However, both the consideration of the El Arish proposal and the 'Uganda' project did show that the Unionist government were at least prepared to consider assisting the Zionists in finding a territorial solution, albeit one which might be partial. In November 1905 Chamberlain wrote to Max Langerman, a South African German Jew who was on friendly terms with the former colonial secretary and a follower of Herzl. Langerman had supported Zangwill's establishment in 1905 of the Jewish Territorial Organisation, commonly known as the ITO, which sought to keep alive the prospect of a territorial solution but which did not exclusively require it to be in Palestine. Chamberlain assured Langerman of his sympathy with the Jewish people and his readiness to give support to any scheme which would offer a hope of relief to their sufferings. He described Herzl's idea as the organisation of a Jewish settlement under the British flag, funded by Jewish bodies, that would 'allow full play for Jewish aspirations without actually creating an *imperium in imperio*', and where under a system of municipal institutions Jewish refugees from tyranny and persecution might develop the resources of a British colony and find a home for themselves.

Chamberlain wrote that this concept appealed to him strongly as being 'the first attempt to solve a problem the existence of which, in its present form, is a disgrace and danger to European civilisation'.[20] Chamberlain did not elaborate on why he considered the treatment of the Jews in eastern Europe to be a danger to European civilisation. It is possible that he feared that the entry of these Jews into western European countries in general, and Britain in particular, would lead to overt anti-Semitism and civil disorder. France had been subject to the Dreyfus Affair from 1894 when a Jewish French Army staff officer was wrongly accused and found guilty of treason. Although freed from prison after five years, a fresh investigation was demanded in 1904, which led in 1906 to Dreyfus's eventual exoneration. The affair had embittered the struggle in France between the supporters and opponents of the republican regime and the affair resonated in France until the Second World War.[21] When he had spoken in support of the Unionist candidate in the Mile End by-election in December 1904, Chamberlain had asked 'how is their salvation to be accomplished without the ruin of our own people at home?'. He stated that he and Herzl had agreed that the best solution to the problem of Jewish aliens was 'to find some country in this vast world of ours where these poor exiles can dwell in safety without interfering with the subsistence of others'.[22]

UNIONIST ATTITUDES

The support expressed in Unionist circles for a territorial solution arose from a number of different reasons which were, however, linked. The Unionists did not wish to permit the continuing of the influx of Jewish immigration into Britain. Whilst a large number of Jews who landed at British ports subsequently sailed to the United States, there remained a large and growing immigrant community which was considered generally by Unionists as an undesirable alien element that would not integrate, would put unreasonable strain upon public finance, and cause social and political unrest.

One of the proposed solutions to this alien immigration was to impose restrictionist legislation which would deny them free entry into Britain, as has been previously examined in Chapter 2. In an attempt to head off such proposals, Herzl gave evidence to the Royal Commission on Alien Immigration in 1902. He did not support the principle of restrictionist legislation but rather proposed the territorial solution as a way in which the problem of Jewish immigration could be solved.

The support of Britain for the establishment of Jewish settlements either in Palestine or elsewhere in undeveloped areas of the globe would, it was argued, absorb an increasing number of those Jews wishing to leave the unfavourable conditions in which they lived in eastern Europe whilst not creating problems of integration in western European (and American) society. The Zionists advocated the thesis that the Jews could not easily assimilate into the Gentile world and indeed their increased presence was itself a cause of anti-Semitism. The removal of Jews to some self-administered territory could be advocated by restrictionists as a legitimate solution which was advocated by Jews themselves (or at least a section of them). Thus, support for a territorial solution found favour with many strident advocates of restrictionism, perhaps most notably Evans-Gordon. He was sympathetic in his cross-examination of Herzl at the Royal Commission hearings, and he was to befriend Chaim Weizmann. Indeed, perhaps ironically, he assisted Weizmann's efforts to move to Britain and obtain British citizenship. Weizmann was to write much later in his autobiography in somewhat glowing terms about the Unionist member for Stepney, whom he considered had been misjudged by Jews. Evans-Gordon had condemned the Tsarist government for its treatment of the Jews and had advocated the suspension of diplomatic relations.[23]

Other Unionist MPs had also expressed their concern at the pogroms in which the Russian authorities had acquiesced or had promoted. The condemnation of Russia may, however, have been motivated more by traditional British antipathy to this Great Power, which was seen throughout most of the Victorian period as the major enemy of the British Empire, rather than by humanitarian concern for Jewish suffering.

The Unionists were particularly concerned with matters relating to the Empire, of which India was seen to be the heart. 'A quarrel with Russia anywhere, about anything, means the invasion of India', Balfour advised Lansdowne in 1901.[24] Throughout the nineteenth century, Britain had viewed the growth of the Tsarist

Empire with concern. The threat, or least the perceived threat, to India came from Russian expansion into Central Asia. Russia was seen as the most likely enemy that Britain would need to face in the first years of the twentieth century. Although the identity of the perceived enemy was to change as the Edwardian decade progressed, particularly after the Entente of 1907, concern for the British Empire remained a prominent theme in Unionist thought.

Support for a Jewish territorial solution could be seen as being of assistance to the British Empire. The establishment of a Jewish colony under the protection of the British flag could assist in the development of existing territory held by Britain. British legitimacy could be strengthened by the growth of such settlements whilst the economic development would increase the viability of the colony itself. Furthermore, depending upon the location of such a Jewish settlement, British protection of the Jews could be utilised in combating territorial claims by rival colonial powers. The rejection of any homeland other than Palestine by the Zionist Congress in Basel in 1905 and the defeat of the Unionists at the 1906 general election, however, effectively precluded any further developments in this matter until the political and geopolitical situation was radically changed by the outbreak of world war in 1914.

Another possible reason for Unionist support for a Jewish homeland was the belief in the alleged power of the Jews in influencing or controlling political decision-making. This opinion was held partially as a result of the number of Jewish financiers who had played some significant roles at various times in European and colonial affairs. The House of Rothschild had financed not only the British war effort against Napoleon but had also assisted Her Majesty's government to acquire the Egyptian interest in the Suez Canal Company, thus securing control of the route to India. Jewish financiers had been seen as playing a leading part in developing Britain's South African interests in establishing a dynamic economy, and had been seen by some as fomenting the South African war.[25] King Edward VII befriended a number of Jewish bankers such as Ernest Cassel and Edgar Spyer and this may have confirmed in the minds of some the power of the Jews in the affairs of state.[26]

The resignation of Balfour and the subsequent general election defeat of the Unionists in 1906 was to lead to the appointment of a number of Jewish Liberal MPs to government positions. Herbert Samuel was immediately appointed the under-secretary of state at the Home Office. One year after H. H. Asquith succeeded Campbell-Bannerman as prime minister, Samuel was elevated to the cabinet. His cousin Edwin Montagu was appointed under-secretary of state for India in February 1910. The following March, Rufus Isaacs was made solicitor-general. Later that year, he was promoted to the post of attorney-general and exceptionally, in June 1912, was given a cabinet seat. The Jewish community, which was already disproportionately represented in Parliament through these appointments, may have appeared to have achieved undue influence in British politics.

UNIONISTS IN THE COALITION GOVERNMENTS AND WARTIME ADMINISTRATION

Until the Lloyd George coalition was formed it had been the Liberal Party which had the dominant role in government policy, but Asquith took into opposition almost all of the leading Liberal politicians who had held senior ministerial rank and also continued to control the Party's finances. Consequently, it was the Unionist Party which supplied the ministers of cabinet rank in the new coalition government. In December 1916 there were some 25 ministers of cabinet rank, of whom 15 were Unionists, three were Labour, and seven were Liberals. Other than the post of prime minister, the only other Liberal ministry of importance was that of munitions, which was held by Addison.

Lloyd George formed a war cabinet to streamline decision-making in the wartime context of government. In December 1916 there were five members. Lloyd George was the sole Liberal, Arthur Henderson initially represented Labour and the other three places were held by Andrew Bonar Law, Earl Curzon and Viscount Milner for the Unionists. In the summer of 1917 the membership was increased to seven with the addition of Jan Smuts from South Africa[27] and Carson, another Unionist.[28] Whilst not formally a member of the war cabinet, Balfour, as foreign secretary attended most of its meetings. The war cabinet met almost daily but many of its functions were hived off in 1917 and 1918. Decision-making was delegated to individual members or small *ad hoc* committees of officials and departmental ministers which assisted them.

The cabinet secretariat was headed by Colonel Sir Maurice Hankey who had been secretary of the pre-war Committee for Imperial Defence. The composition of the secretariat was a confusion of officials, military personnel and politicians. This mixture could, in fact, be combined in its individual members as shown by the appointment as the two assistant secretaries of Colonel Sir Mark Sykes, Unionist member for Hull, and Colonel

Leo Amery, Unionist member for South Birmingham. Another Unionist MP who served in the secretariat under Sykes was Major William Ormsby-Gore, who sat for Denbigh District and also served as Milner's parliamentary private secretary.[29] It was to be the result of these political and politico-administrative changes, brought about by wartime conditions, which would be crucial in the development and execution of British policy in respect of Palestine and Zionism.

HIGH POLITICS

When Ormsby-Gore spoke at the London Opera House meeting to celebrate the issuing of the Balfour Declaration in December 1917 he had said that he rejoiced to see that 'an overwhelming mass of British representative opinion in the House of Commons were now supporting the movement [for a Jewish national home]'.[30] Yet there had been no public debate in relation to the Balfour Declaration in favour of a Jewish national home in Palestine. It was a matter decided behind the closed doors of the Foreign Office and war cabinet. There were no parliamentary debates which considered the principle of support for Zionism[31] and little discussion in the national press.

The discussions and decision-making process had been primarily restricted to fewer than 20 men, including senior civil servants. The principal civil servants were three in number. Ronald Graham, the assistant under-secretary of state at the Foreign Office, who had substantial experience in the Middle East, was the career civil servant primarily involved. In addition, Lord Hardinge, the permanent under-secretary at the Foreign Office, and Sir Maurice Hankey, the secretary of the war cabinet and the Committee for Imperial Defence, played some role, but only of a minor nature.[32] The 14 others who were concerned with the Declaration were all Members of Parliament and ten of these sat in the Unionist interest. Lloyd George and Montagu, the secretary of state for India, were the only Liberals involved. The two other non-Unionists were George Barnes, the Labour Party's representative in the war cabinet, and Smuts, who symbolically represented the imperial dimension in the wartime administration.

The Unionists who were concerned with this matter were the war cabinet members Bonar Law, Carson, Milner and Curzon, together with Balfour, his cousin Lord Robert Cecil, who was under-secretary at the Foreign Office, and Lord Derby, the minister of war. The other Unionist politicians intimately involved were the

MPs Sykes and Amery together with Ormsby-Gore. The decision to issue the Balfour Declaration was, therefore, primarily the result of a debate amongst Unionists.

The personal attitudes of those involved is, therefore, of greater importance than in more widely debated policy decisions. It is thus considered appropriate to examine the attitudes and views of some of the participants in this matter in order to ascertain their motivations in reaching the decision to issue the Balfour Declaration on 2 November 1917.

THE PRO-ZIONISTS

One historian of the Balfour Declaration considered that Lloyd George's role was greater than that of Balfour, as he believed the prime minister to have been even more forward with his Zionist policy than Sykes.[33] This analysis does not appear to match the available evidence nor indeed the expressed comments of Lloyd George. In a letter to Balfour written in August 1918 Lloyd George wrote: 'as to the Jewish policy [Sir Charles] Henry has, I am afraid, misinterpreted the statement I made to him and his fellow anti-Zionists ... I have always been a strong supporter of *your* policy on the question of Zionism'.[34]

Whilst Asquith had noted that Lloyd George was the only other partisan of Samuel's Zionist proposal in March 1915, he considered that Lloyd George did 'not care a damn for the Jews or their past or their future, but thinks it will be an outrage to let the Holy Places pass into the possession or under the protectorate of agnostic, atheistic France'.[35] However, Lord Reading, the former Rufus Isaacs, wrote in February 1915 to Samuel stating that Lloyd George was certainly inclined to be sympathetic as the proposal appealed to the poetic, imaginative, romantic and religious qualities of his mind.[36]

Lloyd George's own account of the origin of the Balfour Declaration, which he described in his *War Memoirs*, was fanciful. In this narrative he suggested to Weizmann, in 1916, that he be recommended for an honour for the services he had rendered to the war effort by his development of acetone. Weizmann said that he wanted nothing for himself but said that he would wish that something be done for his people. 'He then explained his aspirations as to the repatriation of the Jews to the sacred land they had made famous. That was the fount and origin of the famous declaration about the National Home for the Jews in Palestine ... As soon as I became prime minister I talked the whole matter over with Mr Balfour, who was then foreign secretary.'[37]

Balfour had, at the least, acquiesced in Chamberlain's earlier efforts to assist the Jews in finding a territory to establish a Jewish settlement. According to his biographer he was interested enough in Zionism at the end of 1905 to allow his Jewish constituency party chairman, Charles Dreyfus, to organise a meeting with Weizmann. It is possible that he was intrigued by the rejection by the Zionist Congress of the 'Uganda' offer. It is unlikely that Balfour was 'converted' to Zionism by this encounter despite this view being propounded by Weizmann and endorsed by Balfour's biographer.[38] Balfour had just resigned as prime minister when he met Weizmann. Despite his subsequent dramatic defeat at the polls by the Liberals and his ultimate resignation as Party leader in 1911, he was to stage a renaissance politically. His advice was sought by the Liberal administration on matters of defence and with the outbreak of the First World War his opinion was in even greater demand.[39]

In December 1914 Weizmann met Balfour again. Weizmann recorded that Balfour had remembered everything that the two of them had discussed when they had met in Manchester in January 1906. Balfour had expounded to him his views on the Jewish question and said that 'in his opinion the question would remain insoluble until either the Jews here became entirely assimilated or there was a normal Jewish community in Palestine'. Balfour told Weizmann that he had once had a long talk with Cosima Wagner in Bayreuth and 'he shared many of her anti-Semitic ideas'.[40] Indeed, whilst in Germany on other occasions he had expressed anti-Semitic sentiments. Weizmann also reported that Balfour had 'listened for a long time and was very moved – I assure you to *tears* – and he took me by the hand and said that I had illuminated the road followed by a great suffering nation'. Balfour's parting words were, according to Weizmann, 'mind you come again to see me, I am deeply moved and interested, it is not a dream, it is a great cause and I understand it'.[41]

In his introduction to Nahum Sokolow's *History of Zionism* Balfour wrote in September 1918 that 'I have always been greatly interested in the Jewish question that in the early years of this century when anti-Semitism in Europe was at an acute stage I did my best to support a scheme devised by Mr Chamberlain, then Colonial Secretary, for creating a Jewish settlement in East Africa, under the British flag'. He noted, however, that this scheme had a serious defect in that it was not Zionism, but in conversations that he had had with Weizmann in January 1906 he was convinced that history could not be ignored and that 'if a home was to be found for the Jewish people, homeless now for nearly nineteen hundred years, it was vain to seek it anywhere but in Palestine'. He further wrote that 'constant oppression, with occasional outbursts of violent persecution, are apt either to crush their victims, or to develop in them self protecting qualities which do not always assume an attractive shape ... Zionism will mitigate the lot and elevate the status of no negligible fraction of the Jewish race'.

If Zionism succeeded, Balfour continued, it would do 'a great spiritual and material work for the Jews, but not for them alone. For as I read its meaning, it is, among other things, a serious endeavour to mitigate the age-long miseries created for Western civilisation by the presence within its midst of a Body which is too long regarded as alien and even hostile, but which it was equally unable to expel or to absorb. Surely, for this if for no other reason, it should receive our support.'[42]

Blanche Dugdale, who was not only Balfour's niece and biographer but herself an active Zionist, wrote that he 'thought of the Zionists as guardians of a continuity of religious and racial tradition that made the unassimilated Jew a great conservative in world politics, and he felt strongly about the way in which the Jewish contribution to culture and to religion had for the most part been requited by the Christian world'.[43]

It is probable that these are somewhat idealised views of Balfour's attitude which was promoted by those, like Dugdale, who were themselves deeply committed to the Zionist cause. Yet at the Paris peace conference, in July 1919, Colonel Richard Meinertzhagen noted in his diary that Balfour had said to him 'he was an ardent Zionist and that His Majesty's Government was committed to Zionism as our policy in Palestine. His reasons for being a Zionist were complex, but were mainly based on the unsatisfactory position of the Jews in the world ... Balfour went on to say that he himself was not in favour of a British Mandate over Palestine, but that he would not oppose it.'[44] Balfour did not consider that financially Britain's expansion into the Middle East was desirable.[45] He did, however, believe that Zionism could alleviate the continued presence in gentile society of an alien entity that posed a continuing danger to the stability of that society, and it had been Balfour's administration that had enacted the Aliens Act 1905, which restricted Jewish immigrants to Britain.

According to Smuts, it was Milner who worked hardest for the formula of the national home.[46] Samuel, in January 1917, had sent

Milner a copy of his memorandum on the future of Palestine. In his reply Milner wrote that 'it contains suggestions that are new to me. Among the possible alternatives which are reviewed, one which you yourself favour certainly appears to me the most attractive.'[47] Lord Harlech, as Ormsby-Gore had become, recalled that early in their association when he had joined him from Cairo in March 1917 Milner had told him that he was a convinced supporter of Zionism,[48] and Amery described him as a whole hearted sympathiser.[49]

Claude Montefiore reported to his colleagues in the Conjoint Foreign Affairs Committee of the Board of Deputies of British Jews and the Anglo-Jewish Association on 16 May 1917 that 'Milner's own views appear to lie between our formula and the full Zionist scheme. He seems to favour the establishment of a Jewish community in Palestine, or parts of Palestine, under a British protectorate.'[50] Weizmann meanwhile considered that Milner understood 'profoundly that the Jews alone were capable of rebuilding Palestine, and of giving it a place in the modern family of nations'.[51]

Milner, when high commissioner in South Africa, had treated Jews under his administration in a reasonably positive manner. In a letter of July 1902 to the president of the South African Zionist Federation, Milner wrote that 'whatever the conditions of naturalization which may be laid down by law in this Colony [the Transvaal], it is quite certain that they will not contain any discrimination against Jews ... I have no prejudice against Jews as Jews ... Some of the best people I have ever known, some of my closest personal friends are Jews, and Jews intensely devoted to their race and religion.'[52] The following year, at the inauguration of the Jewish Board of Deputies for Transvaal and Natal, he noted that '[t]his great community has its own religion, it has its own race traditions, its own loyalty. There is nothing incompatible in this with the most thorough-going British patriotism.'[53]

However, Milner was not without his prejudices against Jews. In 1899 he had written to Chamberlain of the refugees who had fled from the Transvaal to the coastal towns at the outbreak of the Second Boer War. 'Many of the refugees are not only penniless', he reported, 'but belong to a very undesirable class. They include the loafers and hangers on of society, and those who make a precarious living by mean and in some cases illegal traits – such as the buying of stolen goods and the sale of liquor to natives. A great many of them are the low class Jews known as Peruvians.'[54]

Milner appears to have undertaken the role of mediator or perhaps 'fixer' within the cabinet and sought to allay the doubts and concerns of some of its members about, as Amery put it, 'so novel and quixotic a policy as the official endorsement of Zionism'. Amery recalled that, half an hour before the meeting which took place on 4 October, Milner had looked in from his room in the cabinet offices and told him of the difficulties and showed him alternative drafts which had been suggested, with none of which was he quite satisfied. Milner asked Amery to draft something which would go a reasonable distance in satisfying the objectors, both Jewish and pro-Arab, without impairing the substance of the proposed declaration.[55]

Sykes came from traditional Tory Anglican stock but his mother had converted herself and her son to Catholicism when he was a small boy. He entered Parliament in a by-election in July 1911. He joined an exclusive parliamentary dining club which included among its small membership Lords Robert and Hugh Cecil and Ormsby-Gore. He had become the leading government expert on the Near East and had conducted the negotiations with the French in 1915–16. Sykes had travelled widely in the Near East from childhood, served briefly in the embassy in Constantinople and was thus well placed to take up the role of an expert on the area. He had been sent to the East on a military mission in 1915 by Kitchener. It was, however, only after January 1916, when his negotiations with Picot had been concluded, that he was introduced to Zionism through the medium of the Samuel memorandum.[56] He developed views that supported the aspirations of Armenians, Arabs and Jews, who were to be freed from the yoke of Ottoman rule under the benevolent protection of the Allies in general and the British in particular.

Sykes was introduced to Dr Moses Gaster by Samuel when he wished to increase his knowledge of Zionism.[57] Sykes was to say that the reason that he was interested in the Zionist movement was that he had met Gaster who 'opened my eyes as to what this movement meant'.[58] Some months later, in October 1916, Sykes was introduced to Aaron Aaronsohn, a Palestinian Jew who was active in the Nili spy ring which operated for the benefit of the Allied cause against the Ottoman Turks in Palestine.

It was not until the end of January 1917 that Sykes met with Weizmann and Sokolow for the first time. There followed a meeting when the aims and objectives of the Zionist movement were discussed, which took place at Gaster's home on 7 February 1917. The Zionists were represented by Samuel, Weizmann, Sokolow, Lord Rothschild, James de Rothschild, Joseph Cowen, Harry Sacher and Herbert Bentwich.[59] Sykes attended on the government side alone and had advised that his presence was in a private capacity. Sokolow wrote in his *History of Zionism* that the meeting was a turning point in Zionist history. These discussions yielded a 'favourable result and it was resolved to continue the work'.[60] The following day Weizmann wrote to Vladimir Jabotinsky that he regarded the meeting as 'a historical one ... [I]t is the first time in the history of our movement that we have come so close to the heart of the matter.'[61]

Weizmann considered that Sykes was 'one of our greatest finds' but that he was not very consistent or logical in his thinking, although he was both generous and warm-hearted. 'He had conceived the idea of the liberation of the Jews, the Arabs, and the Armenians, whom he looked upon as the three downtrodden races *par excellence*.'[62] Weizmann also wrote: 'I cannot say enough again on the services rendered us by Sykes. It was he who guided our work into more official channels ... [I]f it had not been for the counsel of men like Sykes and Lord Robert Cecil we, with our inexperience in delicate diplomatic negotiations, would have undoubtedly have committed many dangerous blunders.'[63]

Yet Sykes had not always been well disposed towards Jews. Whilst serving in South Africa during the Boer War, in June 1900, he had written, 'British colonists are liars or Jews'.[64] In another letter in that September, he wrote that the militia would be used 'if there is a dearth of kaffir labour, to dig the mines for the Jews at Johannesburg!'.[65] In May 1901 in another letter that he wrote to his future wife he said: 'if it gives pleasure to some to see sleek, fat Jews and their womenkind talking to one another, I am not one of those'.[66]

Sykes's attitude towards Jews did not appear to have been modified with the passing of the years. He wrote in January 1917 that 'there dwell within this mass [of Russia] six million Jews and such Jews who are outside Russia are not to be seen in the world, repulsive, grasping, griping, fawning, insolent – of course all these faults are the fault of the environment to the [P]ale, the ghetto[;] it is a double tragedy to the Jewish mind oppressed by the undeveloped Russian mind. The Jews of Russia are what the Russians have made them.'[67] There would appear to be in Sykes both a loathing and admiration for Jews. Ormsby-Gore said that Sykes's admiration for practical Zionist effort in Palestine was because it was constructive, and 'was the measure of his real fear and antipathy to the revolutionary energies of anti-Zionist Jews in Constantinople or Russia'.[68]

Amery was converted to the Zionist cause by Sykes. Amery's interests were, at least initially, largely strategical. He was keen on an advance into Palestine and Syria on military grounds, and the idea of consolidating that advance by establishing in Palestine a prosperous community 'bound to Britain by ties of gratitude and interest naturally appealed to me ... but it was not long before I realised what Jewish energy in every field of thought and action might mean for the regeneration of the whole of that Middle Eastern region'.[69] Amery also supported the formation of the Jewish Legion which was advocated by Jabotinsky and Colonel Patterson, who had commanded the Zion Mule Corps at Gallipoli. Amery considered that the effect of raising the Jewish Legion upon Jews in America and elsewhere, who had been largely anti-Entente because of Russia, might be very positive for British interests.[70] Weizmann saw Amery as an important supporter of the Zionist cause who had obtained his enlightened imperialist principles from Milner. 'He was the most open minded of all that group. He realised the importance of a Jewish Palestine in the British imperial scheme of things more than anyone else.' He gave the Zionists 'unstinted encouragement and support' and, in particular, was 'incensed when the leading Jews attacked the scheme openly in 1917'.[71]

THE DECLARATION

The actual sequence of events in respect of the Declaration itself commenced with the invitation to the Zionists to submit a draft declaration. This was sent to Balfour on 18 July by Rothschild, on behalf of the English Zionist Federation. Balfour responded personally, stating that the matter was of the highest importance but feared it might be necessary to refer it to the cabinet. 'I shall not therefore be able to let you have an answer as soon as I should otherwise have wished to do.'[72] The proposed declaration was seen to be moral approval of Zionist aspirations rather than the more detailed programme which had been sent out to Sykes in February. The original drafting of the proposed declaration took place after consultations between the Zionists and Sykes, among others. Ronald Storrs, the Orientalist, worked for a while at Sykes's insistence as an assistant secretary to the war cabinet. 'In the offices and along the passages', he subsequently wrote, 'there were Zionists and rumours of Zionists, and Mark Sykes would burst into my room exultant or despondent according as a draft or an interview with Mr Balfour had been well or badly designed.'[73] Indeed Sykes's approval was seen as vital.[74]

On 23 August Ormsby-Gore wrote to Hankey: 'Lord Milner

would like the proposed "Zionist" declaration brought before the Cabinet as soon as possible', which included a redrafting by Milner that substituted 'establishment' for 'reconstituted', which was considered 'much too strong'.[75] The draft declaration first came before the war cabinet at its meeting on 3 September 1917. In Lloyd George's absence Bonar Law was in the chair; Milner, Curzon and Smuts were also present; Cecil, since Balfour was also absent, together with Derby and Montagu were in attendance. There was no review or discussion of the fundamental reasons for supporting the Zionists. The only reservation was one concerning the need for consultation with the Allies, particularly the United States. Cecil pointed out that this was a question on which the Foreign Office had been very strongly pressed for a long time. 'There was a very strong and enthusiastic organisation, more particularly in the United States, who were zealous in this matter', and Cecil believed that it would be of substantial assistance to the Allies 'to have the earnestness and enthusiasm of these people enlisted on our side. To do nothing was to risk a direct breach with them, and it was necessary to face this situation.' However, the decision taken was to obtain the views of President Wilson.[76]

The only opposition to the policy came from Montagu, who asserted that by supporting and promoting Zionism the British government was betraying Anglo-Jewry. He had written a memorandum entitled 'The Anti-Semitism of the Present Government', in which Montagu maintained that there was no Jewish nation and when the Jews were told that Palestine was their national home, every country would desire to get rid of its Jewish citizens. Furthermore, he considered that Palestine was not a fit place for Jews to live.

On 14 September Montagu wrote that in the cabinet discussion both Cecil and Milner had suggested 'with such force that the views which I held were the views of a minority that I came to believe, and I think the Cabinet must have done so, that the views ... were almost peculiar to myself and a few other eccentric individuals'.[77] Despite this attack on him in cabinet, Montagu circulated another memorandum to the cabinet entitled 'Zionism',[78] together with the letter he had written to Cecil at the Foreign Office.[79] He also wrote privately to the prime minister and lobbied other cabinet ministers.[80] Montagu's paper, in which he had set his views of the Jewish people, their history, character, and aspirations was refuted by a Foreign Office paper entitled 'Note on the Secretary of State for India's Paper on the Anti-Semitism of the Government'.[81] It is, therefore, perhaps indicative of the support for the Zionists by the

Unionists that at the cabinet meeting in September 1917 the only recorded opposition of substance to the Declaration came from a Jewish Liberal member of the government.

However, at the war cabinet meeting on 4 October there was more influential opposition to the proposal which came from Curzon, who 'urged strong objections on practical grounds'. He had visited Palestine in 1883 and said that it was mostly barren and destitute with few large centres of population and that a less 'propitious seat for the future Jewish race could not be imagined'. He also questioned the future of the existing Moslem majority and asked in what occupations the Jews would engage.

Curzon considered that it was a better policy to secure for the Jews already in Palestine equal civil and religious rights than to aim at repatriation on a large scale. He regarded the latter as sentimental idealism, which would never be realised, and that the government should have nothing to do with it. In response it was pointed out that in recent years before the war, Jewish immigration into Palestine had been considerably on the increase and that 'several flourishing Zionist colonies were already in existence'.[82]

Milner submitted an alternative draft which attempted to meet some of the concerns that had been raised by those opposing the proposal which read:

> His Majesty's Government views with favour the establishment in Palestine of a National Home for the Jewish Race, and will use its best endeavours to facilitate the achievement of this object; it being clearly understood that nothing shall be done which may prejudice the civil and religious rights of the existing non-Jewish communities in Palestine, or the rights and political status enjoyed in any other country by such Jews who are fully contented with their existing nationality and citizenship.[83]

However, the war cabinet opined that before coming to a decision it should hear the views of some of the representative Zionists, as well as those who held the opposite opinion. It resolved that Milner's draft declaration should be submitted confidentially to President Wilson, the leaders of the Zionist movement, and to 'representative persons' in Anglo-Jewry opposed to Zionism.[84]

Whilst these views were being obtained Curzon wrote a paper for the consideration of the war cabinet entitled 'The Future of Palestine'. In it Curzon expressed his concern with the meaning of the phrase 'a National Home for the Jewish Race in Palestine' and the nature of the obligations that would be assumed if this object were to be accepted as a principle of British policy. He questioned the likelihood of this policy being successfully realised. He did, however, set out policy objectives that he felt were acceptable, which included the establishment of a European administration and the safeguarding of Jewish and Christian holy places, while guaranteeing the control by a Moslem body of the Mosque of Oman. He stated that equal civil and religious rights should be secured for the Jews (but not to them alone) and he arranged for land purchase and settlement for returning Jews. Curzon wrote that if these objectives could be termed as Zionism then there was no reason why 'we should not all be Zionists and I will gladly give my adhesion to such a policy'. He believed that a pronouncement was demanded as a check or counterblast to the 'scarcely concealed and sinister political designs of the Germans'.[85]

At the cabinet meeting on 31 October, Curzon 'admitted the force of the diplomatic arguments in favour of expressing sympathy and agreed that the bulk of the Jews held Zionist rather than anti-Zionist opinions'. He added that he did not agree with the attitude taken up by Montagu, but did not share the optimistic views held by others regarding the future of Palestine. He feared 'that by the suggested declaration we should be raising false expectations which could never be realized' and attached great importance to the necessity of retaining the Christian and Moslem holy places in Jerusalem and Bethlehem. If this were to be effectively done, he did not see how the Jewish people could have a political capital in Palestine. However, he did recognise that 'some expression of sympathy with Jewish aspirations would be a valuable adjunct to our propaganda', though he thought that 'we should be guarded in the language used in giving expression to such sympathy'.

With the effective capitulation of Curzon, the war cabinet authorised Balfour to take a suitable opportunity of making

> the following declaration of sympathy with Zionist aspirations: His Majesty's Government view with favour the establishment in Palestine of a national home for the Jewish people, and will use their best endeavours to facilitate the achievement of this object, it being clearly understood that nothing shall be done which may prejudice the civil and religious rights of existing non-Jewish communities in Palestine, or the rights and political status enjoyed by Jews in any other country.[86]

THE UNIONIST PRESS

On 24 May the Conjoint Foreign Affairs Committee of the Board of Deputies of British Jews and the Anglo-Jewish Association had issued a statement to *The Times* which publicly opposed Zionism. *The Times* subsequently published letters, which expressed the Zionist viewpoint, from Chief Rabbi Hertz, Rothschild and Weizmann, who had gone to see Henry Wickham Steed at *The Times* after the appearance of the Conjoint letter. Steed was a professed anti-Semite, yet he received Weizmann with the utmost cordiality. 'I found him not only interested in our movement but quite well informed on it', Weizmann recalled. 'He was not only glad to publish the Zionist statements but expressed downright annoyance with the heads of the Conjoint Committee. For a good hour or so we discussed the kind of leader which was likely to make the best appeal to the British public, and when it appeared on the 29th, it caused something like consternation amongst the assimilationists. It was a magnificent presentation of the Zionist case.'[87]

The leading article published on 29 May was entitled 'The Future of the Jews'. The leader supported the contention that Zionism embodied the feelings of Jewry and argued that the non-Jewish world should face Zionist aspirations on their merits. It dismissed the essence of the Conjoint's contention that the Jewish question could be solved merely by removing artificial restrictions upon Jewish activities. It considered that the importance of the Zionist movement, in addition to its territorial aspect 'is that it has fired with a new ideal millions of poverty-stricken Jews cooped up in the ghettos of the Old World and the New. It has tended to make Jews proud of their race and claim recognition, as Jews, in virtue of the eminent services rendered by Jewry to the religious development and civilisation of mankind.' The leader felt that the realisation of Zionist aspirations would, in fact, strengthen the position of those Jews who identified with their countries of residence, and enable them to become more a solely religious community.[88]

There was little further debate in the national press until, on 26 October, *The Times* published a leader entitled 'The Jews and Palestine', which stated that it was no secret that the question of the re-establishment of the Jews in Palestine had been under consideration by the British government, and other Allied governments, for some months. The delay in making a public announcement, it considered, could harm the British and Allied cause and the Germans were attempting to pre-empt British action. *The Times* considered that the only two grounds for not making a declaration were either that the colonisation and development of Palestine by the Jews appeared impractical, or that the Jewish people themselves were opposed to the reconstruction of the national home. But neither of these objections 'stand the test of fact'. The leader concluded that 'further delay on the part of our Government to deal frankly with this important matter would therefore be as inexplicable as its consequences might be dangerous'.[89]

On 9 November, the date on which the details of the Balfour Declaration were made public, the *Pall Mall Gazette* led with an article entitled 'The Promised Land'. The paper gave the Declaration approval but considered that the announcement was 'a little premature'. It considered that there was much merit in the matter and that 'the restoration of Palestine to the Jews will fulfil the centuries old desire of that ancient people. Moreover, it will give them a home for the development of an individual culture, and will not affect other than beneficially the rights which they have won as citizens of countries in which they have made their homes.' It would also provide a refuge for the persecuted and a centre of Jewish life for world Jewry. The leader proposed that the country should become permanently neutralised to prevent its use by unfriendly powers.[90]

No other Unionist paper commented upon the Declaration until after Allenby's successful capture of Jerusalem on 9 December 1917. Then the *Morning Post* carried a leading article dealing with Zionism. The anti-Semitism of certain writers on *The Times* could not compare to the hostility towards the Jews maintained by the *Morning Post*. Its leader argued that the Balfour Declaration was 'a prize for good behaviour, and we shall have to see an end put to the pro-German intrigue now so strong among the German and Russian Jews. We do not desire that the blood of Englishmen should be shed to help people who are taking sides with the enemy.' The paper argued that Palestine could not sustain the current numbers of world Jewry and the land was largely barren and 'as for the Jews, although they are still occasionally agriculturists ... the race as a whole has turned to a more profitable calling'. The *Morning Post* suggested that the poor and oppressed Jews could be sent there to be maintained financially by the wealth of rich Jews. In time 'even a few pioneers ... might, under the protection of the British flag ... create a colony, the nucleus of a Jewish state'. The desire of the Jews to return to

Palestine after 2,000 years was regarded as one of the strangest of phenomena. The paper considered that Palestine would remain a place 'more of pilgrimage than settlement, more of the past than the present, of the dead than the living'.[91]

In contrast to the anti-Semitism of the *Morning Post*, the leader in the *Observer* on 16 December was enthusiastic in joining with 'all that the Jewish race must feel over the rescue of their hallowed shrine and capital'. The capture of Jerusalem, together with the Balfour Declaration, constituted the 'greatest landmark in the history of Israel since the destruction of the Temple'. Zionism would enable Jews to 'perform even greater services than in the past to the progress of mankind'.[92] There was no other comment on the Declaration from the Unionist press. The 'popular' Conservative press was silent. It would, however, enter into the debate when the Palestine Mandate was being considered in the early 1920s.

PARTY ATTITUDES TO THE DECLARATION

While there was some discussion in the press, there were no parliamentary or party debates in respect of the Declaration. It is nevertheless possible partially to gauge its popularity with members of Parliament. The *Zionist Review*, the journal of the English Zionist Federation, invited Privy Councillors, Members of Parliament, editors of periodicals and others to express support for the Declaration. These 'appreciations' appeared as a special supplement to the December 1917 issue of the journal.[93] The *Zionist Review* printed responses from 146 MPs and, with the exception of two Unionists, all were in favour of the Declaration. An analysis of the favourable responses reveal that the 144 MPs comprised 58 Unionists, 63 Liberals, 13 Labour, nine Nationalists, and one Lib/Lab member. Those responding did include some government ministers such as Long and Cecil but excluded others such as Lloyd George and Balfour. Whilst Ormsby-Gore responded, the names of Sykes and Amery were absent; similarly Samuel's name was not included. Thus, any examination of the figures can be, at best, only indicative of the attitudes of the respective parliamentary parties.

In November 1917 the House of Commons comprised 281 Unionists, 260 Liberals, 39 Labour and 90 others. Therefore, approximately 20 per cent of Unionists and 24 per cent of Liberals indicated their support for the Declaration. If these figures were adjusted to include the known Zionist supporters in the Unionist

Party mentioned above, then the percentage of the parliamentary party in the Commons supporting the Declaration would have increased to 22 per cent.[94]

This popular expression of support for the Declaration, particularly by the Unionists, was at a reasonably high level. It is unlikely, however, that many Unionists would have openly opposed a decision of the war cabinet in what was still a critical time in the war, especially as the Bolsheviks had just taken control of Petrograd. Continued Unionist support for Zionism would, in part, be related to events that were taking place in Russia, the genesis of which coincided with the issuing of the Declaration in London in early November 1917.

THE MOTIVATION FOR THE DECLARATION

The existing restrictive legislative provisions, including those enacted at the outbreak of hostilities, and the wartime situation effectively prevented further Jewish immigration into Britain. However, the prospect of renewed mass immigration, particularly in view of the harsh treatment by the Russian authorities of Jews in the war zone, remained an unwelcome possibility to Unionists.

Amery considered that 'an anti-Semitism which is based partly on the fear of being swamped by hordes of undesirable aliens from Russia, etc., and partly on an instinctive suspicion against a community which has so many international ramifications will be much diminished when the hordes in question have got another outlet, and when the motive for internationalism among the Jews is diminished'. He considered that it would be fatal if, 'after the war, the interest of the Jews throughout the world were enlisted on the side of the Germans, as they looked to Berlin as their spiritual home'.[95] Zionism, according to Amery's analysis, would reduce anti-Semitism as the 'hordes' would not look to western Europe as a refuge whilst preventing international Jewry from aligning itself with Britain's enemy and also assisting in the enlargement of Britain's imperial holdings.

Balfour, when writing his introduction to Sokolow's *History of Zionism* ten months after the Declaration, considered that where Jews had been compelled to live among their neighbours as if these were their enemies, they often obtained, with some justification, the reputation of being 'undesirable' citizens. Zionism was for Balfour a potential opportunity to create a refuge for large numbers of those hoping to escape religious and social persecution.[96] The Unionist concern to divert the alien Jewish immigrant resulted in the expression of support for the Declaration by some of those who were, or would become, the most vociferous in advocating the exclusion of aliens from Britain. Joynson-Hicks offered to do 'all in my power to forward the view of the Zionists in order to enable the Jews once more to take possession of their land'.[97] Herbert Nield, Henry Page-Croft and Lord Sydenham, among others, all welcomed the Declaration with sympathetic expressions of support.

The English Zionists advocated British control of Palestine. On 25 April 1917 Weizmann had an interview with Lord Robert Cecil at the Foreign Office at which he set out the case for a British protectorate over Palestine in preference to the other options of condominium or internationalisation. According to Weizmann's account, Cecil mentioned that there would be considerable difficulties in achieving a Jewish Palestine under a British mandate but 'it would strengthen the position very considerably if the Jews of the world would express themselves in favour of a British protectorate'.[98]

At the meeting of the sub-committee of the imperial war cabinet on territorial desiderata on the terms of peace, which took place on 19 April 1917, Curzon said that the French were very jealously attempting to 'peg out claims' to Palestine. It was his opinion that the only safe settlement was that Palestine should be included in a British protectorate. He understood that 'the Zionists in particular would be very much opposed to Palestine being under any other flag or under a condominium'. He also considered that 'the British Government ought to make a very strong effort to secure a clear definition of our position in Palestine'.[99]

The sub-committee reported on 28 April. It concluded that the acquisition by Germany, through control of Turkey, of political and military control of Palestine and Mesopotamia would imperil the communication between the United Kingdom and the East and Australasia through the Suez Canal, and would directly threaten the security of Egypt and India. It was considered of great importance that both Palestine and Mesopotamia should be under British control. It was therefore desirable that the government should secure a modification of the Sykes–Picot agreement with France of May 1916 in order to give Great Britain definite and exclusive control over Palestine, and also take the frontier of the British sphere of control to the River Leuntes and north of the Hauran.[100]

The sub-committee comprised nine members, four of whom were British, with the remainder from the Dominions and Empire.

The British members were Curzon, who was the chairman of the sub-committee, Cecil, the assistant secretary of state at the Foreign Office and acting foreign secretary when Balfour was either ill or absent, Austen Chamberlain, the secretary of state for India, and Long, the colonial secretary. Amery was the secretary of the sub-committee. Thus, the British representation was exclusively Unionist and reflected the Unionist vision of the future of the Middle East.

On 23 August Cecil told Weizmann that he regarded 'the realisation of the Palestine project as of the utmost importance, not only for the Jews but for the English too'.[101] Yet while the Unionists wished to deny control of Palestine to the French or the Russians it was by no means unanimous that Britain should be the protecting power of the Jews there. Balfour, for one, was prepared to accept American control. The imperial consideration was not the overwhelming motivation as has been alleged subsequently.

The position of Russia as an ally had been thrown into question when the Tsarist regime had been overthrown in March 1917. Although the provisional government had expressed its determination to continue as a belligerent there was great uncertainty as to the future effectiveness of such assurances. It would now appear that pro-Allied groups in Russia would need to be encouraged. The pro-Zionists in England maintained that the Russian Zionists and, indeed, the Jewish community in general were an important influence on Russian war policy.

On 31 May, Milner wrote to Lloyd George enclosing a memorandum prepared by Ormsby-Gore. This followed his meeting with a Russian-born Jew named Alshevsky whose purpose had been to urge that British Jews accompany Henderson to Russia in order to counteract pro-German Jews, especially in South Russia. Alshevsky, according to the memorandum, had estimated the Jewish population of Russia as seven million and their power as being enormous owing to the fact that practically all could read and write. Milner wrote: 'I think the enclosed brief note is well worth your *personal* perusal. I have sent a copy to Bob Cecil.'[102]

Ormsby-Gore had written a memorandum in February 1917, whilst on the staff of the Arab Bureau in Cairo, which examined the Zionist movement. In this paper he wrote that 'any suggestion that ... Jewish colonization should be resisted ... would serve to throw the whole weight of International Zionism against us, without bringing any support from those Jews who are anti-Zionist'.[103] The Jews had been accused by British diplomats in

Constantinople prior to the outbreak of the war of being pro-German and of enticing the Sublime Porte to ally itself with Germany.[104] In Washington Britain's ambassador believed that American Jewish bankers were working in the interests of the Central Powers.[105]

Therefore, when the war cabinet met to consider the Declaration on 4 October 1917, it was not altogether surprising to find that Balfour stated that the German government was making great efforts to capture the sympathy of the Zionist movement. 'This movement, though opposed by a number of wealthy Jews in this country', he said 'had behind it the support of a majority of Jews, at all events in Russia and America, and possible in other countries.' He believed that what was at the back of the Zionist movement was

> the intense national consciousness held by certain members of the Jewish race. They regarded themselves as one of the great historic races of the world, whose original home was Palestine, and these Jews had a passionate longing to regain once more this ancient national home. Other Jews had become absorbed into the nations among whom they and their forefathers had dwelt for many generations.[106]

At the war cabinet meeting of 31 October, which finally approved the draft Declaration, Balfour said he believed that everyone had now agreed that, from a purely diplomatic and political point of view, it was desirable 'that some declaration favourable to the aspirations of the Jewish nationalists should now be made'. He considered that the vast majority of Jews in Russia and America, and indeed worldwide, now appeared to be favourable to Zionism. 'If we could make a declaration favourable to such an idea', he believed, 'we shall be able to carry on extremely useful propaganda both in Russia and America'.[107] This view received the assent of his colleagues. However, events which were to take place in Russia, just a short time after the Declaration was made, were to nullify any anticipated advantage the British government had hoped to achieve by this pro-Zionist move.

Conservative Attitudes towards Jews in the Great War and the Russian Civil War

The announcement of the British government's support for the Jewish national home in Palestine was overshadowed by the news from Russia. The provisional government had been overthrown by a Bolshevik *coup d'état*. The overthrow of the Tsarist regime the previous March had been met by the Allies with some apprehension, but the decision of successive provisional government administrations to remain in the war and to continue to fight against the Central Powers had given some reassurance. The Bolshevik coup, however, came at a time when the Allies on the Western Front were under increasing pressure from the German forces facing them and whilst the American troops were only just arriving in France in significant numbers. The Bolsheviks' political platform was peace, bread and land reform. The first of these aims was the one which most immediately threatened the Allied war effort.

The reaction by the Conservative press to the events in Russia was not unnaturally hostile. The withdrawal of Russia from the war was seen as a move to assist the Central Powers rather than a domestic policy to rebuild Russia. Lenin had been transported by the Germans in a sealed train from Switzerland to Russia and thus the link was clearly demonstrable.

The antipathy towards the Tsarist regime by Russian Jews had already been noted in British political and press circles. Russian Jews who were living in Britain had manifestly refused to volunteer to join the war effort to support, as they saw it, an oppressive anti-Semitic regime in Russia. Jews in many parts of the Russian Empire which had been overrun by troops of the Central Powers had assisted in provisioning their purported enemies. Thus it was a relatively easy assumption to make that Lenin and the Bolsheviks were German agents and if they were German agents they had to be Jews. The call by the Bolsheviks for an armistice was met in the leader columns of *The Times* with the assertion that Lenin and several of his associates were in the pay of the Germans and were adventurers of German Jewish blood.[1] The following January the *Morning Post* went further in this vein. According to its leader, a part of Germany's war plan was to engineer a revolution in England, the agents of which were mainly German and Russian Jews who the leadership of the Anglo-Jewish community had failed to stop.[2]

LOYALTY OF THE JEWS

The Conservative press had since the outbreak of the war raised doubts as to the commitment to the war effort and indeed loyalty of sections of the Jewish community. It was perhaps remembered that the *Jewish Chronicle* had, at the end of July 1914, expressed the hope and desire that Britain would not enter the war but its patriotic call to arms the following week was ignored.[3] The view not to enter the war was expressed by many other non-Jews at the time, most notably liberal editors such as C. P. Scott. The Conservative distrust of Liberal commitment to the war was perhaps no less great but very few Liberals, with the prominent exception of Haldane, were accused of being German sympathisers and/or agents. In November 1914 the *Morning Post* published an article alleging that the loyalty of Jews of German origin was to Germany.[4] In 1915 the Crown, at the instigation of Sir George Makgill, a Scottish baronet who questioned the allegiance to Britain of Jews of German origin, brought an action in the courts, requiring Sir Ernest Cassel and Sir Edgar Speyer to show by what authority they claimed to be Privy Councillors since they were not natural-born British subjects.[5]

Sir Alfred Mond, the Jewish Liberal MP for Swansea, was the subject of a number of virulent attacks which led him to take actions for libel against some of his detractors. The Conservative caucus in his constituency even passed a resolution stating that Mond 'was not a fit and proper person to represent any British constituency in the Imperial Parliament'.[6] Jewish Conservatives were not spared either. Arthur Strauss, the Unionist member for Paddington North, was called upon to resign in April 1915 as he was German by birth.[7]

The *Jewish Chronicle* alleged in a leader dealing with the establishment of the first coalition government of the war that 'those who were most prominent in forcing the present crisis ruled out all Jews from the new Cabinet'.[8] It said the story had emanated from a reliable source, although it was to be refuted by Herbert Samuel.[9] According to Mond's biographer, Hector Bolitho, his appointment to the coalition government by Lloyd George was despite 'great prejudices against him'. Lloyd George recalled that 'there was nearly a Conservative revolt. They said Mond was a German Jew.'[10]

In the same issue of the *Jewish Chronicle* 'Mentor' commented on Northcliffe's agitation for coalition and the anti-Semitic stance of *The Times*. Israel Zangwill was to write in 1916 that *The Times* 'attributes to Jews or Jewish influence every enemy manoeuvre'.[11] In July 1917 *The Times* attacked the appointment of Montagu as secretary of state for India. Montagu had already been subject to an assault earlier that month from the *Morning Post* which described him as 'a political financial Jew'. In August the *Jewish Chronicle* was forced to lead with a rebuttal of the 'persistent anti-Jewish campaign which is being waged in an increasing section of the British Press', which specifically included the *Morning Post* and the *Evening Standard*.[12]

The *Daily Mail* had also carried anti-Jewish articles which focused on the East End of London. In November 1916 it revealed the presence of East End 'shirkers' who avoided military service, and in March 1918 it alleged that Jews were fleeing the East End owing to enemy bombing raids. The unwillingness of many Jewish immigrants from the Russian Empire to join the forces which were allied to the oppressive Tsarist regime caused embarrassment to the establishment of the Anglo-Jewish community and to Samuel, who was the home secretary. In the summer months of 1916 parliamentary questions were raised by those wishing to see the deportation of those 'friendly' aliens who did not join the British military.[13] This was perhaps another facet of the debate which had so tortured the Liberal Party when it had to face the increasingly loud calls to enact conscription legislation.[14]

The accusation that Jews were German agents was to persist until the end of the war. In April 1918 a *Morning Post* article, 'The Jews and Eastern Europe', argued that the German solution to the Polish question was a Poland without access to the sea and with 'the Yiddish Jew' acting as the German intermediary for the sale of German goods in Russia and 'the exploitation of Russian national resources by the Germans'.[15] In July the *Morning Post* urged the British government to remove all German-born Jews in government service and advocated the removal of Speyer and Cassel from the Privy Council. The leader continued by reminding its readers that it had recently drawn attention to 'several Jews in

Government offices who were actually carrying on a Press Campaign in favour of German settlement in Poland. These more modest flames should also be weeded out.'[16]

JEWISH BOLSHEVISM

If the *Morning Post* saw the Jews as fulfilling a vital role for the Germans in what was formally Russian Poland, *The Times* had in February 1918 identified the Jews as the key element in the Bolshevik revolutionary government. Its correspondent stated that 'renegade Jews' were to be found on practically every revolutionary committee, be it civil or military and that they 'are largely to blame for the present hopeless state of affairs'. The Jews had introduced an element of bitterness in the revolution and, he continued, the Jews were 'most numerous among the Bolsheviks'.[17] By December the revolution had become 'Trotsky's Evil Regime' and the description of the revolutionary Jew had become reminiscent of an anti-Semitic cartoon. The *Times's* special correspondent in Petrograd described the chief judge of the court as 'an obese Jewess with oiled locks who lolls in her seat'.[18]

In its portrait of Bolshevik leaders, Trotsky was described by *The Times* correspondent as 'a Jew of the Jews'.[19] In its leading article in April 1919 *The Times* stated that most of the Bolshevik leaders were Jews and that nearly 75 per cent of the commissars who had central control were Jewish, whilst the Jewish officials of the Soviets were 'legion'.[20] In November and December 1919 *The Times* published letters from a number of writers, including those using aliases which alleged Jewish responsibility from Bolshevism. Israel Cohen, a journalist and Zionist activist, responded in a letter printed on 12 January 1920, and this led to an ongoing correspondence that month with 'Testis' who had written a rebuttal three days later.

Both *The Times* and the *Morning Post* were to report on what *The Times* described as a Bolshevik 'secret conference' held in London in January 1919. It recorded the refusal of admission by the organisers of several potential delegates stating that one of these was a Jew who was a member of a Jewish Workers' Society.[21] The *Morning Post* indicated that the exclusion reported in *The Times* would have been an exception as it maintained that the language that the gatherings almost universally used was Yiddish. The audience, it reported, was almost entirely composed of 'Semitic types' and went on to record that very few of the participants were British.[22]

The day following these reports the *Morning Post* leader accused Jews in Britain of complicity in the murders and the revolutionary propaganda of Bolshevism. The leading Bolsheviks in Russia were again stated to be Jews who had exercised fiendish cruelty. In Britain Jews had been enfranchised, allowed to live anywhere and 'can sit in Parliament'. Anglo-Jewry's leadership, it maintained, 'have much more than a proportionate share in the honours, dignity and power of Government'.[23] In March 1919 the *Morning Post* leader maintained that Bolshevism in both Russia and Germany was organised and supported by Jews who had 'officiated at these orgies of Bolshevism'.[24]

The following month its leader stated that Britain was fighting Bolshevism in opposition to a very strong group of German-Jewish and Russian-Jewish capitalists who were 'secretly working for the Bolshevik cause'. Bolshevik Jews were at the centre of the Russian revolutionary government and they had 'powerful friends in all the allied countries who are helping them'.[25] When writing of the downfall of the short-lived Bolshevik regime in Hungary, the paper asserted that Bela Kun and almost all of his government were Jews. These included some from Germany which it alleged were German agents whilst others were 'just as obviously agents of Lenin and Trotsky'.[26]

The attitude of the *Morning Post* to the plight of Jews in the newly reformed Polish state was, not uncharacteristically, unsympathetic. It sought to minimise the anti-Semitic actions of the Poles towards their Jewish citizens. In March 1919 it editorialised that there had been no pogrom 'of any consequence' and that those Jews who had been attacked were profiteers.[27] In April it maintained that an unseen hand was stifling the 'infant Poland in its cradle' and that this was being undertaken in the interest of German-Jewish capitalism.[28] It considered that there was a 'plot against Poland' which was being maligned for murdering Jews. It argued that were this to be the case the 'warm-hearted democracies' might be turned against Poland whilst the 'great power of Jews the world over would certainly be mobilised against Poland'.[29] It viewed the appointment of Sir Stuart Samuel, the former Jewish Liberal Member of Parliament for Whitechapel and President of the Board of Deputies of British Jews, to lead a commission to Poland to investigate the position of minorities to be a policy which deliberately insulted the Polish state whilst ingratiating the British government with the 'Jewish vote'. The *Morning Post* issued a warning to the Anglo-Jewish community that it was 'a nation with a foreign policy of their own', which was hostile to the friends of England, and 'that is what, in the end, Englishmen will not stand!'.[30]

The Times was less unsympathetic to the plight of Polish Jewry. It published articles by Cohen who had visited the country on behalf of the Zionist organisation. It argued that anti-Semitism was bad not only for Jews but for the Polish state as well. However, it implied that the Jews' desire for status as a different nationality was possible justification of the Polish belief that Jews were not loyal to the new state.[31] In July 1919 the *Times* correspondent in Poland minimised the extent of persecution suffered by the Jews. In an article entitled 'The Unpopularity of Jews' it was argued that Jews had killed Poles as well as Poles having killed Jews. The hostility to Jews in Poland was compared to the feeling which it was alleged was aroused by the behaviour of 'the low East End Jewish population during the Zeppelin raids'. This antagonism was justified by the allegations that Jews were prominent in the Bolshevik revolution in Russia and the terror which followed. Furthermore, the Jews had assisted the Germans when they had occupied Poland in the war and also the Jews had carried out profiteering in Poland.[32]

Both *The Times* and the *Morning Post* appeared to subscribe to the notion that Jews were responsible for Bolshevism with its alleged links to Germany. Furthermore, the Jews were not only revolutionaries but capitalists who were exploiting gentiles. The *Morning Post* leader in November 1919 perhaps best encapsulated this view of Jewry when it stated 'Bolshevism is a movement led and organised by Jewish revolutionaries, and that these revolutionaries form a secret organisation which is spread over the whole world. They have at their command enormous sums.'[33]

THE PROTOCOLS OF THE ELDERS OF ZION

The canard of a world Jewish conspiracy was to receive prominence when *The Protocols of the Elders of Zion* was published in English in February 1920. This work of vicious anti-Semitism was a reworking of a French political satire which became a tract utilised to stir up hatred of Jews in the Russian Empire by the Black Hundreds and other groups. A Tsarist government secret enquiry revealed the spuriousness of the Protocols. According to Norman Cohn's account in *Warrant for Genocide*, Nicholas II instructed that the *Protocols* be dropped as propaganda as 'one cannot defend a pure cause by dirty methods'.[34] However, with the advent of the Bolshevik revolution and particularly the murder of the Tsar and his family at Ekaterinburg in July 1918, the *Protocols* began their career as a international anti-Semitic tract. The discovery by the Whites of a version of the *Protocols* amongst the personal possessions of the dead Tsarina and the drawing of a swastika in her room led to an interpretation that the Jews were responsible for the deaths of the imperial family. The Whites were to use anti-Semitism and the *Protocols* as propaganda during the civil war.

The English edition of the *Protocols* was entitled *The Jewish Peril*. *The Times* devoted a long article to the book in May 1920.[35] The piece speculated on the authenticity of the *Protocols*. The implication was that the work could well be genuine as the 'uncanny note of prophecy' had already been fulfilled in parts and 'in parts far gone in the way of fulfilment'. The writer asked whether the British, having escaped the control of Germany by 'straining every fibre of our national body', were only to fall into a 'Pax Judaica'. *The Times* printed letters from both sides of the argument and therefore could maintain a neutral position. Indeed it was Philip Graves, at that time a correspondent of *The Times*, who exposed the forgery in August 1921.

Another Conservative journal took up the story; the *Spectator* gave over a substantial part of its edition on 15 May to articles dealing with the issue. The journal considered that the *Protocols* were Jewish in origin but were the 'fantasies of a mad conspirator'. It considered that although it bore little relationship to reality the book could spread panic and chaos.[36] In June the *Spectator* considered the question of whether or not there existed 'on the Continent or even here ultra-revolutionary secret organisations inspired and controlled by the Jews' and concluded that 'their goals continue to arouse a lot of interest, even anxiety'.[37] The following month its assault turned specifically to Anglo-Jewry by attacking Jewish politicians in Britain.[38]

By October, even though it had questioned the importance of the *Protocols*, the journal demanded the establishment of a Royal Commission. It considered that if the findings confirmed a danger from Jews then the granting of citizenship to Jews should be exercised only with the greatest care. The paper considered that 'we must publicly expose these conspirators, tear off their hideous masks, and show the world how ridiculous this social plague is, even though harmful and dangerous'.[39]

The *Morning Post* had no reservations in its attitude towards the *Protocols*. The editor of the paper, H. A. Gwynne, had received a typewritten version in the autumn of 1919. Gwynne sent copies of this document to several people for their opinion. These included

Rudyard Kipling, Leo Maxse, Sir Basil Thomson, who was head of the Special Branch at Scotland Yard, and Lady Bathurst. However, it was not until July 1920 that the *Morning Post* ran a series of 17 articles, with editorial comment, which expounded and supported the view that the 'Jewish Peril' was authentic. In September 1920 these articles were to appear in book form under the title *The Cause of World Unrest*. All the contributors were staff members of the *Morning Post*, save Nesta Webster.[40] The attacks on Jews by the *Morning Post* were to continue; in December it ran both an article and an editorial which maintained the allegation that the Jews ruled Russia.[41]

THE NORTHCLIFFE PRESS

The attitudes, both during the First World War and in the revolutionary climate which followed, adopted towards Jewry by *The Times* and other newspapers owned by Lord Northcliffe may in part be understood by an examination of the views of Northcliffe and his staff. Northcliffe's biographer and nephew Geoffrey Harmsworth wrote that his uncle was susceptible to what he described as the ancient fear of Jewish willpower with its enormous unconcern for other people's ideas.[42] Wickham Steed, the foreign and subsequently the managing editor of *The Times*, noted the result of an editorial meeting of the paper on 31 July 1914 which followed an interview with Lord Rothschild that had taken place with the paper's financial editor at the banker's request. It was alleged that Rothschild had urged *The Times* adopt a policy of British neutrality. Northcliffe, according to this narrative, asked Wickham Steed for his view of the Rothschild demand. The reply was that 'it is a dirty German-Jewish international financial attempt to bully us into advocating neutrality and the proper answer would be a still stiffer leading article tomorrow'. Lord Northcliffe replied: 'I agree with you. Let us go ahead.'[43]

According to Harmsworth, Rothschild and his brother Leopold then went to Printing House Square to see Northcliffe at a meeting arranged by Lloyd George. Again, they advocated neutrality as a result of information they had received regarding Germany's naval and military might. This was seen as an indication of the attitude not only of the Rothschilds but also that of the Liberal government which was far from convinced that intervention in the European war was desirable.[44] The attitude of *The Times* towards a declaration of war was similar to that of the Conservative leadership which urged urgent action by Asquith.[45]

According to another biographer of Northcliffe, the press lord engaged, at least with his staff, in 'Jew baiting'.[46] As has been previously noted he also appeared to have an unrealistic comprehension of the number of Jews in the world. He is reported to have considered that in 1919 there were 1,500,000 Jews in London alone.[47]

Wickham Steed's account of the 'intervention' of Rothschild in *Through Thirty Years* indicated the anti-Jewish attitude that he held.[48] The *Times* correspondent in Russia, Robert Wilton, identified himself with the extreme right wing. In his book, *The Last Days of the Romanovs*, published in 1920, Wilton maintained that the Bolsheviks were simply Jewish agents of the Germans and the revolution was nothing but a Jewish-German invasion of Russia.[49]

The Northcliffe papers' attacks on Jews mirrored the concerns that the Conservative Party held in respect of the conduct of the First World War prior to the second coalition government when the Liberals lost effective control.[50] The more pronounced and in some ways even more insidious attacks on the Jews as the leading force behind the Bolshevik revolution began at the time when the loss of the Russian ally in the East increased the concerns felt that Britain and its remaining Allies were in great danger in losing the war to the Germans. The incompetence and unjust nature of the Tsarist regime could, like the incompetence of many of the British and French generals on the western front, be ignored and the blame for failure placed at the feet of a minority which had many detractors and few friends.

THE *MORNING POST*

The *Morning Post* represented the extreme right of Conservatism and its hostility towards Jews was extreme. It found itself constantly at odds with the coalition administrations, which by the nature of their composition, were not the advocates of Tory policies dear to the hearts of the proprietor and editor of that paper. The owner of the *Morning Post* was Lady Bathurst whose family had acquired the title in the mid-nineteenth century, and she had succeeded to its ownership following the deaths of her father and brother; her editor from 1911 to 1937 was Howell Arthur Gwynne.

Gwynne did not value highly the attributes of aliens. The paper, under his editorial control, had opposed foreigners in general and Jews in particular. His attitude can be illustrated by his comments in a private letter to his proprietor which was written in January 1918. In it he described one of the German air raids on London. 'All the Englishmen were steady and amenable to discipline', he wrote, 'but the Jew and the Belgian and the Russian aliens made one truly ashamed of one's manhood.' He reported that he had pulled out by the scruff of the neck and kicked into the street a Russian Jew who, according to Gwynne, had pushed aside to the wall a girl of 12 or 13 in his anxiety to get to safety. 'This is the only way', he wrote, 'to deal with those people.'[51]

The *Morning Post*'s correspondent in Russia at the time of the revolution was Victor Marsden, who like the *Times* correspondent had lived for many years in Russia. He also had much sympathy with the views of the reactionary element in Russian politics which included anti-Semitism. In fact, Marsden was to produce a new translation of *The Protocols of the Elders of Zion.*[52]

THE *DAILY TELEGRAPH*

The *Daily Telegraph*, the other 'quality' Conservative paper with substantial circulation, did not indulge in similar forays of what may be regarded as questionable racial stereotyping at best or anti-Semitic attack at worst. In view of the major shareholding in the newspaper held by Lord Burnham, otherwise Harry Levy-Lawson, it is perhaps not surprising that a different view prevailed.[53]

INTERVENTION AND SUPPORT FOR THE WHITES

The attitude of Conservative Members of Parliament towards the Jews and revolution was not manifested significantly in the House until after the Coupon election in December 1918. However, in February 1918 Pemberton Billing, an independent Conservative, had said that Trotsky and Lenin were both of Jewish origin; this remark reinforced the impressions reported in the press.

After the Coupon election Lloyd George again returned to the House of Commons as prime minister. The composition of the coalition had changed and the balance of numerical power in the House had moved significantly to the right. At the same time the position of Lloyd George appeared to have been strengthened, having 'won' the war and the election which followed. The dominance of the prime minister over the coalition administration was resented by many Unionists in and out of the Commons. Opposition to the government was to increase in the time following January 1919 and was ultimately to result in the abandonment of the coalition and the Unionist leaders who remained loyal to it in October 1922.

However, one policy of the administration which did find favour in large measure with the Unionist right wing was intervention in Russia. In November 1917 the *Morning Post* had called for direct intervention by Britain to assist in the suppression of the Bolsheviks and their replacement by Russians friendly to the allies.[54] Allied intervention began in the following March when a company of Royal Marines were landed in Murmansk in North Russia and in April when a handful of British and Japanese troops were disembarked from warships in Vladivostok harbour, in the Russian far east.[55] What had begun as actions to secure Allied war materiel and possibly to revive the Eastern Front against the Central Powers were to become an active participation in Russia's civil war. Ultimately troops from Britain, France, United States, Japan, Czechoslovakia, Poland and Serbia were to participate in fighting Bolshevik forces. These allied troops, excluding the Poles, were to number some 100,000 men. Britain had its troops in north Russia, the Transcaucas and Siberia. Support for British intervention came most strongly from a government minister who was still purportedly a Liberal. Churchill, whose journey of return to the ranks of the Conservative Party was not to be completed until 1924, was more vociferous than almost any other politician in advocating the anti-Bolshevik crusade. As minister of war, he was well placed to project these views.

Intervention was manifested not merely by the presence of Allied troops on Russian soil but included naval blockades, supply of materiel and finance to the anti-Bolshevik regimes and armies which emerged on the boundaries of the Russian heartland. These varied in nature and political composition. In north Russia the British commanders Poole and Ironside were to encounter a Social Revolutionary government. Similarly in Siberia the Social Revolutionaries held governments in Ormsk and Irkusk. In the Ukraine, nationalists, monarchists and anarchists struggled against each other and the Bolsheviks. In the Donbas region Cossacks opposed Bolsheviks, Ukrainians and sometimes monarchists. Increasingly as the civil war progressed the democratic forces of opposition to the Bolsheviks were replaced by the extreme right military which held a vision of a renewed Tsarist empire.

Deniken and later Wrangel in the south, Kolchak in Siberia, Iudenich in the north-west and the Cossack Atamans Semenov and Kalmykov became the conduits through which the British opposition to Bolshevism was manifested. Not only were these leaders politically on the monarchist right but they led officers and men who were frequently undisciplined, brutal and corrupt. One leading historian of the Russian civil war has said that all of Denikin's generals encouraged pogroms against the large Jewish population in south Russia and allowed their officers and men to rob and rape freely.[56]

White anti-Semitism particularly manifested itself after a Red victory. Kolchak's supporters, following Bolshevik successes against them in May and June 1919, undertook a pogrom against the comparatively small Jewish population of Ekaterinburg in July that claimed some 2,000 casualties.[57] However, a White victory might also result in a reign of terror against Jews. When the north-western White army captured Pskov in May 1919, General Bulak-Balakhovich threatened the Jews with pogroms unless they paid huge ransoms.[58] It was, however, in the Ukraine that the most sustained and brutal attacks upon the Jews were perpetrated. In the period 1917–21 it has been estimated that in the Ukraine some 2,000 pogroms were experienced.[59] The attacks on the Jews increased significantly when Denikin's forces entered the Ukraine in September 1919. These attacks took place on a hitherto unprecedented scale and have been described as some of the most brutal acts of persecution in the history of the Western world.[60] On a single day at the end of August 1919 the Whites in the Jewish settlement of Kremnchug raped 350 women, including those who were pregnant or had just given birth and even those women who were dying, whilst some four weeks later in Fastov nearly 2,000 Jews were killed and more than 200 buildings destroyed in a pogrom which lasted five days.[61]

REACTION TO WHITE ANTI-SEMITISM

It was a Labour MP, Robert Richardson, the member for Durham-Houghton-le-Spring, who asked the government what action was being taken by Britain to prevent the persecution of Jews by the Kolchak regime.[62] Less than a month later, the Unionist member for Islington East, Lieut. Alfred Raper,[63] enquired as to the number of Orthodox priests killed by the Soviet government in central Russia and 'whether a single instance is known of the said government having dealt in the same way with any Jewish Rabbi'. He further asked what action was being taken to stop the 'pogrom of the Christian population of Central Russia'. He then reeled off a list of names, asking the under-secretary of state for foreign affairs whether they were leading Soviet officials. The list was as follows: 'Messrs Trotsky, whose real name is Bronstein; Zinovieff, real name

Appelbaum; Kamenev, real name Rosenfeldt; Radek, real name Sobelson; Yofee, Steklov, real name Nakhamkes; Sokolnikov, real name Brillant; Posem, Unshlikt, Grinberg, Skripruk and Litvinov, real name Finklestein.' Colonel Josiah Wedgwood, a long time philo-Semite who now sat in the Labour interest for Newcastle-under-Lyme, intervened to enquire if it was Raper's intention to stir up anti-Jewish feelings and provoke pogroms in Russia.

Raper, however, was not to be discouraged. He then asked: 'Is it not a fact that the majority of these men are of Jewish origin, and further that these Jewish criminals, who every decent Jew disowns, constitute the National Government of Central Russia?.' Lt-Col. Walter Guinness then raised the allegation of the relationship between Bolshevik Jews and the Germans by inquiring whether these men did not have strong German connections and stating that 'the efforts they have made to conceal their German origin are very strong evidence of their underground connections with our former enemy'.[64]

Only four days later, Raper was again asking questions in the House to the effect that Jews, who according to his figures represented some 2 per cent of the population, controlled the national government of Russia. Sir Hamar Greenwood, the under-secretary at the Home Office who was answering questions for the government, concurred with the proposition that the Jews were in control of the Soviet regime. Raper suggested that 'measures' were taken to 'enlighten the Country as to the real character of these Bolshevik Jews'. Wedgwood again rose to counter this attack by proposing that Raper be prevented from asking prejudicial questions.[65] In the debate on the Consolidated Fund Bill the following day Raper again alleged that Russia's government consisted mainly of 'a band of discredited international Jews'. He advocated British intervention in order to prevent 'this poison virus from penetrating further into the veins of the world'.[66]

There were no Unionist protests in the House at the treatment of Jews by the Whites. In November 1919 Lt-Col. L'Estrange Malone, the Liberal member for Leyton East, spoke in the debate on the army estimates, calling for the end of what he termed 'absurd copy' in the press concerning the Jewish question in Russia. He not only castigated this 'absurd attack' which was made without real knowledge of the facts, but also highlighted the ideological differences within the Russian Jewish community between communists and Zionists. Indeed he, like a number of other politicians, saw the future of eastern European Jewry as one dominated by either communism or Zionism.[67] Malone was to return to his defence of the Jews in the Supply debate on army estimates in February 1920, when he condemned the aid given to the Whites in view of the atrocities which they had perpetrated, especially against Jews.[68]

J. E. Swan, the Labour member for Durham Barnard Castle, had also raised the issue of a White pogrom in a question to the prime minister in December 1919. It fell to Bonar Law, the Unionist leader, to respond. He acknowledged that the pogrom in Kiev between 18 and 20 October had been carried out by Cossack and Volunteer Army troops. The government, he advised the House, had already instructed the British high commissioner 'to report fully on alleged pogroms in South Russia, and the British Military Mission has already received instructions to do all in its power to prevent such excesses'.[69]

In addition to the atrocities carried out by the White armies, the Poles, who fought the Bolsheviks from April 1919 until October 1920, had no love of their Jewish neighbours and pogroms ensued. As has been previously stated, the government sent out to Poland a commission under Sir Stuart Samuel. Its report, which was published in June 1920, was not entirely sympathetic to the Jews as in part it was written by Capt. Peter Wright, a Foreign Office official with prejudices against the Jews. In July Lt-Col. Sir Frederick Hall, the Unionist member for Camberwell Dulwich, spoke in the House about the report. He implied that there were no grounds that existed to support the allegations of massacres and ill treatment of the Jews and that 'exaggerated reports' to that effect had been circulated from German and Bolshevik sources. He further implied that the Jews had been employed by the Germans to 'promote and support their tyrannical measures when they invaded Poland in concert with Lenin and Trotsky'.[70]

JEWISH–BOLSHEVIK CONSPIRACY VERSUS ZIONISM

The theme of the Jew as a Bolshevik was to play its part in the ongoing debate regarding immigration and the rights of aliens. Whilst the attitude of the Conservative Party towards alien immigration is considered elsewhere, it should be noted here that opponents of immigration would, among other accusations, identify Bolshevism with aliens, and aliens with Jews. As R. A. Carter, the Unionist member for Manchester Withington, put it in the debate on the second reading of the Aliens Restriction Bill in April 1919: '[the alien] should not have the power to vote, because he would be able to turn that to the detriment of the country ...

You never hear of any disturbance, rioting, or anything of that kind without a fair sprinkling of aliens. Bolshevism, of course, is introduced in England almost entirely by aliens.'[71]

This conspiracy theory was to be perpetuated in the minds of some Conservative activists well beyond the period when British troops faced Bolshevik forces in Russia. In their monthly periodical, entitled *The Ilford Monthly*, Conservatives in Ilford, Essex, published a series of articles during 1926 on the alien question. This included assertions that Eamon de Valera was a Jew (so that Sinn Féin was, presumably, a manifestation of the Jewish 'Hidden Hand') and that the Labour Party was mainly controlled by 'the million or more' alien Yiddish-speaking Jews in the country. In that same year Sir Alan Burgoyne, the Conservative MP for Aylesbury, had alleged in the House of Commons that Russian Bolshevism was Jewish.[72]

The danger of Jewish Bolshevism also appeared to be real to many of those who were sympathetic towards Jewry. To them the choice available to Jewry was either Bolshevism or Zionism. This analysis had been argued at the time when the Balfour Declaration was under discussion in 1916 and 1917. In part it had been promoted by the Zionists themselves. They had wanted to create the impression that world Jewry in general and Russian Jewry in particular could offer the Allies important influence in promoting the Allied cause in the war. This could be achieved if the Allies supported Zionism, which would lead to the emergence of the Zionists as the predominant and influential party in Russian Jewish politics. Milner and Amery appeared to be influenced by this in their support of Zionism, as has been examined in Chapter 3.

This analysis was voiced in the House of Commons by L'Estrange Malone. He said that 'I believe that the Zionist movement, when it matures into actuality, will be one of the predominant factors, if not the predominant factor, in changing profoundly, like trade and commerce, the whole internal constitution of the Russian Soviet administration.'[73]

In stark contrast to his attacks on the Unionists' Aliens Bill 15 years earlier, Churchill in the same debate, in November 1919, identified Lenin as a German agent sent to Russia in

> the same way that you might send a phial containing a culture of typhoid or of cholera to be poured into the water supply of a great city ... [H]e gathered together the leading spirits of a formidable sect, the most formidable sect in the world, of

which he was the high priest and chief. With these spirits around him, he set to work with demoniacal ability to tear to pieces every institution on which the Russian State and nation depended.[74]

The allusion to poisoning drinking water was one of the familiar accusations against Jews which had been levied since the Middle Ages. If there was any doubt as to the identity of the 'most formidable sect' this was clarified by the secretary of state for war in a speech that he made in Sunderland on 3 January 1920, when he attacked English socialists who, he said, 'believe in the international Soviet of Russian and Polish Jews'.[75] Churchill wrote to his government colleague H. A. L. Fisher reaffirming the views expressed in that speech and further stated that 'I am afraid the facts established only too clearly the predominance of Jews in the Bolshevik movement'. He added, somewhat menacingly, that 'it is my firm belief that the Jews in this country would be well to admit the facts more openly than they do and to rally to the support of those forces in Russia which give some prospect of setting up a strong and impartial government'.[76]

In February 1920 Churchill wrote an article in the *Illustrated Sunday Herald* entitled 'Zionism versus Bolshevism: A Struggle for the Soul of the Jewish People'. He divided Jews into three categories: those who were loyal citizens of their respective countries; those who wished to build up the Jewish homeland in Palestine; and those 'international Jews' who were seeking to create a 'worldwide communistic state under Jewish domination'. He saw the fundamental struggle as being between Jewish communists and Zionists and that the outcome would be of great importance to the rest of the world.[77]

The world Jewish–Bolshevik conspiracy versus Zionism was the theme of a pro-Zionist article, entitled 'The New Palestine', which appeared in the *Popular View* in May 1921. This journal was distributed with *Home and Politics* which was published by the Women's Unionist Organisation. The anonymous article (by 'An English Visitor' to Palestine) considered Zionism the antidote for Bolshevism.[78] 'It is often argued', stated the author,

that the Jews are organising a world-wide conspiracy – that Trotsky found in the Jews the most ardent supporters of Bolshevism. The latter may be true. Any oppressed and downtrodden section of a nation naturally becomes the centre of intrigue and revolution. But once in Palestine the Bolshevik

Jew starts his new lease of life, he forgets his Bolshevism and becomes a colonist. He waves a red flag one day and starts orange cultivation the day after. It is well known that Trotsky has taken stern measures to repress the Zionist movement. Surely it is plain common sense that the restoration of the Jewish nation to Palestine is the best antidote to Bolshevism, for whereas the latter is international, the former is the most intense expression of national aspirations.[79]

Zionism had become the corollary of Bolshevism in the eyes of some British politicians. Support of Zionism would not necessarily require a suspension of the belief in the world Jewish conspiracy. Two pro-Zionist Unionist ministers, Milner and Robert Cecil, were identified in March 1918 as being the propagandists of the anti-Bolshevik faction in the cabinet.[80] Furthermore, some other politicians, possibly encouraged by Arab anti-Zionist propaganda, identified Zionism with Bolshevism. This tactic would be employed by elements of both the Conservative press and the Conservative right in the arguments surrounding the mandate for Palestine which took place in 1922 and is examined in Chapter 6.

— 5 —

The Conservatives and Jewish Immigration, 1918–29

The general election of December 1918 was perhaps the most exceptional of British twentieth-century parliamentary elections. The electorate had increased, as a result of the Representation of the People Act 1918, to almost 21.4 million, of whom 8.4 million were women; this compared with an electorate of 7.7 million in December 1910. Furthermore, the endorsement of every Coalition candidate by Lloyd George and Bonar Law signified the split in the Liberal Party, and identified supporters of a government that had won a war that appeared to be in danger of being lost only a few months previously.

The Coalition manifesto called on the new electorate to return to government the administration that had achieved victory over the Central Powers and which sought to deal with the consequential results that could 'only be surmounted by the good sense, the patriotism, and the forbearance of our people'. The Coalition considered its 'fundamental object' was to promote the unity and development of the Empire and to achieve conditions in Britain which would 'secure plenty and opportunity to all'.[1] As the campaign progressed, the patriotic appeal by the Coalition became increasingly identified with the pledge to exact punishing reparations from the defeated Central Powers.

The mood of the electorate was to support a government that could be identified as representing their patriotic interests. They returned the Coalition with 478 seats in Parliament. The result was a victory primarily for the Unionist Party who not only had 335 Coalition members returned (compared with 158 Coalition Liberal and 10 Coalition Labour members) but also 23 non-couponed Unionists elected. In the East End of London redistribution had resulted in a reduction of constituencies from 11 to eight. All but Whitechapel and St George's[2] were won by the Coalition, and of these three were taken by the Unionists.[3] There were no specific local issues in respect of aliens which emerged during the short election campaign despite the agitation that had taken place in the area during hostilities. However, practically every member of the Coalition, nationally, told their electorate that they would support the government in removing aliens from the country.[4]

ALIENS RESTRICTION (AMENDMENT) ACT, 1919

In March 1919 Bonar Law received a deputation of Unionist MPs who obtained an undertaking that the government would introduce a new Aliens Restriction Bill before the end of the month.[5] The *Pall Mall Gazette* in mid-March carried both an article and leader column advocating anti-alien restrictions[6] whilst the *Morning Post* led with a highly critical item entitled 'The Jews as a Nation' in which it questioned the loyalty of Jews as citizens.[7] The government introduced the Aliens Restriction Bill in April, with the second reading taking place on 15 April.

There were clear racial and xenophobic comments made by some Unionist members during the debate. Sir Ernest Wild, who sat for the East London seat of West Ham, Upton division, described aliens as 'parasites', maintaining that the industries of tailoring, cabinet-making and boot-making were being subverted by aliens and that at least half of the vice in London was due to them.[8] Lt-Col. W. Greene, the member for Hackney North, maintained that aliens had inferior standards of life, health and decency from those of 'our own people' and R. A. D. Carter, who represented the Withington division of Manchester, considered that former aliens should not be given the right to vote as civil disturbances were caused, at least in part, by them. Col. Charles Burn, the member for Torquay, considered that enemy aliens were the instigators of crime and comprised some of the greatest criminals and that the white slave trade was primarily controlled by Germans.[9]

This xenophobia was repeated in the autumn when the committee stage of the Bill was taken. Wild stated that parts of East London were 'infested' by aliens and that vice and crime were fostered by them. Sir Herbert Nield, who represented the Ealing division of Middlesex and was a member of the executive of the National Union of Unionist Associations, portrayed the criminal alien as adroit and clever and capable of escaping from 'open-handed' English justice. The Independent Noel Pemberton-Billing was even more forthright, calling for the preservation of his country and seeing it 'saved from the Asiatic'. Ormsby-Gore called this naked anti-Semitism and Jew baiting, but nevertheless said that 'there is something to be said for keeping them out'.[10]

Both Wild and Ronald McNeill considered that the Coalition victory in December 1918 was due largely to the pledge that 'we were going to keep our country for our own people'. McNeill said that at popular meetings during the campaign all other issues had paled before that policy commitment. They proposed an amendment to the Bill which would restrict the employment of aliens to no more than a quarter of any work force, with requirements to report to the police placed on employers. The amendment was defeated by 205 votes to 130 votes but almost a third of the Unionists in Parliament had voted for the amendment.[11]

Another Unionist backbench amendment sought to make even more draconian the proposed draft Order in Council which set out the criteria for exclusion. This produced the opinion of its seconder that it was mainly the children of aliens and 'cross breeds' who became the special care and consideration of local authorities.[12] Yet another Unionist bemoaned the inadequacy of the previous Act which did not keep out indigent aliens who were unable to speak English and were unwelcome.[13] This amendment was opposed by a Manchester Unionist, Major-General Hurst, who considered it would adversely affect British trade and considered that it had always been 'the glory of England to open her doors to all comers from every country who may be fit for British citizenship'. This speech evoked the response from Joynson-Hicks that he wished to 'dissociate myself entirely from the hideous and selfish speech to which we have just listened'.[14] Nevertheless, the amendment fell but received 102 votes in favour to 157 against. Ninety-eight Unionists had supported the amendment.[15]

The government were, however, defeated on an amendment the following day. The amendment was concerned with foreign pilotage but its significance was much wider. The Unionist rebels were able to obtain the support of almost all the Labour vote (40 voted with the rebels) as well as 14 Coalition Liberals, three Asquith Liberals and eight others. Neville Chamberlain was one of the Unionists who voted against the government. The Unionist vote against the government amendment was 120. This was almost double the Unionist vote for the government which was only 66. In addition, 45 Coalition Liberals and two Coalition Labour voted for the government with the support of two Asquith Liberals and one Labour member.[16] The Coalition once again was forced to meet with anti-alienist hard-liners. The meeting took place the following day when Lloyd George and other ministers met with nine members including Sir Edward Carson, Joynson-Hicks, Neild and Wild. The conference lasted over three hours and the rebels exacted concessions from the government to make the Bill more severe. As a result, new proposals were introduced to exclude aliens from employment in the Civil Service and to provide for the deportation of all enemy aliens except where a licence of exemption had been obtained.[17]

The Aliens Restriction (Amendment) Act came into force on 23 December 1919. In addition to the provisions agreed at the conference on 24 October it provided for the continuation and general extension of the emergency powers enacted in the Aliens Restriction Act 1914. Any act by an alien calculated or likely to cause sedition or disaffection was punishable by up to 10 years imprisonment. Industrial unrest which was promoted or attempted by aliens could result in imprisonment for three months. No former enemy alien could enter the country for a five-year period, nor acquire land or an interest in key industries until 1921. Any person aiding, abetting or harbouring an alien contravening the Act would also be guilty of an offence and liable to imprisonment of up to one year.[18]

The passing of this Act was, no less than the Aliens Act 1905, a seminal event which illustrated the attitude of the Unionist Party towards the Jewish community. The speeches of many Unionist members in the debates were more xenophobic than those which had been made in 1904 and 1905 when alien immigrants were still settling in Britain in relatively significant numbers; the reaction of Conservatives to events in Russia in 1917 and in other parts of Europe following the end of the Great War, which were examined in the previous chapter, was probably a significant factor in this increased xenophobia. The radical Unionism which had promoted tariff reform now found itself able to exact harsh measures against, primarily, the Jewish community which had made Britain its home since 1880. The general elections of 1910 and 1918 had increased the number of Unionist members in the Commons who supported this more radical approach to conservatism. Although tariff reform as an issue in its own right was dormant within the Conservative and Unionist Party between 1913 and 1923, its impact on the style and philosophy of Conservatism was far from inert.

The landed interest in particular, which symbolised Victorian Conservatism, had its representation in the parliamentary party significantly reduced. In 1914 it still represented 23.3 per cent of Unionist members in the Commons but after the Coupon election it had dropped to 16 per cent and by 1924 it had been reduced to 12.5 per cent. The professional and business interests after the 1918 election represented the occupations of nearly three-quarters of Unionist MPs, and these groups would continue to comprise between 70 per cent and 75 per cent of the parliamentary party throughout the 1920s and 1930s.[19] It is considered here that this change in composition resulted in a Unionist Party which was more radical in its conception of Conservatism and thus more receptive to the imposition of structural, that is, legislative, anti-Semitism, albeit coded in format, than was the high Toryism of late-Victorian Britain. This change was brought about by the growth of tariff reform and survived it.

RESTRICTIONIST RESPONSES OF CONSERVATIVE LOCAL GOVERNMENT

The Unionists in control of local government where aliens lived were able to impose their own restrictions. The London County Council was controlled by the Municipal Reformers from 1907 until 1934. During the First World War they had refused to award contracts to firms controlled by enemy aliens and refused educational scholarships to foreign-born children of enemy alien parentage. This discrimination was further extended in March 1918 to refuse scholarships to any child not born in Britain. In 1920 the LCC refused to employ anyone who was not a natural-born British subject. In 1923 the Council resolved to give priority in housing to British citizens and two years later proposed not to allow any lettings to aliens.[20]

THE CARLTON CLUB VOTE AND THE ELECTIONS OF 1922 AND 1923

In October 1922 the Conservative Party abandoned coalition politics and withdrew from the government. The voting at the Carlton Club on Pretyman's motion can be examined and compared with the vote against the government's amendment during the debate on the Aliens Restriction Bill which was discussed above. Excluding those members who were government ministers in 1919, there were 81 Conservatives supporting the motion to withdraw from the Coalition who had voted on the amendment, and of this number 56 had opposed the government amendment. Thus, almost 70 per cent had already expressed their disapproval of the Coalition by a Commons vote three years earlier. This would appear to indicate the strength of anti-alienism amongst those Conservatives who were to dominate Parliament until they lost their status as the largest party in the House of Commons in 1929.[21]

With the isolation of the 'coalitionist' Unionists who did not serve in the new administration, the success of Bonar Law in the ensuing general election in November 1922 led to the promotion of prominent anti-alienists who joined the government of the 'second-class brains'. Joynson-Hicks became secretary at the Overseas Trade Department and McNeill was appointed under-secretary at the Foreign Office.

The general election of 1922 did not see the issues of either tariff reform or immigration control as part of the Conservative platform. However, Bonar Law did state that the Conservatives would make retrenchment an essential part of their programme, to assist trade within the Empire.[22] This reference was a precursor to the renewal of tariff reform, which had laid dormant since 1913, as a Conservative policy. The future of Palestine was, however, an issue and is discussed in Chapter 6. The election resulted in the return of 345 Conservative MPs. The two wings of the divided Liberal Party had 106 MPs elected, which was less than the 142 Labour members.[23] Only one Conservative was returned for an East End constituency, Sir William Prescott at Mile End. The Conservatives were able to retain seats further east, such as East Ham. It was, in part, from such seats on the periphery of dense Jewish settlement that the Conservative attacks on anti-alienism would be maintained in Parliament.

The general election did, however, have one notable incident of direct anti-Semitic behaviour when the sitting Conservative member for Putney, the Jew Samuel Samuel, was opposed by an independent Conservative candidate, Brigadier-General Prescott Decre. Samuel described the object of the opposition against him by the supporters of Prescott Decre as 'purely anti-Semitic'.[24] Samuel was returned but the opposition to a sitting Conservative by another Conservative was reminiscent of the attacks on Arthur Strauss in 1915.

In February 1923 the Conservative member for East Ham North, Charles Crook, moved a motion in the Commons that it was of 'the utmost importance that a strict control shall be maintained over alien immigration'.[25] The call was only partially economic, for Crook wished to maintain the racial integrity of Britain which, he stated, had been formed from the stock of the Saxons, Normans, Danes and Celts. He was seconded by Lt-Col. Sir Joseph Nall who sat in the Conservative interest for Manchester Hulme. He was concerned particularly to exclude what he called the 'alien revolutionary agitator'. They were supported by the veteran anti-alienist Sir Herbert Nield who considered that Stepney had been 'positively ruined by the incursion of these aliens', where one would find advertisements and public notices printed in Yiddish. William Bridgeman, the home secretary, stated that the government's policy was to 'keep out people whose entrance into this country endangered the employment of British workmen'.[26] The motion was carried by 212 votes to 107. Both Nall and Crook had been elected in the intakes of 1918 and 1922. The ranks of anti-alienists were therefore renewed in the elections of those years and subsequently in 1924, when the number of Conservatives MPs rose to 419. The quality of these members was questioned by a contemporary, describing them as having 'no go – no intelligence – no soul – utterly valueless to arouse enthusiasm or to impart ideas'.[27]

The general election called by Stanley Baldwin in December 1923, following the formal readoption by the Conservatives of tariff reform at the National Union Conference in Plymouth at the end of October 1923, resulted in the reduction of Conservative seats in the Commons from 344 to 258. Although the Conservatives were still the largest party, Liberal support for Labour led to the first Labour government. However, it only survived until October 1924 when, at the general election, the Conservatives were re-turned with the largest number of seats in the Commons they had ever achieved.

THE 1924 GENERAL ELECTION

The election of 1924 was fought by the Conservatives on a number of planks. The Labour Party was attacked for its defence of left-wing causes such as the Campbell case and the Russian Treaty, which Baldwin described as emanating from its 'extremist section'.[28] The other main plank was limited tariff reform, labelled 'safeguarding of industry'.[29] Anti-alienism re-emerged as a Conservative election policy. Baldwin, in the course of a radio broadcast on 16 October, said that he wanted to examine the 'laws and regulations as to the entry of aliens into this country for in these days no alien should be substituted for one of our own people when we have not enough work at home to go round'.[30]

McNeill, speaking in Canterbury later in the month, said that the previous Conservative administration had exercised the 'greatest possible discrimination regarding the character and antecedents of aliens coming to this country' whilst the Labour government had withdrawn this control and allowed any number of aliens to enter Britain. He also said that the Conservatives had proposed an amendment on a housing matter which would have given preference to Englishmen, but the Socialists and Liberals had defeated this proposal so that 'if two persons were competing for a house, and one of them was an Englishman and the other a Polish Jew or Russian Revolutionary, the preference would not be given to the Englishman'.[31] McNeill was reappointed under-secretary of state at the Foreign Office when Baldwin formed his new administration in November.

SIR WILLIAM JOYNSON-HICKS

More significantly for those concerned with aliens was the appointment as home secretary of Joynson-Hicks. The new home secretary addressed the issue of alien immigration at a Primrose League demonstration in Croydon less than two weeks after his appointment. He stated that his administration of the existing legislation 'will be based on one main principle – that the Alien who desires to come to this country must come in for the good of the country, first, last, and at all times'. After receiving cheers from his audience he continued by saying that 'no man shall be admitted to the rights of Great Britain and to the privileges which residents of this country enjoy unless I am satisfied that his coming will be of benefit to this country. The second great principle I will lay down', he stated, 'is that any man or woman alien who, by his or her conduct, disgraces himself or herself, or breaks the laws of this country, shall be at once sent back to his or her country.'[32]

The Times ran a series of articles on 'Alien London' from 27 November. In its leader on the same day *The Times* stated that foreign Jews 'do not form a desirable element in our population and still less a desirable element in our electorate'. These Jews were accused not only of aloofness but also of 'oriental arrogance'. They were alleged to live in inconceivable filth and squalor and were 'naturally alive to the eloquence of the Red Apostle, possibly forming a "nucleus" of serious mischief'.[33] The *Times* leader two weeks later maintained that aliens carried the seeds of disease in their bodies and that they brought with them unclean and insanitary habits of life.[34] Little had changed in the stereotype image which had previously been used by the anti-Semitic right in its description of Jews.

The issue of alien restriction came before the Commons in the debate on the Expiring Law Continuance Bill which included the proposed renewal of the Aliens (Restrictions) Act. John Scurr, the Labour member who, in 1923, had relieved the Conservatives of their remaining parliamentary seat in the East End at Mile End, wished to see a modification of the restrictions imposed on aliens. He was accused by Joynson-Hicks of wanting to allow lunatics, the diseased, paupers and people seeking work to flood England with the 'whole of the alien regiments from every country in the world'. The home secretary went on to say that the aliens who previously had been admitted to the country had 'flooded our markets and industrial centres from all parts of the world, particularly from Russia'. However, he said he was not proposing to exercise his powers harshly by expelling them en masse. It was only those who committed offences who were to be considered by the home secretary for expulsion. He added that because of the levels of unemployment he would not under any circumstances allow the entry of any alien seeking work.[35]

Joynson-Hicks's policy in respect of alien immigration was set out in a news item in the *Daily Mail* entitled 'Britain First – Home Secretary's Order to Aliens Officers'. The paper quoted a letter from Joynson-Hicks to Col. John Gretton, the Conservative MP for Burton, who had been chairman of both the Unionist Business Committee and the Unionist Reconstruction Committee. In it Joynson-Hicks advised that he had instructed his officials, while administering the provisions of the Order with tact and fairness, 'to exercise at the same time all possible strictness in every case and remember that when any doubt arises the benefit should be given to this country rather than the alien'.[36] Joynson-Hicks demonstrated his concern to ensure his officials implemented his directives by carrying out visits to ports of entry such as Dover, which he inspected in January 1925.[37] A further debate on aliens took place in the Commons during the following month. Among those speaking was the Conservative MP for Worcester, William Green. He was concerned not only to prevent aliens gaining employment in Britain but wished to maintain racial purity. 'I feel', he said, 'that it is absolutely essential to preserve the purity of our race and prevent contamination with the riff-raff ... of Eastern Europe, the stiffs of the Mediterranean and the dead-beats of the world.'[38] Joynson-Hicks, from the government benches, took a less strident approach to the position of aliens already in Britain whilst maintaining his position on further admissions. However, he described the 900 Jewish transmigrants, held in a detention camp in Eastleigh after the United States government had refused them entry owing to quota regulations, as 'the class of people who come from the east of Europe that we do not want, and America does not want them either'.[39]

The Jewish community was extremely concerned with Conservative policies towards aliens, a very large proportion of whom continued to be Jewish. The Board of Deputies of British Jews sent a deputation to see the home secretary in February 1925 which included Samuel Finburgh, the Jewish Conservative member for Salford North. The deputation wished to see the lifting of the restrictionist regulations on those aliens who had resided in Britain for years. Joynson-Hicks gave the Board of Deputies little comfort. He found it necessary on this, and on other occasions, to deny that he was anti-Semitic, but stated he would not admit more aliens. He further advised them that naturalisation was a very high privilege which could be earned by anglicisation, especially if there had been war service.[40]

The leadership of the Jewish community had thus been rebuffed by the government. In its leader column the following week the *Jewish Chronicle* opined that 'the Government represents a party, the large majority of whom are anti-alien in the sense of generally disliking foreigners, and despising anyone who does not happen to have been born in this country with a long English lineage to boot. It contains, too, if not a large, then a noisy and active element, formed of those who have identified themselves with anti-Semitic agitation in this country.'[41]

Joynson-Hicks, despite his protestations, can be considered one of the most important anti-Semites within the Conservative Party.[42] He had come to blows with the Jewish community as early as 1906, when he fought, unsuccessfully, the general election at North-West Manchester against Churchill. Joynson-Hicks's official biographer considered that the campaign meetings were all well mannered and convivial except among the Jewish community, who provided him with his most unruly audience. When he addressed them on the Aliens Act, some members of the audience 'rushed to the front and hurled defiant yells at the speaker. One even invaded the platform.'[43] He fought the seat again in April 1908 when Churchill's ministerial appointment as President of the Board of Trade required that he submit to re-election. Joynson-Hicks again defended the Aliens Act 1905, declaring that he was not going to pander to the Jewish vote on this matter.[44] On this occasion Joynson-Hicks was victorious, but it did not endear to him the Jewish community, whom he now considered his opponents.

He spoke at the dinner of the Maccabeans (a Jewish fraternal society) three weeks after his election. He told his Jewish hosts that he 'could say that they were a delightful people, that the Jews were delightful opponents, that he was very pleased to receive the opposition of the Jewish community, and that, in spite of all, he was their humble and obedient servant. He could say that, but it would not be true in the slightest degree. I have beaten you thoroughly and soundly, and I am no longer your servant.'[45] His subsequent career in politics displayed that his attitude to the Jews had not undergone any significant change since that time.

Joynson-Hicks objected to Jews taking up issues of particularist interest such as naturalisation. He was opposed to organised Jewish pressure groups which were held together by 'racial instincts and by interests which were unimportant in relation to the great political issues of the country whose nationality they had adopted'.[46] If such sectarianism continued it would be going a very long way to creating anti-Semitism.

Joynson-Hicks considered that in the elections of 1906 and 1908 the Jewish community, 'almost to a man', were his 'desperate and unforgiving enemies'. In January 1910 he did not apologise to the Jewish community for his previously expressed views and comments. Despite the substantial increase in Unionist representation in the Commons following the first general election of 1910, Joynson-Hicks lost his seat. He was to fight the December 1910 election at the two-member constituency of Sunderland. He was to lose again, this time, perhaps ironically, with a Jewish Unionist colleague, Samuel Samuel. He re-entered Parliament the following year when he successfully fought the Brentford by-election.

Joynson-Hicks, as home secretary, controlled the naturalisation of resident aliens. In 1924 these numbered some 272,000, of whom 90 per cent had lived in Britain since before the First World War.[47] When he met with the Board of Deputies delegation he outlined his policy on naturalisation. 'If an alien, whether Jew or Gentile, who has lived here for fifteen or twenty years, who has brought up his family as English and learned the language – and especially served during the War – desired to become a citizen of this country, there was no reason why he should not be naturalized and every reason why he should.'[48] Joynson-Hicks was advocating an assimilationist approach, which denied the retention of ethnic identity.

His views were expounded again to the Jewish community in an interview that he granted to the *Jewish Chronicle* in April 1926. 'The chief test which I apply before I decide to grant a naturalization certificate', he said, is whether the applicant has, as far as can be judged, become an Englishman at heart and has completely identified himself with English interests. I will give an example. If two brothers came to this country and one of them settles in a district where only aliens live, continues to speak his native language, marries a woman from his own country, sends his child to a school where only foreign children are kept, keeps his account in a foreign bank, employs only foreign labour, while the other marries an Englishwoman, send his child to an English school, speaks English, employs British labour, keeps his account in a British bank, it is the second brother and not the first who will obtain naturalization.[49]

He reiterated his policy again the following year in the Supply debate in the Commons. He stated that although he was speeding up the processing of naturalisation applications he had not made naturalisation easier. If a man who had lived in Britain 10 or 20 years was not 'in his heart and mind an Englishman ... I do not want him'. He continued by stating that unless

I am satisfied that a man, however long he has lived in this country, has become a real Englishman, desiring to put his roots deep down here and desirous of having his children educated as English boys and girls and, in fact, desirous of making England his home for the rest of his life, and with no thought of returning to a foreign country, wherever it may be, in my view he is not entitled to the proud privilege of being made a British citizen.[50]

It is not clear exactly what Joynson-Hicks considered to be a 'real Englishman', but it is probable that this would not have included Jews who retained attachment to Jewish (particularly Yiddish) culture or professed Zionist sympathies.[51]

Joynson-Hicks was a strident Christian in politics as well as in his private life. His passion extended to conversion work. He was a patron of the Barbican Mission to the Jews which was active in the East End of London. It is argued here that someone who wished to see the conversion of Jews to Christianity would not have any sympathy with their desire to retain their cultural identity. It is probable that, whatever else Joynson-Hicks believed, he would have considered that a 'real Englishman' was a Christian, and possibly a member of the Church of England. Indeed, even if Joynson-Hicks had forgotten to uphold

Englishness, he would have reminded on the occasion when it was believed he was considering the appointment of Lord Reading, the former Rufus Isaacs, as chairman of a commission to enquire into police methods. The home secretary was lambasted by the Party chairman, J. C. C. Davidson, who asked: 'Why are the only qualifications sought for those of the clever Oriental?'.[52]

Joynson-Hicks was attacked in the Commons for his alien and naturalisation policies not only by the Liberal and Labour opposition but also from his own backbench. Finburgh found it necessary publicly to criticise the home secretary in the November of that year. Finburgh considered that it was unjust to victimise people merely because they had not obtained naturalisation prior to 1914. He argued that most had attempted to become British citizens but the Home Office had placed obstructions in their path. Joynson-Hicks challenged Finburgh to produce evidence of any anti-Jewish bias.[53] Whilst Finburgh was not able to make an effective response to this challenge, in fact a memorandum, which had been written in February 1925 by the Home Office's principal assistant secretary, Sir John Pedder, noted that the Conservative government had attempted to increase the period of residence to ten years before an applicant would be considered for naturalisation. The Home Office had already adopted a policy of unofficially requiring residence for a period of 15 years and over for Russian cases, who were mainly Jews, despite the statutory period of only five years.[54]

The Jewish community traditionally had dealt with government in an informal and private manner. The publicity exposing the failure of the Board of Deputies delegation, the *Jewish Chronicle* leader on the nature of the Conservative government, and the backbench attack by Finburgh illustrate the alienation of the Jewish community by the Conservative administration.

Joynson-Hicks attempted to make permanent the statutory provisions for alien restriction by introducing the Alien Restriction (Amendment) Bill. This proposed legislation would obviate the need for the annual renewal of the provisions of the 1919 Act. The measure passed through all its stages in the House of Lords in July 1927 and received its first reading in the Commons that month. However, in November the home secretary had to postpone the measure owing to other government business.[55] He was not able to reintroduce the measure before he lost office with the fall of the Conservative government in 1929.[56]

Conservative antagonism towards aliens was not, however, diminished. Sir Frederick Hall suggested in August 1928 that convicted aliens should be flogged and thereafter deported.[57] In February 1929 the Central Council of the National Union of Conservative and Unionist Associations adopted a motion, by acclaim, that the government impose a direct tax of £10 a head per annum on all aliens employed in a wage-earning capacity.[58] It is, therefore, not inconceivable that, had the Conservatives been returned to office in May 1929, legislation which further diminished the rights of aliens would have been brought forward.

Anti-alien agitation continued to be an issue which concerned the political right. In 1928, Lt-Col. A. H. Lane, who upon Joynson-Hicks's appointment as home secretary, had been a member of a delegation that had urged him to take strident measures against aliens, published *The Alien Menace*, which went into a second edition that year, with the addition of a foreword by Lord Sydenham of Combe, a prominent anti-Semite of the radical right. Lane's polemic, which was subsequently expanded into a third edition in 1932, argued that the 'whole fabric of British life and inspiration is being steadily undermined by the effect of the Alien's presence, his propaganda, and the practices he has brought with him to this country'. According to Sydenham, naturalisation did not change the habits, morals and outlook of the individual who remained an alien. 'His descendants', he wrote, echoing the views expressed in 1905 by Balfour, 'unless and until they have been racially absorbed, continue to be Aliens.'[59]

6

The Conservatives and the Palestine Mandate, 1920–29

Among the more satisfactory items to emerge from the Inter-Allied Conference at San Remo in the spring of 1920 was, according to *The Times*, that Great Britain was to receive the mandate for Palestine, to be considered in terms of the Balfour Declaration which had proposed a national home for the Jews.[1] *The Times* was also enthusiastic when Herbert Samuel was appointed as High Commissioner for Palestine. 'He will carry with him to Palestine the goodwill of all who understand the high importance of stating the Jewish question in its true terms', the *Times* leader wrote, 'enabling Jews, as Jews to stand on a sound footing among the great peoples of the earth.'[2]

This enthusiasm for both the San Remo Conference and Samuel's appointment as High Commissioner was not universally shared in Conservative circles. In the House of Commons debate on the San Remo Conference in April 1920 Earl Winterton, whilst paying lip-service to the Balfour Declaration, stressed the 'rights' of the existing Palestinian inhabitants. The Jews, he observed, represented less than 10 per cent of the whole population, the majority of whom were in the towns 'engaged in the small retail trade, money lending occupations of that kind'.[3]

Winterton had previously questioned the parliamentary secretary for war in respect of the riots that had occurred in Jerusalem. Although the riots were instigated by Palestinian Arabs against Jews, Winterton suggested that the cause was 'six of one and half a dozen of the other'.[4] However, a number of Unionist MPs such as Brigadier-General Richard Colvin, who sat for Epping, Arthur Mills, the Unionist member for North Down, and Lt-Col. Wilfred Ashley, the member for Fylde North Lancashire, raised the issue of protection of the Jews from Arab rioters and/or were concerned with the treatment of Jabotinsky, who had been imprisoned by the military authorities and sentenced to 15 years' imprisonment for organising Jewish self-defence.[5]

Samuel's appointment was questioned by Brigadier-General Herbert Surtees, the Unionist member for Gateshead. He asked in the Commons what actions were to be taken to placate the Arab population in view of the appointment of Samuel, a practising Jew, as High Commissioner. Lt-Col. Henry Page-Croft, the Unionist member for Bournemouth, asked whether the Palestine government was 'in perfectly safe keeping in the hands of Sir Herbert Samuel', whilst Joynson-Hicks expressed concerns regarding payment of Samuel's salary from the Palestine revenue.[6] This was the beginning of Conservative opposition to the Palestine Mandate and to the commitment made in the Balfour Declaration.

The substantial measure of Unionist backbench support for the Declaration, which was evident November and December 1917, can be attributed, at least in part, to the requirement of Party solidarity, particularly in a time of war. By 1920 the necessity for such solidarity was no longer seen by all Conservative MPs as being critical. This was particularly so in relation to such matters as Palestine. Disillusionment with the Lloyd George administration was increasing, particularly among the die-hard element of the Conservative Party. Supporters of the Balfour Declaration were probably aware of this growing discontent as, in April 1920, they formed the Palestine Parliamentary Committee with Lord Robert Cecil as chairman and Ormsby-Gore as secretary. The committee's main object was to support the efforts of the government to give effect to the Balfour Declaration.[7]

The military government which, until the summer of 1920, administered Palestine was not particularly enamoured with the Balfour Declaration. The military administrators, in particular, found that the Jews did not fit into the stereotype of those to be governed by the British. The Zionists were educated, highly politically motivated and saw the British occupation of Palestine as merely a stage on the way to Jewish national revival. The Arabs, by contrast, more neatly fitted into the character of a 'native' population whose leaders could be dealt with by flattery and bribery, whilst the masses were primarily illiterate peasants.[8] Furthermore, there was an increasing concern in Britain with the economic consequences of the First World War and the financial burden that the mandate had added to the war debt that had arisen.

The economic cost of administering the Palestine Mandate was to become a recurring theme with disgruntled Unionists who saw this as one way of attacking the Coalition administration. Hall raised the issue in July 1920,[9] but he made a more concerted attack in December 1920. Hall maintained that an enormous amount of money was being expended by the British government for which Britain was receiving no benefit. Sir Harry Brittain, the Unionist member for Acton, Middlesex, also implied there was no return to Britain for its expenditure and suggested that the country relieve itself of its financial responsibility. Page-Croft asked that the government give an undertaking that the establishment of the Jewish national home would not involve any permanent expenditure for the British taxpayer.[10] However, it was in the House of Lords that the first substantive debate took place in relation to the mandate for Palestine and the Balfour Declaration.

THE LORDS' DEBATE OF JUNE 1920

The debate was initiated by Lord Sydenham, who was a noted anti-Semite and prominent in the anti-alien movement during the 1920s. As has been previously seen, he was also one of many Conservative politicians who had welcomed the Balfour Declaration in 1917. Sydenham maintained that the British position in Palestine had deteriorated since it had been occupied by General Allenby in 1917, owing to the machinations of the Zionist Commission which resided in Jerusalem. He alleged that the Jews had no regard for the interests of the Moslem and Christian populations and, indeed, that they were responsible for the riots that took place in Jerusalem earlier that year. 'It appears', he said, 'that the Moslems came without firearms, which seemed to show that they did not intend any harm to the Jewish population. On the other hand, the Jews had firearms, which were provided to them by Lieutenant Jabotinsky.'[11]

Sydenham characterised the Jewish immigrants as 'Russian Bolsheviks'. He also considered that Christianity was under threat in Russia primarily from the Bolshevik commissars of which, he observed, it had been stated that 90 per cent were Jews. 'Unless the Government now cry a halt', he argued, 'there will be a rush of Bolsheviks from Russia and Central Europe which might drive Christianity out of the land of its birth.'[12]

Another Conservative peer who had supported the Balfour Declaration in 1917 was Lord Lamington. He now considered that support for the Jewish national home was in contravention with commitments made by Britain to the Arabs and that Palestine was of no commercial interest to Britain. Although acknowledging that 'we are undoubtedly under a great debt to those of the Jewish persuasion for carrying on the usages, customs and government of civilisation', he regarded with alarm Britain taking any course which would, in his view, lead to disaster in Palestine and bring no good to the Empire.

Curzon replied for the government, reassuring Sydenham and others that the British civil administration would not result in Jewish control, nor the expropriation of Arab lands for Jewish settlement, and that emigration would be restricted to the economic capacity of the country. Curzon was, in any event, a reluctant supporter of government policy in Palestine, and Sydenham considered that Curzon's statement had satisfied his concerns and withdrew his motion.

In March 1920 a draft wording of the proposed mandate was circulated at the Foreign Office. Curzon wrote on the draft paper that the document 'reeks of Judaism in every paragraph and is an avowed constitution for a Jewish State'. He went on to write that 'this mandate has been drawn up by someone reeling under the fumes of Zionism. If we are all to submit to that intoxicant, this draft is all right ... but I confess I should like to see something worded differently.'[13]

THE PALESTINE PARLIAMENTARY COMMITTEE

The Zionists and their supporters were concerned with not only the terms of the proposed mandate document but also the boundaries of Palestine, with particular reference to the northern boundary with French-controlled Lebanon. Weizmann was in correspondence with Balfour, Ormsby-Gore and Lloyd George regarding the northern boundary.[14] This concern led the Palestine Parliamentary Committee to forward to the cabinet secretary a motion which urged the government to include within the terms of the mandate recognition of the historic connection of the Jewish people with Palestine and of the status of the Zionist Organisation, the policy of development of Palestine into a self-governing commonwealth, and the inclusion within Palestine of the lower part of the River Yarmuk.[15] *The Times* carried a leader in October 1920 proposing the Litani River as the northern boundary of Palestine.[16]

Although it was not agreed that the Litani River should become the northern boundary of Palestine, the supporters of the Jewish national home could take some comfort in the changes made in the Lloyd George Coalition in January 1921, when responsibility for Palestine was transferred from the Foreign Office under Curzon to the Colonial Office under Churchill, whose deputy with responsibility for the Middle East department was Ormsby-Gore.

THE MODIFICATION OF COALITION POLICY

In July 1921 the mandates for both Mesopotamia and Palestine were questioned by Joynson-Hicks. He considered that Palestine had been conquered by the British for the Arabs and not really to allow Jews to go there and to settle. He also criticised the appointment of Jews to senior positions in the civil administration and considered that the 'debt of honour' should be cancelled because of the economic conditions in Britain.[17]

This view had been expressed early in the debate by Esmond Harmondsworth, the Conservative member for the Isle of Thanet, who considered that it was a mistake for taxpayers in Britain to be asked to finance a national loan for the Jews. He considered that, since 'they are the richest nation in the world', they should pay for it.[18] This attitude was in line with the anti-waste campaign which was being run by Harmondsworth's father, the press baron Lord Rothermere, whose Anti-Waste League had won two by-elections in Conservative-held seats. Harmondsworth's uncle, Lord Northcliffe, signalled a change in the policies of his newspapers when a leader in the *Daily Mail* attacked the Palestine Mandate, principally on the basis of cost. At a meeting in February 1921 Ormsby-Gore criticised the stand now adopted by Northcliffe, arguing that it would result in the return of Palestine to the Turks.[19] The *Daily Mail* returned to the subject in May 1921, when it maintained that the British taxpayer was forced to fund Zionism.[20]

Owing to the internal disagreement on the emphasis of policy, and also perhaps because of a growing campaign by Conservative backbenchers and the Tory press, the government commitment to Jewish national revival in Palestine was modified. This was brought into public focus when Churchill stated in Jerusalem during his visit in April 1921 that the establishment of a national home did not mean a Jewish government to dominate Arabs. He argued that changes to the form of government would take a considerable time and that 'our children's children would have passed away before that is completed'.[21] This statement had been preceded the previous month by Amery's speech at a dinner given by Kerem Hayesod in London when he stated that he did not think that the aim of the Jewish national home was 'a political state as such'. He considered that, in due course, Palestine would become a 'free self-governing community' as part of an inevitable evolutionary process which was being followed by all lands in the British Empire.[22]

In November 1921 the Palestinian Arab delegation, which had come to Britain the previous August, held a lunch at the Hotel Cecil attended by several peers, MPs and other notables including Sydenham, Sir Charles Yale and Sir Michael O'Dwyer.[23] A further meeting took place in March 1922, which was supported by Lords Lamington, Sheffield, Islington, Ampthill and Sydenham as well as Joynson-Hicks.[24] In May a further luncheon was held at Claridges, given by the National Political League for the Palestinian Arab Delegation. Those who attended included Lt-Col. John Pretyman Newman, the Conservative MP for Finchley, and Lt-Col. Francis Freemantle, the Conservative member for St Albans. The other Conservative MP at the luncheon was Joynson-Hicks, who spoke, calling the Balfour Declaration 'one of the mysteries of modern politics' which had been 'engineered by the Zionist Organisation'.[25]

NORTHCLIFFE AND *THE TIMES*

In February 1922, Northcliffe had visited Palestine. Helen Bentwich, wife of Norman Bentwich who was the Chief Legal Officer of the civil administration in Palestine, considered that Northcliffe was the most difficult of the political personalities who briefly visited Palestine at that time. She considered that he was 'unbalanced in his statements and actions' and was 'obsessed with the fear of Moslem reactions (in India) to the situation in Palestine'.[26] Northcliffe's attitudes were expressed in a statement he issued in Cairo in which he suggested that there was a risk of Palestine becoming a second Ireland. He argued that there was resentment by British residents and 'native' Palestinian Jews to 'the arrogance and swaggers of the new arrivals from the ghettos of Central Europe'.[27] *The Times* now joined the assault on Zionism. In its leader in April 1922 the paper called for the appointment of an impartial commission to examine the 'painful' situation in Palestine and called for the abolition of the Zionist Commission.[28] Two weeks later, a further leader called again for the abolition of the Zionist Commission. It proposed that the whole problem should be reduced to modern and practical dimensions and solved by the tried methods of 'impartial British administration'.[29] This was a demand by *The Times* for Palestine to be administered and dealt with in the traditional way of British colonial rule by its regulation of 'native' populations.

In June the *Times* leader labelled political Zionism as 'aggressive and intolerant'. It questioned whether or not Britain should defend the Jews against the growing discontent of the Arab majority in Palestine whilst the Zionists consolidated their 'political supremacy'. It now considered that the pledge to give a national home to the Jews was in defiance of broad British interests in the Middle East.[30] The following month there were two leader columns in the paper calling for the removal of Jewish officials in the British administration in Palestine.[31]

THE SUPPLY DEBATE IN MARCH 1922

Meanwhile, the parliamentary attacks on the mandate continued. In the Supply debate in March 1922 Frederick MacQuisten[32] said that it was a great mystery to the average Briton, especially if he were unemployed, to see 'good money going for the benefit of people who he always thought knew far more about money than he did'. He did not feel that Britain was bound by the Balfour Declaration. MacQuisten had met with the Palestine Arab Delegation and repeated their allegation that a great many of the Jewish immigrants were undesirable Russian Jews with Bolshevik tendencies.[33] Viscount Curzon, the Conservative member for Battersea South, asked whether Churchill was aware that 'the large majority of the Jewish immigrants to Palestine had been released from the ghettos of Eastern Europe and saturated with Bolshevik ideas'.[34] This allegation of Bolshevism would continue to be raised both generally by Conservatives in respect of Zionists and specifically in relation to the concession to Pinhus Rutenberg to build an electrical power station. Rutenberg was accused by Captain Charles Foxcroft[35] as being 'known in Russia as a dangerous world revolutionary'.[36]

THE LORDS' DEBATE IN JUNE 1922

In the House of Lords the opponents of the Palestine Mandate had a noted success in a debate initiated by Lord Islington.[37] The thrust of Islington's argument was that the Arabs were being discriminated against by the British authorities, who were dominated by the Zionists. Whilst the language he employed was reasonably moderate, the sense of anti-Semitism was, on occasion, not far below the surface. Islington compared the refusal by the authorities to allow certain officers in the Australian Army, who had fought in Palestine, to settle there whilst '25,000 alien Jews from Eastern Europe had been introduced into the country' within the previous two years. Islington considered that Parliament was not committed to Zionism and had never given its decision in regard to it. Furthermore he believed that it was not 'the proper function of His Majesty's Government to spend money of the British taxpayer' for the purposes of establishing a Jewish national home.[38]

Sydenham spoke in the debate in a far more overt racist tone than Islington. He described the immigration of Jews into Palestine as the dumping down of '25,000 promiscuous people on the shores of Palestine, many of them quite unsuited for colonising purposes, and some of them Bolsheviks, who have already shown the most sinister activity'. He argued that it could not have been necessary to give the contract for the concession for the production of electricity to a 'revolutionary Russian Jew, who really, of course, hails from Germany'.[39]

The now ennobled Balfour made a striking defence of both the Declaration which he had issued on behalf of the government and the policies of the British administration in Palestine towards the Jewish national home. However, his arguments failed to convince Lord Willoughby de Broke, who said that, whilst he had no prejudice against the Jews, his prejudice was in favour of the British people, who were 'going to be asked to pay for all of this'.[40]

The motion against the Palestine Mandate was carried by 60 votes to 29. Those supporting the resolution included: the Earl of Middleton, a former Unionist secretary of state for India; the Earl of Shaftesbury, who in November 1922 became Lord Steward of His Majesty's Household; Viscount Goschen, a junior Unionist minister during 1918 in the Coalition government; Viscount Hutchinson, junior minister of the War Office under Balfour's premiership; and Lord Carson, who, as Sir Edward Carson, had served in the war cabinet. Some Liberal and Labour peers supported the motion but, in view of the composition of the Upper House, it was the number of Conservative peers who supported the motion which enabled it to be carried.

THE COMMONS' DEBATE IN JULY 1922

The government's defeat on 21 June in the House of Lords was followed by a debate in the Commons less than two weeks later, when a motion was proposed by Joynson-Hicks to reduce the salary of the secretary of state for the Colonies. This was a procedural device to introduce a motion opposing the Palestinian Mandate and the concession for the supply of electricity in Palestine. Joynson-Hicks, who admitted his prior support in 1917 for the Balfour Declaration, now considered that it was not consistent with pledges which had been made to the Arabs. The problem was not, he argued, the Balfour Declaration but the 'real trouble is the way in which the Zionists have been permitted by the Government, or with the connivance of the Government, practically to control the whole of the Government of Palestine'. Joynson-Hicks propounded what was, in effect, a conspiracy theory by which the administration of Palestine was manipulated and controlled by the Zionists.

The Rutenberg concession was attacked by Joynson-Hicks. Rutenberg had made only one of a number of offers which had been put forward but, he argued, those others were not from Jews and were therefore rejected. Furthermore, Rutenberg was 'a man whose character is at least the subject matter of very grave concern'.[41] Joynson-Hicks's arguments were rebutted by Lord Eustace Percy, who was to become a junior minister in the Bonar Law administration. He defended the Coalition government's position, arguing that Joynson-Hicks's stand would give the Arabs the impression that with enough agitation the British would clear out of Palestine. Percy maintained that such attacks on the conduct of the British colonial administration had not been made in the past by the members of the Tory Party as it would undermine colonial administration. He considered that Palestine was, in its essence, a part of the British Empire and 'the British Empire can never continue so long as you weaken British Administration by enquiring into it and investigating it at every possible moment'.[42]

This proposition did not prevent the opponents of the mandate from arguing that it was the Jews who were the effective rulers of the country, not the British administration. Joynson-Hicks had also attacked the appointment of Samuel as high commissioner and the other Jews who were employed in the British administration of Palestine. Sir John Butcher[43] considered that the British had spent 'enough blood and treasure in liberating the people of that country' and that it was wrong not to allow the British to develop the territory rather than allow the Jews to obtain economic and political power.[44]

The anti-Zionists' position was substantially reliant upon their argument of Jewish political domination and power in Palestine. The alleged 'control' of the colonial administration was grossly overstated. Although the high commissioner was himself Jewish, only 50 out 360 senior officials were Jews and there were 566 Jews in the total of 2,130 junior officials.[45] This 'Jewish power' was seen as having been manifested in the Rutenberg concession. However, the allegation that special consideration was given to Jews in respect of the concession was demolished by Lt-Col. Sir John Norton-Griffiths, the Conservative MP for Central Wandsworth and an industrialist. He stated that the proposed concession had been 'hawked all over London and refused by house after house'. He dismissed the value of the concession, saying: 'I would not give a bob for it now.'[46]

The anti-Zionists argued that the cost of Palestine was a continuing drain on the British taxpayer but ignored the reduction in cost which had actually been achieved. In 1920 the costs were at a level of £8 million but were reduced to £4 million in 1921, and an estimated £2 million for 1922. Furthermore, it was anticipated that the costs would be reduced to approximately £1 million by 1924.[47]

The plea that the rights of the Arabs for self-determination were denied by the British government because of its commitment to the Jewish national home would have been a more credible argument had it not been advanced by die-hards who, when faced with demands by the Indian population for greater self-government, vehemently attacked the British government for making any move in such a direction. Hence the demand for Arab self-determination was a hollow cry which was without conviction and taken up by the die-hard Conservatives as an attempt to legitimise their anti-Semitic opposition to the policy of re-establishing the Jewish national home.

Those opposed to the policy set out in the Balfour Declaration were willing to renege upon the pledges and promises which were made to the Zionist movement by the British and other Allied and associated powers in respect of the re-establishment of the Jewish national home in Palestine. These promises were made, according to Churchill, because it was considered that the Jews would be of value in the struggle to win the First World War. The support which the Jews could give the Allied powers, all over the world, and particularly in the United States and in Russia, 'would be a definite, palpable advantage'.[48]

The appeal made to the Commons by the government that it should not abandon the undertakings given to the Zionists proved to be overwhelmingly successful. Joynson-Hicks's motion was defeated by 292 votes to 35. The limited number of MPs who supported the anti-Zionist motion included a number of outspoken members who had been prominent in the anti-Semitic, anti-alien campaign. These included Sir Frederick Banbury, Viscount Curzon, Rupert Gwynne, Rear Admiral Sir W. Hall, Ronald McNeill and Major Joseph Nall, in addition to Joynson-Hicks, who had become the leading anti-alienist in the House of Commons. However, the level of support for the anti-Zionist position amongst MPs was possibly understated in the Colonial Office amendment vote on 4 July 1922. Pretyman Newman and Seddon did not have their votes recorded but both of them, together with Freemantle, had attended the luncheon for the Palestinian Arab Delegation given by the National Political League at Claridges Hotel in May 1922, to which reference has already been made.[49]

THE CHURCHILL WHITE PAPER

The government's success in the vote on Joynson-Hicks's amendment may have been at least partly because of the further modification of its policy towards Zionism which was expressed in the Churchill White Paper issued in June 1922. The White Paper stated that it was not the government's aim to create a wholly Jewish Palestine. Jewish immigration into Palestine was not to be allowed to be so great in volume as to exceed the economic capacity of the country to absorb the new arrivals. Furthermore, the Palestine administration would ensure that persons who were 'politically undesirable' were excluded from Palestine. It was intended that a committee of the proposed new Legislative Council would confer with the administration upon matters relating to the regulation of immigration to the country. It was also made clear that it was not the intention of the British government to allow the Palestine Zionist Executive (formerly known as the Zionist Commission) to share any general administrative power in the country.[50]

THE CONSERVATIVE PRESS

The Conservative press had moved increasingly against Lloyd George and the concept of coalition politics.[51] Opposition to the Palestine Mandate enabled an attack to be focused on the Middle Eastern policies of the Lloyd George government, which were perceived as being pursuant of a Liberal, rather than Conservative, tradition in respect of the treatment of Turkey. Lloyd George's support for the Greeks in their war against the Turkish Nationalists proved to be an ill-fated policy when the armies of Greece were rebuffed and defeated by the Kemalist forces in central Turkey.

Furthermore, the appeal for economy and in particular the anti-waste platform demanded the withdrawal of Britain from the 'costly commitment' of maintaining its military forces and civil administration in Palestine as well as its military commitment to Mesopotamia. After Northcliffe's death, his brother, Lord Rothermere, acquired the *Daily Mail* and it became a vehicle for the dissemination of his anti-waste campaign. It proved to be particularly successful in the defeat of Sir Herbert Jessel, who was the Jewish Conservative candidate in the St George's, Westminster, by-election held in June 1921. Rothermere's *Daily Mirror* and *Daily Mail* both attacked the Palestine Mandate on grounds of cost and called on Jessel to denounce the Jewish national home.

Beaverbrook also abandoned his support for the Lloyd George Coalition and used the *Daily Express* and *Sunday Express* to oppose the government. His newspapers included overtly anti-Semitic attacks in respect of the commitment to the Palestine Mandate. Weizmann was described by the *Daily Express* as 'the most wonderful of the mystery men' who had persuaded Britain to spend millions of pounds to enable the Jews to take over the control of Palestine. He had, the paper alleged, 'a genius for exerting a hidden mastery over the minds of our simple British politicians'.[52] The Jews were also equated to Bolsheviks.[53] These attacks were a continuation of the Tory press's obsession with the theory of the world Jewish conspiracy.

The *Daily Express* special correspondent in Palestine, W. E. Whittaker, in his articles described the Jews of Palestine as having 'more experience of the gutters of the great cities of the East of Europe than of agricultural land'.[54] In February 1923 the *Sunday Express* proclaimed that 'at the expense of the British taxpayer a Zionist Government, with a Jewish Governor, has been established in Palestine', for which British soldiers had fought and died.[55]

The downfall of the Lloyd George Coalition enabled the opponents of Zionism to attempt to influence Conservative policy and to obtain a commitment to withdraw from the Middle East. Beaverbrook proposed that Britain withdraw 'bag and baggage' from these commitments in his article in the *Sunday Express* at the beginning of 1923.

The *Daily Mail* published a series of articles in 1923 by its special correspondent, J. M. N. Jeffries, entitled 'The Palestine Deception'. In these articles it was argued that the undertakings given in the Balfour Declaration were in flagrant contradiction of the pledges given by McMahon in 1915 and Allenby in 1918 to the Arabs. It was contended that power was increasing in the hands of the 'Judaeo-Slavs' who were socialists, at best, and communists, at worst. These articles were full of accusations implying that Britain had been deceived by the Jews and that it should withdraw from

Palestine (and Mesopotamia). This would avoid embarrassment, war and ruinous expenditure.[56]

The *Spectator*, under the editorship and proprietorship of Strachey, allied itself with the die-hard opponents of Lloyd George.[57] Strachey, who had opposed home rule for Ireland and the nationalist movements in India, allegedly supported self-determination for the Palestine Arabs, who were 'persons who not unnaturally want self-determination, not Hebrew domination'. The Balfour Declaration encouraged the immigration of 'hostile aliens'.[58] Bolsheviks had been depicted by Strachey as 'either Jews or Atheists'.[59] Immediately following the general election in 1922 he called on the Conservative government to withdraw from Palestine and to resist Jewish pressure. The government, he wrote, should not be afraid to offend international Jewry as 'we should never get on satisfactory terms with Jewish financiers by showing ourselves afraid of them'.[60]

The *Morning Post* remained the leading newspaper supporting the die-hards of the Tory right. The paper had questioned the loyalty of Jewish Liberal politicians. At the end of 1921 it added Mond, now the minister of health, to its list, which included Lord Reading (the former Rufus Isaacs), Samuel and Montagu.[61] The paper was prominent in promoting the theory of a world Jewish conspiracy, which in part equated Bolshevism with the Jews. Consequently, it had attacked Jewish financiers as aiding the Germans and the Bolsheviks.[62] The *Morning Post* argued that Jewish power was so great that 'Jewry and the British Government have now become almost interchangeable terms'.[63]

For the die-hards, the Jews were seen as the purveyors of power which was exercised against the true interests of Britain. This could, in their eyes, be identified with the pursuit of policies by the Coalition government which were counter to those expounded by the Tory right. Home rule for Ireland was a particularly sensitive issue to the Conservatives. The settlement reached by the Coalition administration with the Irish Nationalists at the end of 1921 was seen as a betrayal of the Union. Thus the perceived role that Mond and Montagu had played in framing the settlement would have been viewed as proof of the insidious nature of Jews.[64]

BONAR LAW AND THE GENERAL ELECTION OF 1922

Following the Carlton Club vote and the fall of Lloyd George as prime minister, Bonar Law formed the first solely Conservative administration since the resignation of Balfour in 1905. Bonar Law appointed the Duke of Devonshire as colonial secretary with Ormsby-Gore as the under-secretary of state. Ormsby-Gore had detached himself from supporting the Coalition some months before and had urged Bonar Law to re-establish his leadership of the Conservative Party. His appointment, therefore, may be seen as a reward for loyalty to the Party rather than a covert statement by Bonar Law of support for the Palestine Mandate.

Bonar Law's general election address expressed the hope that the negotiations for the settlement of the Near Eastern crisis would result in a 'true and lasting peace, conducing both to the political tranquillity of the Near and Middle East, with which so many of our Imperial interests are bound up, and to the personal security and happiness of the inhabitants of all races and creeds in the regions which have been the scene of so much disturbance and suffering'.[65] Beaverbrook wrote to Bonar Law advising him that he could not follow the Conservative leader's approach to Mesopotamia and Palestine. He advised Bonar Law that he felt so strongly on the Middle Eastern question that he was going to 'try to bring public pressure to bear on the Conservative candidates in the constituencies to pledge themselves to the bag and baggage policy of evacuation in Mesopotamia and Palestine'.[66] The following day the *Daily Express* advised its readers to ask candidates whether they were 'in favour of clearing out of Mesopotamia, Palestine and Constantinople, not if or as commitments permit, but absolutely and at once'. The next day it urged that 'every [parliamentary] candidate must be pledged to evacuation' and there was 'only one Near Eastern policy for the British taxpayer – to insist his Government should clear out "bag and baggage"'.[67] It was estimated by the Zionist Organization that 26 candidates supported the 'bag and baggage' campaign, of whom 17 were elected.[68]

The *Daily Mail* called on Bonar Law to effect 'a drastic revision of our commitments in the Near East, Palestine, Mesopotamia and Constantinople'.[69] It was at an election meeting in Leeds that Bonar Law addressed the press campaign to withdraw from Palestine and Mesopotamia. He said that whilst he understood the feelings relating to the potentially immense expenditure to these commitments he would not make a definitive pledge. 'All I can say is, we will examine it carefully, but in examining it we cannot, with our record as a nation behind us, consider merely what will pay us today. We must consider to what extent we are bound by obligations.'[70] Three days later, when addressing an election meeting in London, he again raised the issue of withdrawal from Palestine and Mesopotamia. 'I wish', he said, 'we should never have gone there. We will certainly examine it.' He acknowledged that he had personal responsibility for the policy to accept mandates for Palestine and Mesopotamia as he had been part of the Coalition government at the time. His commitment to examine the policy, with 'a perfectly open mind', was subject to consideration of 'not merely what will pay us best at the moment, but what obligations we have incurred which we cannot pay'.[71] The *Jewish Chronicle* report stated that Bonar Law had said that he would not be stampeded on the issue of the Palestine Mandate by Beaverbrook and Rothermere.[72]

The Conservatives were returned with 345 MPs, a majority of 75 over the two wings of the Liberal Party, the Labour Party and other minor parties, and less than two weeks after polling day Esmond Harmondsworth wrote to Bonar Law. He expressed the view that the prime minister, in his speech, had stated that there were no obligations binding Britain to Mesopotamia and Palestine and his promise to reconsider the whole question 'turned a very considerable number of votes to the Conservative side and saved many seats where there were very small majorities and possibly even in others where the majority was larger'. Bonar Law swiftly responded by writing that what he had said was not that 'there were no obligations but that I did not admit, without examination, that the obligations existed'.[73] The prime minister's insistence that there was a difference between Harmondsworth's view of his undertaking and that which he actually expressed was not the result of any personal policy commitment to retain the mandates. He privately wrote to Curzon that as far as Mesopotamia was concerned 'you know how keen I am if we can get out of it'.[74] Curzon, who had been reappointed by Bonar Law as foreign secretary, was more disturbed about the Palestine Mandate and the Jewish national home, which he had opposed in cabinet in 1917.[75]

CONSERVATIVE SUPPORT FOR THE JEWISH NATIONAL HOME

There were, however, Conservatives who expressed the opposite view at this time. Amery, who had been appointed First Lord of the Admiralty by Bonar Law, whilst wishing to reduce expenditure in Palestine saw 'no reason whatever for abandoning the general line of policy which we have adopted, of the going back on pledges and undertakings which we have formally and publicly given'. Neville Chamberlain, the postmaster-general, wrote that he considered that Britain was 'definitely pledged to the Balfour Declaration, and I should therefore certainly oppose the proposal to go back upon that Declaration'. His half-brother and former party leader, Austen Chamberlain, could not conceive that the new government would repudiate the pledge given by Balfour or alter the policy pursued by the previous government in regard to Palestine. Acceptance of the mandate, he wrote, 'imposes obligations on this country which I am confident all British Governments will feel bound to fulfil'.

Sir Lamington Worthington-Evans, the former secretary of state for war, stated that 'the British government has given a pledge and will not break it'. Sir Robert Horne, the previous Chancellor of the Exchequer, believed that it would not be the British way to evacuate Palestine or Mesopotamia until they had been put in order and that order had been solidified. In addition to these Conservatives of cabinet rank statements were made by 27 Conservative MPs pledging their support for the fulfilling of the obligations to the Jews entered into by the British government. Two Liverpool Conservatives, Sir Watson Rutherford and Sir Leslie Scott, had supported Zionism in their election addresses.[76]

THE CONSERVATIVE GOVERNMENT REVIEW OF POLICY

A fundamental reassessment of Britain's policy towards the Palestine Mandate and the Jewish national home caused great concern to those Conservatives, such as Ormsby-Gore, who supported the Balfour Declaration. As the under-secretary of state for the colonies he was able to bring before the cabinet the history of the negotiations which led up to the Declaration in November 1917.[77]

In February 1923, Devonshire circulated a memorandum to the cabinet outlining the policy pursued by the Coalition government since 1917. It was stated that the object of the Balfour Declaration was to enlist the sympathies on the side of the Allies of influential Jews and Jewish organisations world-wide; the policy was a legacy not of the Coalition but of the First World War and Britain had committed itself publicly to the Zionist policy, which had been strengthened by the wording of the mandate for Palestine. The pledges given in 1915 by McMahon and in 1918 by Allenby did not include Palestine, despite assertions to that effect made by anti-Zionists in the 1920s. However, it had become necessary in June 1921 to explain the meaning of the Balfour Declaration, which disclaimed all intentions of setting up a Jewish state.

The White Paper of June 1922 made further advances towards the Arab viewpoint by the explicit dissociation of the British government from 'extreme' Zionism and clarifying that the Zionist

Organisation under the mandate did not involve participation in the government of Palestine. Furthermore it had proposed that a committee of elected members of the Legislative Council (which would have an Arab majority) would have a direct voice in the control of immigration.[78]

The Arab Delegation had returned to London following the downfall of the Coalition government. It was hopeful that it would be successful in reversing, rather than revising, British policy in Palestine. It had obtained support mainly from Conservative politicians and Tory newspaper proprietors, who were opposed to the Lloyd George administration. The Conservative government excluded those Unionist ministers who had been close to Lloyd George and his policies, but perhaps even more significant was that the Arabs' main protagonist in the Commons, Joynson-Hicks, was now a member of the cabinet. The press campaign, which has been examined above, had continued in the first half of 1923. Devonshire, therefore, wanted the cabinet to consider the policy to be adopted by the Bonar Law administration.

It was not until the end of June 1923 that a cabinet committee was established to advise the government in respect of the future policy to be adopted in regard to Palestine. Devonshire chaired the committee but its most influential member was Curzon, who effectively wrote its report.[79] In addition to Curzon, two of its other members, Derby and Amery, had been closely involved with the Balfour Declaration. The remaining members were Peel, Hoare, Lloyd Greame, Wood, Novar, Worthington Evans and Joynson-Hicks.[80]

The committee reported in July 1923 and only took evidence from Samuel, the high commissioner for Palestine. Some of the committee, notably Joynson-Hicks, had considered that the Balfour Declaration was 'both unnecessary and unwise'. However, no member of the committee seriously advocated the reversal of British policy. It was considered that 'it is well nigh impossible for any Government to extricate itself without a substantial sacrifice of consistency and self-respect, if not honour'.

There were other reasons which the report outlined. These related to imperial considerations. Opinion was mixed as to the strategic value of Palestine to the Empire. One of the considerations behind the original Declaration was its value as a base for protecting the route to India. The settlement in Egypt in 1922 was seen as weakening the position of Britain in this respect and consequently the retention of Palestine became more significant. Had the Conservatives decided to abandon the mandate, either another Allied power, France or Italy, would have stepped in, or else the Turks under Atatürk would have reclaimed their lost territory. These alternatives were unacceptable to the Conservatives.

The proposed solution was to retain the mandate but to weaken the Zionist dimension further by establishing an Arab Agency to mirror the Jewish Agency which had been set up in accordance with the terms of the mandate. However, it was proposed that Zionist consent should be obtained as it should not appear that a breach of faith had occurred since this could result in the withdrawal of inward funding by Jews, which was seen as essential not only for the Jewish 'colonies' in Palestine but for the future development of Palestine as a whole. The cabinet accepted the report, satisfied that they were innocent of any breach of faith to either the Arabs or the Jews.[81]

THE PRO-ARAB MEMORIAL

The committee had been subject to further pressure from the supporters of the Palestine Arab Delegation. A memorial had been organised to present to the committee requesting that it 'reconsider the Palestine question in the light of the Arab demands'. All the signatories were Conservative MPs and by mid-July 85 of them had signed the memorial.[82] By 2 August the total had reached 111.[83]

The list included some well-known antagonists of the Jews such as Frederick Banbury, Lord Curzon, Henry Page-Croft and Herbert Neild. The list did not include any former ministers but five of their number, including Curzon and Page-Croft, were to hold junior office subsequently and Hugh O'Neill was to chair the 1922 Committee from December 1935 until July 1939.[84] However, the absence of ministerial office holders did not detract from the size of support for the memorial. The number of signatories represented almost 40 per cent of the Conservative backbenchers. It thus demonstrated the level of anti-Zionism, if not anti-Semitism, within the parliamentary party. Devonshire's departmental memorandum to the cabinet in February had postulated that the reason for the opposition to the Jewish national home was not the ostensible reasons outlined in the press and in parliamentary debate but the far more potent influence of anti-Jewish prejudice. This was considered to be a 'powerful force even here, and it has been intensified in recent years by the vague belief in a world-wide Judaeo-Bolshevik conspiracy against civilisation'.[85]

It is argued here that the influence of the backbenchers with the Conservative administration was limited. However, the memorial came at a time when the government was reassessing its position and therefore a charge of disloyalty could not readily be sustained against those advocating a reversal of existing policy. The memorial demonstrated that the Conservative Parliamentary Party was not enthusiastic, at the very least, to maintain any pro-Zionist policy. The further modifications to the pledge made in 1917 in respect of the Jewish national home, particularly by the proposal to establish an Arab Agency, were possibly made not only to satisfy the anti-Zionists on the committee but also to reflect wider Party opinion. Indeed, the pro-Zionists had feared worse.[86] The Balfour Declaration, in its totality, had not been abandoned.

THE REVISED CONSERVATIVE POLICY

In his address to the Imperial Conference in October 1923, Devonshire reaffirmed that the government's policy in Palestine was based on the Balfour Declaration. He emphasised the advances made both by the previous Coalition government and the current Conservative administration to meet the Arab viewpoint. A solution to the 'Jew–Arab controversy', he reported, 'has still to be found' but he would continue to carry out Britain's obligations, despite the Arabs' refusal to co-operate in elections to the Legislative Council.[87]

Indeed the Arabs also rejected the offer of the Arab Agency in Palestine.[88] This rejection had caused a partial reassessment of the views towards the mandate. The *Times* leader in October 1923 reaffirmed its earlier support for the Balfour Declaration by declaring that 'we cannot break our pledges to the Jews or our obligations to the League of Nations'.[89] The cabinet accepted that the government should not proceed further with political concessions to the Arabs.[90] Devonshire made the government's position clear to Samuel when he instructed him that it would not renew its offer to the Arabs and that in future any overtures towards co-operation must come from them.[91] The settlement of Conservative policy in July 1923 and the continuing Arab rejection of the movement by the British towards their position led to the effective depoliticisation of the mandate.

THE DECEMBER 1923 GENERAL ELECTION

Unlike the general election of November 1922, that of December 1923 did not see Palestine as an issue. The Zionist Organisation considered that there had been 130 anti-Zionist MPs returned to the House of Commons in November 1922. These were reduced in the new House, as, of that number, 16 did not seek re-election and a further 38 were defeated, including five of the 16 'bag and baggage' men.[92]

THE CONSERVATIVE GOVERNMENT FOLLOWING THE OCTOBER 1924 GENERAL ELECTION

In October 1924 the Conservatives were returned to government with a majority of 223 over all other parties. As in 1923, Palestine was not an election issue. Leo Amery became secretary of state for the colonies and Ormsby-Gore returned to the post of under-secretary. There was little parliamentary or national press coverage of Palestine. In April 1925 Amery went to Palestine as part of his Middle East visit. On his last day in Jerusalem he meet with delegations from both the Arabs and the Jews. He told the Arabs that the Balfour Declaration had been considered by the war coalition which produced the policy, reconsidered by the Conservative government which followed and also confirmed by the Labour government in 1924, in addition to the nations represented in the League of Nations. 'I am sure, therefore, that the gentleman here', he told them, 'do not really expect that the British Government could change its policy on this matter.' He told the Jews that the Arabs would always be the largest element of the population of Palestine and that the Jewish national home would have to live with the Arab national home.[93] Amery's own assessment of his visit was that he had done 'good work in Palestine on the whole', being sympathetic to the Arabs but making it clear that there would be no general change of policy.[94]

The Conservative government's perception of its Palestine policy was reviewed by Amery at the Imperial Conference held in October 1926. He considered that its 'steady and impartial' policy had resulted in a greatly improved political situation. Although the Arabs were opposed to the Balfour Declaration they realised that the British government had not embarked upon a policy of displacing the native population by a 'horde of Jewish immigrants' and were realising further that Jewish capital and settlers had contributed to the growth of the Arab population as well as the Jewish community.[95]

Supporters of the Jewish national home were nevertheless concerned with the direction that government policy might take. They formed, under the leadership of Finburgh, an all-party parliamentary committee supporting the Balfour Declaration. There were 61 members who initially joined the committee, of which 37 members were Conservatives. This number represented only 10 per cent of the Conservative backbench members. It included two Conservatives who had previously signed the anti-Zionist memorial.[96] Six of their number had, or would in the future, serve as ministers of the Crown.[97] This committee did not achieve any perceptible change in the government's policy to the mandate as Amery continued with the existing policy, which had emerged in the summer of 1923 and taken form in the autumn of that year. It is possible that the reason for the formation of the committee was to oppose any pressure to change policy by the Conservative backbenches, which were perceived by some pro-Zionists to have remained hostile to declared government policy.[98]

There was to be no change in that policy in the remaining period of the Baldwin administration. Support for loan guarantees and loans for Palestine was equivocal – not least from Churchill who seemed to change his mind, to the dismay of Amery.[99] Yet the colonial secretary, particularly after the end of the recession which affected Palestine in the mid-1920s, was optimistic for the future of the mandate. In November 1928 he wrote to that vociferous opponent of the mandate, Beaverbrook, that 'even Palestine is turning the corner and you will see that we will make something of it yet'.[100] However, it was not clear quite what that 'something' was to be. Amery envisaged the Jews would be like the Scots. Palestine was to be made the centre of western influence in the Middle East. The Jews would be used, 'as we have used the Scots, to carry the English ideal through the Middle East and not merely to make an artificial Hebrew enclave in an oriental country'.[101] Ormsby-Gore, however, in the debate on the civil estimates in April 1929 rejected this view when it was propounded by Wedgwood. The under-secretary of state saw the aim as making Palestine a distinct Jewish civilisation that was 'purely Jewish and Palestinian Jewish at that', and that the Zionist aim was to create in Palestine the physical and economic conditions which would nurture such a culture.[102]

There was to be no internal debate between the political heads of the Colonial Office in respect of the purpose of the mandate as the general election held on 30 May 1929 resulted in Labour emerging as the largest party in the Commons. The second minority Labour government followed and it was for this administration to deal with the results of the riots which occurred in Palestine in August 1929.

7

The Conservatives, Anti-Semitism and Jewish Refugees, 1933–39

The coming to power of the National Socialists in Germany at the end of January 1933 quickly led to the beginnings of organised state violence against those opposed to the Nazis. By 30 March the Anglo-Jewish community had staged a protest meeting, which passed a motion appealing to the British government to grant the right of asylum, without the distinction of race or creed, to the victims of 'these unparalleled atrocities'.[1] The following day, Locker-Lampson sent a letter to Hitler deprecating his decision to discriminate against German Jews which, he argued, would damage British sympathy for Germany.[2] *The Times* echoed this view in its leader on 9 April arguing that the Nazis' anti-Jewish policy had not advanced their prestige in England.[3] The previous year Robert Boothby, the Conservative member for East Aberdeen and Kincardine, had told Hitler that if he beat up the Jews 'it wouldn't go down at all well in England', where, he added, in a possible reference to the appointments of Samuel as home secretary and Reading as foreign secretary, 'we encourage them to govern us'.[4]

A protest meeting in Whitechapel on 1 April was organised with Members of Parliament present and presided over by Lord Mount Temple.[5] A meeting was also held the following month in Hendon which was attended by the Conservative MP for Sheffield, Hillsborough, Joseph Gurney Braithwaite.[6] On 27 June a large protest meeting was held at Queen's Hall which expressed its abhorrence at the anti-Jewish persecutions in Germany, and its sympathy with the victims of Nazi repression. It attracted a large cross-section of British public life, including members of both Houses of Parliament. There were 13 peers present and 50 MPs. The Conservatives were represented by three peers and 26 MPs; in addition, a letter of support was received from Lord Salisbury.[7] However, neither the Party, nor its affiliated bodies, would formally join any protest demonstrations against the treatment of Germany's Jews. When the Junior Imperial League was approached by a Jewish youth organisation to support a proposed demonstration, its chairman expressed the view that 'there would, no doubt, be many people who sympathised, but did not think that a Party Political Organisation should take part in such a gathering, and that there was a limit to the interference in Foreign Governments'.[8]

Austen Chamberlain, who was one leading Conservative who had remained hostile to Germany, said at the annual meeting of the Birmingham Unionist Association that the stirring of religious persecution and racial proscription was shocking and it revealed a spirit of intolerance which he had hoped had left the world. He considered that Europe was now more filled with fear and more sensitive to imminent danger.[9] Locker-Lampson and Sir Patrick Hannon, the member for the Moseley division, also spoke on the subject of Jews in Germany. Amery recorded that this met with much applause from the members. This he found interesting as there were not many Jews in Birmingham. He considered that it was the feeling of 'fair play' rather than specific Jewish sympathy that had moved his fellow Conservatives present.[10]

Sympathy with the plight of the Jews in Germany was expressed by some Conservatives in the Commons. In the debate on the adjournment on 13 April, John Morris, the member for Salford North, had placed on the order paper a motion deploring the continued persecution of the Jews and requesting that the government make 'friendly representations' to the German government to respect the numerical weakness and defenceless position of the Jews. The government, however, would not find time for discussion of the motion.[11] Owen Temple Morris, the member for Cardiff East, asked the colonial secretary whether he proposed to take any additional measures to enable German Jewish refugees to settle in Palestine, to which there was no substantive government response.[12] In July Locker-Lampson introduced the 'Nationality of Jews Bill', which proposed to promote and extend citizenship in Palestine for Jews who were deprived elsewhere of their citizenship. He considered that it was un-English and caddish to bully a minority and that Britain should 'stand by Jewry in its trouble'. The Conservative sponsors in addition to Locker-Lampson were Rear-Admiral Murray Sueter, Sir William Sugden, Sir Patrick Hannon and William Stewart. However, the Bill did not proceed beyond its first reading.[13]

CONSERVATIVE ANTI-SEMITISM – THE MEMBER FOR TOTTENHAM NORTH

The opposite view to that expressed by Locker-Lampson was expounded by Edward Doran, the Conservative member for Tottenham North who had been elected in 1931. In December 1932, he had raised the issue of Jewish immigration and naturalisation in the Commons.[14] By March 1933 he was calling for the prohibition of German Jews entering Britain, arguing that 'hundreds of thousands of Jews are now leaving Germany and scurrying from there to this country'.[15] This 'invasion of undesirable aliens', he opined, was causing great resentment and anxiety. His solution was to expel these Jews before serious trouble developed.[16]

Doran expressed his attitude towards Jews at a meeting in his constituency in May. He was opposed to Jews who were concerned with the film industry, music halls, theatres, tailors' shops, 'selling tobacco at cut prices, fires and fraudulent bankruptcies'.[17] Doran's virulent anti-Semitism was not, however, shared by his constituency Conservative Association. Its chairman wrote to one concerned constituent that the Association's members unanimously regretted Doran's anti-Semitic agitation.[18]

Doran was called to give an account of himself before the Association. However, when the meeting took place in August, the MP was absent in Canada. A letter from him reiterated his anti-Semitic views. Although the meeting was subject to heckling and disorder by Doran's supporters, a resolution was declared carried which not only officially reprimanded the MP but expelled him from the Association, which undertook immediately to adopt a new prospective parliamentary candidate.[19] Furthermore, at the National Union of Conservative Associations' conference the following year it was the Tottenham North constituency that placed on the order paper the motion which 'respectfully' urged the government to create 'further provision in favour of persecuted German Jews of good character, that they may emigrate into the British Empire'. However, the motion was withdrawn on the authority of the mover who, the conference report related, was unable to attend.[20]

GOVERNMENT POLICY

Doran's attempts to prevent the entry of German Jews into Britain had led to a statement of the government policy by the home secretary, Sir John Gilmour. 'It is not within the contemplation of the law that there should be discrimination against aliens on grounds of religious belief or racial origin', he stated in the Commons in March 1933. 'But', he continued, 'there are adequate powers under the Aliens Order to protect this country from any undesirable influx of aliens.' The principle upon which the admission of aliens was administered was, he reconfirmed, that 'the interest of this country must predominate over other considerations'.[21]

The concern of the Jewish community for the fate of their German co-religionists led to an undertaking being given to the government that no Jewish refugee would become a charge to the state. The formula was that 'all expenses, whether in respect of temporary or permanent accommodation or maintenance will be borne by the Jewish community without ultimate charge to the state'. It was anticipated that this undertaking would be limited both in time and numbers; only some 3,000–4,000 refugees, it was estimated, would seek temporary refuge in Britain before migrating elsewhere.[22]

The cabinet decided in April not to alter the existing criteria for the admission of aliens but resolved to consider further extensions on temporary stays provided the Jewish community did maintain its undertaking. The cabinet also considered that it would be in the public interest to try to secure for Britain prominent Jews who were being expelled from Germany and who had achieved distinction in science, medicine, industry, music, or art. It was believed that this would not only obtain for Britain the advantage of their knowledge and experience but 'would also create a very favourable impression in the world, particularly if our hospitality were offered with some warmth'.[23]

The home secretary stated in the Commons that financial independence was only one of the factors considered when granting leave to land was made and that the interests of Britain 'must predominate over all other considerations'. However, he added that each case would be carefully considered on its individual merits and that 'no unnecessary obstacles are placed in the way of foreigners seeking admission'.[24]

The cabinet committee which was established to consider the plight of the refugees suggested that if the position further deteriorated in Germany the matter should be considered by the League of Nations Office for Refugees.[25] The position did, in fact, continue to worsen in the summer months of 1933 and in October a high commissioner for refugees (Jewish and other) coming from Germany was appointed by the council of the League of Nations.

The commissioner was responsible to a governing body consisting of representatives of 12 governments interested in German refugees. Lord (Robert) Cecil, the strongly pro-Jewish and pro-Zionist former Conservative cabinet minister, who now sat in the Lords as an independent peer, was proposed by Anglo-Jewish bodies, with the support of the Archbishop of Canterbury, as the British representative. The government appointed Cecil, notwithstanding opposition from the Colonial Office.

Sir John Simon, the foreign secretary, in his letter of appointment to Cecil set out the government's position. It did not wish any recommendations to emerge from the governing body which would 'provoke resentment in Germany'. Britain could not contemplate making any financial contribution either in connection with the office of high commissioner or for any schemes to assist refugees. There would be little scope for immigration into Britain's colonies as they were predominantly tropical and agricultural. Furthermore, the government could not depart from the existing immigration policies in Palestine which were determined by the economic absorptive capacity of the country. Simon also advised Cecil that 'owing to the acute unemployment in the United Kingdom, there are no prospects for Germans seeking employment in commerce or industry' and that there was 'little or no possibility of finding useful openings in this country for more refugees of the professional classes'.[26]

Although precise statistics are not available it is estimated that, during 1933, 300–400 refugees entered Britain each month. This figure dropped to about 100 persons per month in 1934.[27] The government, after some initial relaxation in the admission of refugees, thereafter again restricted the numbers of Jews entering Britain.

BRITISH FASCISM

The rise of native fascism did not attract the attention of the Conservatives in the same way that Liberal and especially Labour politicians viewed with concern the activities of the Blackshirts. This in part may have been because of the constituency aspect of MPs' activities. The majority of Jews lived in constituencies which were represented by the Labour Party at Westminster. However, the infamous Olympia meeting, which took place on 7 June 1934, did produce what may be considered to be a definitive reaction by Conservatives. The 12,000-strong meeting was attended by many who were merely curious to see the phenomenon of British fascism; it included a number of Conservative MPs.

The meeting witnessed violence between largely Communist anti-fascists and Oswald Mosley's blackshirted stewards. Whilst the debate regarding the extent of the violence and its causes still continues, what is clear was the contemporary reaction to it. Amery recorded that Geoffrey Lloyd, Baldwin's parliamentary private secretary who attended the meeting, was in a state of great indignation about the brutality. He considered that this seemed to be the general view of Conservative MPs who went there.[28] Three other Conservative MPs, William Anstruther-Gray, the member for Lanarkshire North, Harry James Scrymgeour-Wedderburn, who sat for Renfrew West, and Terence J. O'Connor, who represented Nottingham Central, immediately following the meeting had a letter rushed to *The Times* which appeared the following day. In this letter they wrote of the 'wholly unnecessary violence inflicted by uniformed Blackshirts on interrupters. Men and women were knocked down and were still assaulted and kicked on the floor.' They continued that 'these methods of securing freedom of speech may have been effective, but they are happily unusual in England, and constitute in our opinion a deplorable outrage on public order'.[29]

The defenders of the Blackshirts did include other Conservative MPs such as Michael W. Beaumont, who wrote to *The Times* dissenting from the views expressed earlier by his three colleagues.[30] But Mosley received comparatively little support from within the Conservative Party.[31] Opposition to the activity of the British Union of Fascists (BUF) was to increase, and the banning of uniforms for political parties followed the violence in the provinces and the 'Battle of Cable Street' in London's East End in October 1936. The Public Order Bill was introduced in the Commons on 10 November and became law the following month. Mosley's biographer, Robert Skidelsky, considered that the Bill received support from the large 'law and order' brigade of Tory backbenchers in part because of Mosley's 'betrayal' of Conservatism by joining the Labour Party, whilst the wearing of uniforms 'definitely raised hackles'.[32]

Whilst this may have been a reason for some, it is argued here that Conservatives generally saw fascism as a foreign political ideology which had little place in the British system of governance. The methods employed by Mosley and his followers were not considered to be the 'English' way of conducting political action. Harold Nicolson had begged Mosley in November 1931 not to become involved with the fascists. He told him 'that fascism is not suited to England. In Italy there was a long tradition of secret societies. In Germany there was a long tradition of militarism … In England anything on those lines is doomed to failure and ridicule.'[33]

Fascist attacks, both metaphorically and physically, on Jews were perceived as the type of behaviour which took place in continental Europe, particularly in eastern Europe, but not in Britain.[34] Even the virulently anti-Semitic journal *Truth*, which was secretly controlled by Sir Joseph Ball, the director of the Conservative Research Department, did not approve of the attacks by Mosley's 'gangsters' on 'poor little Jewish shopkeepers'. *Truth* considered that 'the average Englishman' felt that persecution and violent attacks were disgusting things, 'even if the victims are only Jews'.[35] The BUF were also supporters of Hitler's Germany which did not sit well with the attitude of many Conservatives.[36] Whilst some, such as Austen Chamberlain and Duff Cooper, were anti-German, many other Conservatives simply did not really like 'foreigners'. Whilst this attitude led to a natural inclination towards anti-Semitism, it also blunted its vehemence.

The disgust with which the activities of the fascists were regarded produced a resolution of the annual meeting of the central council of the National Union which asked the government to consider introducing legislation outlawing racialist political propaganda.[37] At a dinner at the Savoy Hotel in May 1937 Oliver Stanley, the President of the Board of Education, told his audience that the tragic events befalling Jewry, so long as they occurred overseas, could only be deplored. However, 'when the challenge was being made to a century-old tradition of freedom and tolerance', he did not think that anyone could keep silent.[38]

THE ANSCHLUSS AND THE CONSERVATIVE RESPONSE

The issue of Jewish refugees, other than in the context of Palestine, played almost no role on the national political stage until the Germans marched into Austria and annexed it in March 1938. As the crisis in Central Europe deepened, the concern for her Jewish population increased. Daniel Sommerville, the Conservative member for Willesden East, asked if the government would take international action together with other interested powers to seek better treatment for European Jewry under threat of persecution.[39] Victor Cazalet, the Conservative member for Chippenham, 11 days after the Anschluss, asked whether the government would be prepared to offer immediate citizenship to a certain Austrian who had resided in Britain for some time. Sir Samuel Hoare stated the government's position as one of pursuing the policy of offering asylum, as far as practical, but that it was essential to avoid creating an impression that the 'door is open to immigrants of all kinds'.[40]

Locker-Lampson, however, proposed an overt policy to assist Jewish victims of Nazism by introducing a motion to bring forward a Bill to extend Palestinian nationality to them. The motion was passed on the casting vote of the Speaker. However, of the 144 votes in favour, only ten came from government supporters: of these eight were Conservatives, one independent Conservative and the other, a National Liberal. In addition to Locker-Lampson, the other Conservatives who supported the proposal were Vyvian Adams, the member for Leeds West, Colonel Sir George Courthope, the member for Rye, Peter Eckersley, who represented Manchester Exchange, Sir Nicholas Grattan-Doyle, who sat for Newcastle-upon-Tyne North, Sir John Haslam, the member for Bolton, Sir Cooper Rawson, who represented Brighton, and Rear-Admiral Sir Murray Sueter, the member for Hertford. Daniel Lipson, the Jewish independent Conservative for Cheltenham, and George Morrison, the Liberal National for the Scottish Universities, were the other National Government MPs who supported the motion.[41] The following month Neville Chamberlain refused time to discuss the matter[42] and no more was to be heard of this novel attempt to save Jewish lives until consuls of neutral countries adopted the practice during the ensuing world war.

Another proposal had been raised in the Commons by Ian Hannon, who sat in the Conservative interest for Wolverhampton, Bilston. He asked that a scheme of settlement be made in British colonies. The government, however, considered that there was no suitable territory for large-scale settlement owing to climatic and economic factors.[43]

The actions of the Nazis in their treatment of Jews who held British nationality incensed Brigadier-General Edward Speirs, the Conservative member for Carlisle. He asked, on more than one occasion, that the prime minister should protest at such treatment.[44] Another Conservative backbencher, Richard Porrit, who sat for the Heywood and Radcliffe division of Lancashire, asked Chamberlain what steps were being taken to protect the property of British Jews in Germany.[45]

One of the most passionate Conservative advocates of the Jewish cause was Victor Cazalet. In a letter to the editor of *The Times*, following his visit to Vienna, he wrote that none of the reports of

Austrian Jewry had exaggerated their plight and their hopeless future. 'Unless some action is taken soon', he stated, 'a proportion of the shame may legitimately be felt by those outside the boundaries of the Greater Reich.'[46] In July he co-signed a further letter to *The Times* protesting against the Nazis' attempts to destroy 'one of the most gifted races in Austria and Germany' and urged that the British government give full support to the Evian Conference on refugees.[47]

In the adjournment debate at the end of July, Cazalet said that it was impossible to exaggerate the situation of hundreds of thousands of Jews, and others, in central Europe and that there were 'wholesale indiscriminate arrests of Jews going on in Vienna'. He perceptively stated that 'we can all understand one act of cruelty, but what we cannot conceive is a definite official policy that is driving thousands of people to choose suicide as the only release from their problems'. Cazalet advocated Jewish settlement, in addition to that in Palestine, in central and eastern Africa. He recalled Joseph Chamberlain's offer to the Jews of a settlement in East Africa and told the Commons that the Jews 'would rather fight the tsetse fly in Central Africa than the Nazi regime in Germany'.[48]

However, the Conservative Party in the Commons remained, at least in substantial part, hostile to Jewish immigrants or refugees. Sir Ralph Glyn, the member for Abingdon, asked if it were intended that precautions were to be taken to prevent 'the entry of undesirable persons' who could take advantage of the 'present special circumstances'.[49] Page-Croft required the reassurance of the home secretary that there would be no variation in government policy that, as long as there remained high unemployment, 'there will be no wholesale importation of refugees allowed'.[50] Glyn and Sir John Withers, who sat for Cambridge University, sought details of how many Jews had been allowed into Britain and of these, how many had been naturalised.[51] Sir Philip Dawson, the member for Lewisham West and chairman of the Anglo-Italian Parliamentary Committee, enquired if the home secretary proposed to take action to limit alien competition from refugees.[52]

GOVERNMENT POLICY

The Conservative leadership in the government was, therefore, under conflicting pressures from within the Party. In the July 1938 adjournment debate Winterton stated that the government had adopted a 'middle-course' policy which was defined as the treatment of each refugee as sympathetically as possible but without indiscriminate admission. This policy, he added, had the support of the private refugee organisations who, up to this time, had vetted, supported and organised the refugees admitted to Britain.

Winterton advised the Commons that the Evian Conference on Refugees had concluded that the only practical solution to the problem was 'infiltration, not mass migration'. The reasons that he gave for this approach was that 'we live in an age of intense suspicion, acute nationalism, and every sort of restriction of an economic character'. He considered that the impracticability of mass-migration was the result of the changes in admission policies that had already been adopted by the Dominions and the United States, which had previously had 'open door' policies. This, he considered, was not anti-Semitism. Those countries taking part in the conference would continue to limit immigration to their 'absorptive capacity', but Winterton hoped that this would be more liberally interpreted.[53]

The government had already considered its approach to the increasingly pressing issue of the refugees immediately following Germany's occupation of Austria in March. Hoare reported to the cabinet that he anticipated that more refugees from Austria would seek refuge in Britain. He felt 'great reluctance in putting another obstacle in the way of these unfortunate people'. The cabinet agreed that the matter should be dealt with by a committee under the chairmanship of the home secretary. This committee was instructed to 'bear in mind' those matters raised by Hoare 'regarding the importance of adopting as humane an attitude as possible'.[54]

There appears from this cabinet decision to have been the beginning of a substantive change in the way that the Conservative leadership was to view the admission of Jews into Britain. As has been discussed previously, Conservative immigration policy since the Aliens Act 1905 had been to keep immigrants out of Britain, particularly those emanating from eastern Europe. Although the 1905 Act had been amended at its committee stage to accommodate those immigrants who were the subject of religious or political persecution, the operation of the Aliens Order by Conservative and Conservative-dominated administrations had not generously interpreted this provision.

The treatment of Jews by the Nazis, which had reached a new pinnacle of inhumanity after the Anschluss, evoked sufficient disgust to allow a reappraisal of Conservative immigration policy.

It is possible that central European Jews, most of whom were well educated, middle class, and practised western European mores, although not English, were seen as generally less threateningly alien than those who had fled directly from eastern Europe in the earlier part of the century. It is also possible that the central European Jews, businessmen and professionals, were seen as wealth creators and opponents to the socialism which had been seen as the hallmark of many of the earlier eastern European Jewish immigrants.

Another reason for this change may have resulted from the Conservatives' policy towards Palestine and the Jewish national home, which is examined in detail in Chapter 8. It is possible that there was a realisation that the pressure to prevent Jewish immigration into Palestine might be greater than the pressure to exclude Jews from Britain.

However, it was clear to the government that Jewish immigration into Britain would need to be carefully managed in order to avoid arousing increased anti-Semitism. Hoare's cabinet committee had been charged by the whole cabinet with 'avoiding the creation of a Jewish problem in this country'. This was made potentially more difficult as a result of the pressure on Jews to emigrate following the events which occurred in Germany during November 1938.

KRISTALLNACHT

On 7 November, Herschel Grynszpan, a Jew, fatally shot Ernst von Rath, the third-secretary at the German Embassy in Paris. On the night of 9/10 November Nazi formations attacked thousands of Jews, and smashed and looted Jewish property. There were 91 persons killed and some 20,000 arrested, most of whom were sent to concentration camps. One hundred and seventy-seven synagogues were destroyed and 7,500 shops attacked and plundered. On 12 November a collective fine of one billion Reichsmarks (approximately £84 million) was levied on the Jewish community in respect of von Rath's murder. Jewish insurance claims were forfeited to the state. On 3 December a decree was passed which 'aryanised' remaining Jewish property, and Jews were, from 1 January, forbidden to function in the German economy.

Notwithstanding the trauma inflicted upon German Jewry, Robert Turton, the Conservative member for the Thirsk and Malton division of Yorkshire, asked the home secretary to refuse readmission of aliens who left the country as they 'clearly have no desire to live in the country of their adoption'. He also requested that aliens be excluded from London.[55]

However, the general reaction amongst Conservatives to the persecution of the Jews was indignation. Even Henry 'Chips' Channon, the Conservative member for Southend, who had visited Germany in the summer of 1936 and had become an admirer of the Nazi regime, considered the German actions 'short-sighted, cruel and unnecessary'. He confided to his diary that he could no longer cope with them and he considered that they had lost all sense of reason. Hitler, he considered, had made Chamberlain's task more difficult.[56]

Owing to the events of *Kristallnacht* the appeasement policy of Chamberlain's government came under the spotlight only two months after the Munich conference. Harold Macmillan thought that *Kristallnacht* had more effect in swinging opinion away from 'the rosy views of appeasement' than any other event. 'The natural decency of the British people', he wrote, 'was deeply shocked.'[57] Although the opinion of an arch anti-appeaser and written some 25 years after the events, this view cannot be easily dismissed. On 18 November 1938, Lord Zetland, the secretary of state for India, spoke in Torquay at a meeting in support of the government. He said that he was 'obliged to confess that my hope [of the Munich conference] has been rudely shaken by the events in Germany of the past week'. He assured his audience that the government were giving the problem 'their most serious consideration and that they will be prepared to find a haven of rest for some at least of [the Jews] within the confines of the British Empire'.[58]

The issue of the Jewish problem had been discussed during the meeting of the cabinet committee on foreign policy which had met on 14 November. Chamberlain opened the discussion by stating that 'we are not in a position to frighten Germany'. However, there was a 'very general and strong desire that something effective should be done to alleviate the terrible fate of the Jews of Germany'. Stanley raised the suggestion of settlement in British Guiana. Chamberlain said that the opening up of an undeveloped country was a long and expensive business and that the settlement of 250,000 Jews would take a very long time.[59] He considered that the most suitable places for the mass settlement of Jews within the Empire were to be found only in the Dominions. However, the Dominion governments had been reluctant to accept mass immigration. The committee decided that the United States government should be approached to consider the assignment of part of Britain's immigration quota of 60,000 to enable German Jews to emigrate to America.[60]

At the cabinet meeting on 16 November Halifax reported that United States Ambassador Kennedy had advised that the German pogroms had created anti-British feeling in the United States. It was suggested that as Britain was near at hand it should have been able to take effective steps to stop the persecution. This attitude of the Americans appeared to have concerned the foreign secretary. Halifax felt obliged to point out to his colleagues that he attached great political importance to providing support for Jewish relief. He suggested that Britain might make some part of the Empire available for settlement. Chamberlain thought that in addition to offering an overseas territory the government could make a considerable contribution towards the problem by allowing Jews to enter Britain as a temporary refuge.[61]

Walter Elliot thought that it was vital to take immediate action and he warned that a political campaign of agitation, such as that undertaken by Gladstone over the Bulgarian atrocities, could be mounted. He also appealed to his colleagues' self-interest by reminding them that many of the refugees would prove to be valuable citizens as had others in the past. However, Hoare had said that it was the Jewish representatives who were averse to allowing a very large number of Jews to enter Britain, or allowing entry to those whom they had not approved. The reason for this view was given as the fear of 'an anti-Jewish agitation in this country'. The home secretary opined that the government was going as far as public opinion would allow.[62] He clearly did not share the view expressed by his pro-Jewish colleague Elliot and it was arguably Conservative rather than general public to favour Jewish entry into Britain opinion which was the cabinet's primary concern. Any policy to favour Jewish entry into Britain which the government contemplated would be vigorously opposed by those who considered the Jews to be not only undesirable but also a menace to western civilisation.

CONSERVATIVE ANTI-SEMITISM – THE MP FOR THE PEEBLES AND SOUTHERN DIVISION

One such Parliamentarian was Captain Archibald Maule Ramsay who had become the Conservative MP for the Peebles and Southern division of Midlothian and Peebles in 1931.[63] He had been educated at Eton and Sandhurst and was severely wounded in the First World War. He appears to have become aware of what he considered to be the dangers of communism during the course of the Spanish Civil War in 1937. He later explained that in 1938 he became aware that Bolshevism was Jewish. He became sympathetic towards Germany and virulently anti-Semitic. During 1938 he joined the Co-ordinating Committee, a group of right-wing organisations opposed to communism, some of which were anti-Semitic. The committee ceased to exist in early 1939 and Ramsay formed the Right Club which, he wrote, was 'to oppose and expose the activities of Organised Jewry',[64] but the first objective was 'to clear the Conservative party of Jewish influence'.[65] Ramsay was also a member of the Nordic League, an association of 'race-conscious Britons'.[66]

Ramsay did not, however, pursue his anti-Semitism in the Commons until after the outbreak of war. After the resignation of Leslie Hore-Belisha as secretary of state for war, Ramsay tabled a motion, which still appeared on the order paper months later. He argued that the 'national publicity services' were under the control or influence of powerful organisations which were systematically biased 'against any nationalist cause, Christian or Mohammedan, and favours internationalists and Jews'.[67] In May 1940 he said in the House that 'the essential characteristic of the Comintern is that it is not Russian but International-Jewish' and that the press was 'Jew-ridden'.[68] This speech was only a few days before Ramsay was interned in Brixton Prison, under Regulation 18B, where he remained until September 1944.

Ramsay's anti-Semitism and that of his wife did cause him some constituency problems. One section of the Unionist Association was reported in February 1939 as having been by 'no means pleased' with his anti-Jewish speeches and the adverse publicity he brought to the constituency.[69] Another report stated that an official of the Association had said that exception had been taken to Ramsay's statements initially by the younger element but had then spread throughout the division. It was said to be a logical assumption that a section of the members would insist that he either withdraw his remarks or resign the seat.[70]

However, W. Thorburn, the chairman of the Unionist Association, stated that it was his opinion that if Ramsay was 'honestly convinced that there is a sinister attempt to undermine the social and political life of the country, he is surely entitled to warn his constituents'.[71] A meeting of the Unionist Association's executive, the following week, 'solidly supported Captain Maule Ramsay'.[72] This support was repeated at a general meeting of the Association in March when Ramsay strongly defended his anti-Semitic statements. The reception he was accorded by the meeting indicated that he had their confidence and strong support and at its conclusion he received 'an extremely cordial vote of thanks'.[73]

The treatment of Ramsay contrasts sharply with that meted out to Doran by the Tottenham North Unionists in 1933. There, those supporting their anti-Semitic MP were in a minority, whilst in Peebles the opposite was the case. The failure of the Peebles Conservatives to condemn the views and actions of a man who would, the following year, be considered a danger to the state in time of war was either an act of their blind ignorance of the nature of their MP or a fundamental sympathy with the attitudes and beliefs that Ramsay expounded.

CONSERVATIVE ANTI-SEMITISM IN THE 1930s

If Ramsay could arguably be described as an extremist backbencher of little or no influence in the Party, the same could not be said of (Sir) Joseph Ball, who, as mentioned earlier, was the director of the Conservative Research Department. He was also a personal friend of Chamberlain with whom he went on fishing holidays.[74] Ball's background was in military intelligence and he joined the Party in 1924. In 1936 he was able to acquire the publication *Truth* which had been a liberal journal founded in 1877 with a circulation of about 10,000. The acquisition was covert; he used the financial support of Lord Luke of Pavenham, who acquired the shares on behalf of the Conservative National Publicity Bureau.[75]

Truth was, not unnaturally, a supporter of Chamberlain's government and a severe critic of his opponents. It maintained a consistently anti-Semitic tone. However, it opposed Italy's fascist anti-Semitic laws and was not particularly pro-Arab in its commentary on Palestine.[76] It did suggest, however, that three Jewish Labour Party opponents of Chamberlain, Harold Laski, George Strauss MP and Victor Gollancz, should be given permits to enter Palestine 'so we may be rid of them'.[77] Jews were portrayed as being inclined towards criminal activity. 'The Hebrew flock numbers more black sheep than prize winners', it said in May 1938.[78] The next month the following comments appeared: 'In Great Britain there are I believe only 350,000 Jews, although this is difficult to credit when one walks through the West End on a Saturday night. Yet it is no exaggeration to say that, of every ten swindles that come under the notice of *Truth*, an unduly high proportion are operated by Jews.'[79]

As a supporter of appeasement, *Truth* found it convenient to play down the extent and severity of Nazi persecution of Jews in Germany and Austria. Notwithstanding the numerous reports from non-Jewish observers in central Europe, it alleged that such accounts were nothing more than the 'Hun' atrocity stories similar to those which had been circulated after the German invasion of Belgium in 1914.[80]

Truth opposed Jewish immigration, which was described as an 'invasion' that could become a fifth column working against British interests. Great Britain, in general, and London, in particular, were said to be 'crawling with foreign undesirables'.[81] Jewish refugees were characterised as being prosperous, arrogant and ungrateful. In June 1939 it stated that 'one of the mysteries of this present time is how the refugees who are pouring into Great Britain manage to present such a well fed, well dressed, and cheerful – not to say arrogant – appearance ... Our uninvited guests cut a much more prosperous figure than our own people in the depressed areas, or our thousands of unemployed blackcoats.'[82]

Truth was not consistent in its attitude towards anti-Semitism. In August 1939 it argued that one of the reasons that both Jews and Gentiles should oppose the indiscriminate admission of refugees was because it could lead to a violent manifestation of anti-Semitism in Britain, 'where, at best, that feeling is always only just below the surface'.[83] However, three months later it declared that one of the main causes of the survival of anti-Semitism in Britain was the 'uncouth and ungrateful behaviour' of the more affluent Jewish refugees from central and eastern Europe. 'Those people have excited anti-Semitic feeling', it wrote, 'where, prior to their seeking and getting asylum in this country, it did not exist at all.'[84] Even if it was unable to decide upon the nature of anti-Semitism in Britain, the journal was certainly attempting to ensure that it did not dissipate.

What is also clear is that Chamberlain was aware that *Truth* was secretly controlled by Ball.[85] It is, therefore, almost impossible not to believe that Chamberlain was fully aware and, at least, tacitly approved of the journal's policies, including its virulent anti-Semitism. Chamberlain had, according to Neville Laski, the president of the Jewish Board of Deputies, never expressed a word of sympathy for the Jews in Germany, even on a purely private occasion when nothing of what had been said would be reported.[86] If one can infer from this that Chamberlain was anti-Semitic, he was hardly alone in this belief within the Conservative Party. Halifax subsequently admitted to a close friend many years later that he had 'always been rather anti-Semitic'.[87]

Channon confided to his diary comments about Jews which were probably shared by many of his Conservative colleagues. He described Jewish Conservative MP Philip Sassoon as having an Oriental mind 'with all its vanities' and his Liberal National colleague, Hore-Belisha, as an 'imaginative Jew [and] his mentality is a Hollywood one'. He also described Hore-Belisha as 'an oily man, half a Jew, an opportunist, with the Semitic flair for publicity'. He subsequently wrote that he would become '"the Jew boy"', bungling and self-important'.[88] At the League of Nations head-quarters in Geneva Channon believed that Russians and Jews 'intrigued with and dominated the press' and spread rumours of impending war. These Jews, he considered, were furious that, as a result of the Munich agreement, there would be no war.[89] Channon also considered that the French Prime Minister, Leon Blum, was 'the real architect of many of our woes' and he thought that it was 'revolting to see the Churchill gang kowtowing to this Jewish agitator'.[90]

Jews were not considered to be civilised in the same way as the British upper classes. Channon considered that the servants at Sassoon's Hertfordshire country house were casual and almost rude; 'but this ... often happens', he wrote, 'in a rich Jew's establishment'.[91] Nancy Astor, when rebuked by another Conservative for her actions at a meeting of the foreign affairs committee, retorted 'only a Jew like you would dare to be rude to me'.[92]

As mentioned earlier, one particularly offensive comment in the Commons produced an incident in April 1938. Commander Robert Bower, the Conservative member for the Cleveland division of Yorkshire, shouted to Emanuel Shinwell, the Labour MP for Seaham,[93] to '[g]o back to Poland'. Shinwell, who had grown up in Glasgow, had in fact been born in the East End of London. According to Channon's account of the incident, Shinwell, shaking with fury, got up, crossed the House, and went up to Bower and smacked him very hard across the face. Although both men apologised to the House, everyone was shocked. Channon's verdict on Bower was that he was 'a pompous ass, self-opinionated, and narrow'.[94] Although this was one incident of Conservative anti-Semitism which did not go unanswered, its perpetrator, notwithstanding Channon's views, would not expect to be ostracised by his colleagues. In fact, the view of one Conservative historian was that there was a strong anti-Semitic element in the Party and that the espousal of the Jewish and Zionist causes put politicians such as Boothby, Churchill and Cazalet beyond the pale.[95]

THE NON-DISCLOSURE OF GOVERNMENT POLICY

It was clear that the cabinet were mindful of anti-Semitism in Britain and Hoare was to reveal this anxiety in the Commons in late November 1938. The cabinet believed that there would be a considerable danger in publicly revealing a figure for immigration that would be allowed. The figures that have been released are, therefore, probably unreliable. On 21 November Chamberlain told the House that about 11,000 refugees had been admitted and remained since 1933.[96] It is difficult to reconcile this with the subsequently published statistics.[97] It is, therefore, considered that there was probably a deliberate policy to avoid reporting accurate information in respect of the numbers of Jews who were admitted to Britain.

The Commons debated the 'deplorable treatment suffered by certain racial, religious and political minorities in Europe' on the evening of 21 November. Samuel Hammersley, who had been returned for Willesden East at a by-election the previous July,[98] believed that the international community, which had previously dealt with the mass migration of the Greeks from Asia Minor, could find a solution to the problem of German Jewish refugees. He considered that a great deal of exaggeration took place when assessing 'absorptive capacity'. He believed that more Jews could be admitted to Palestine and also into the colonial Empire. He did not, however, suggest increased immigration into Britain itself.[99]

Similarly, Commander Sir Archibald Southby, the Conservative member for Epsom Surrey, considered the solution to Jewish settlement primarily lay elsewhere than Britain. He told the House that it should not lose sight of the fact that 'there exists in the minds of many of our own people a very real fear lest there should be a tremendous influx into this country of refugees who are unable to maintain themselves and who would compete with our own citizens for a livelihood'. He also reminded the Commons that there were 'in London alone about 250,000 Jews'. Whilst Southby did not appear to object to the entry of self-supporting Jewish refugees of good character he was concerned to 'safeguard the occupations of our own folk'. He believed that the solution to the problem of the Jewish refugees would need to be found outside not only Britain itself but also outside Palestine, the Dominions or the Colonies.[100]

In his reply to the debate Hoare reminded the House that Britain was a thickly populated industrial community with a very large number of unemployed and that there was an underlying current of suspicion and anxiety about large-scale alien immigration. He said that there was the making of 'a definite anti-Jewish movement'. His prohibition of demonstrations in parts of London was part of his attempt to stamp it out. He had also, he argued, to be careful to avoid 'anything in the nature of mass immigration which, in my view, would inevitably lead to the growth of a movement which we all wish to see suppressed'.

He admitted, however, that a larger number of visas had been granted than would appear from the figures given earlier in the day by Chamberlain. He also stated that during the previous ten days the Foreign Office passport control offices in Germany had been 'strained to breaking point'. However, although pressed by Captain William Shaw, the Conservative member for Forfar, he refused to effect a quota, arguing that many people would think the number too large whilst others would think it too small.[101]

In order to avoid the appearance of allowing mass immigration, the home secretary stated that the government would look 'sympathetically and favourably' upon applications for entry from trans-migrants, who would only look to Britain as a temporary refuge. He held out the prospect that these could, in part, settle in the colonial empire, whilst others would move on after a period of training in Britain. He also advised the House that he would allow the immigration into Britain of Jewish and other 'non-Aryan' children whose maintenance could be guaranteed.[102]

He concluded his speech by praising the Jewish community in Britain and the other religious bodies working with them in refugee relief. He wished them 'every success in their mission of mercy', adding that he would do his utmost 'to facilitate their work, to extend its scope and to show that we will be in the forefront among the nations of the world in giving relief to these suffering people'.[103] Hoare had given the impression by his closing remarks that the government was only encouraging the private charitable works of the Jews and the churches in Britain. The increasing role of the government in allowing into Britain substantially more Jewish refugees was minimised by the categorisation of many of them as non-permanent immigrants.

THE CONSERVATIVE OPPONENTS OF GOVERNMENT POLICY

Conservative MPs who were opposed to the admission of refugees pressed the government to reverse its policy. Rear-Admiral Tufton Beamish, the Conservative member for Lewes, maintained that every refugee admitted into the country was an incitement to foreign regimes to rid themselves of those they considered to be racially or politically undesirable and that this made great difficulties for Britain.[104] Howard Gritten, the Conservative member for Hartlepool, asked on both 8 and 15 December when the government would limit the 'enormous influx of aliens' in view of the 'great numbers of British unemployed'. When told that the admissions policy was designed not to aggravate adversely current unemployment, he asked whether the government intended 'to continue its special favours to its friends the Jews'.[105] Major-General Alfred Knox, who represented Wycombe, Buckinghamshire, had asked whether the prime minister would consider the possibility 'of setting aside some part of England as a national home for the English',[106] while Major John Stourton, the member for Salford South and a member of Ramsay's Right Club,[107] asked if the home secretary's attention had been drawn to the 'growing public indignation against the policy of admitting further refugees'.[108]

The government refused to change tack and continued to refuse to be drawn as to numbers of Jews who were being admitted. When asked by Stuart Russell, the Conservative member for Darwen, Lancashire, what numbers of adult and child refugees from central Europe the government envisaged as being within the absorptive capacity of the country, Lloyd said that it was 'limited' but that 'it would be impracticable and undesirable to fix and announce some maximum figure'.[109] Similarly, when the Conservative member for Kensington South, Sir William Davison, asked what the total number of Jewish refugees that had been admitted, the conditions of their admission and how many were in paid employment, he received a non-informative answer. Osbert Peake, who was now the under-secretary at the Home Office, replied that it was not possible to distinguish refugees by their religious or racial origins and that the majority had been allowed into Britain on a temporary basis, pending emigration to another country.[110]

THE GOVERNMENT'S PUBLIC CAMPAIGN

At the same time, outside Parliament, the government used Winterton, who had latterly been the Chancellor of the Duchy of Lancaster and chairman of the Inter-Governmental Committee on Refugees, to promote its partially surreptitious refugee policy. Speaking at Cambridge in early February 1939 he attacked those promoting the 'anti-alien outlook', accusing them of being

ignorant of economics and un-Christian.[111] Eight days later in
Bristol, Winterton said that in the highly industrialised and thickly
populated country of Britain the opportunities for integrating
refugees into British national life were strictly limited and the best
hope of an ultimate solution was their settlement in colonies and
overseas territories. However, he said, he could not accept that a
limited settlement of refugees of a different race or religion in
Britain, or to a much greater extent in the colonies, would be
prejudicial to British interests. It was, he considered, 'necessary to
reassure public opinion that there was no question of such a body
of foreigners coming to Britain and injuring British standards of
life or conduct'.[112]

At the end of April, Winterton was obliged to address the fact
that a large number of Jews had by now been admitted to Britain.
In a speech made at the town hall at Worthing in Sussex he said
that it would be a mistake to assume that because Britain was not
in a position to absorb permanently a large number of refugees it
was not prepared to see 'considerable numbers of trans-migrants
in this country'. He confirmed that the home secretary would be
prepared to admit, under proper safeguards, 'a very much larger
number of refugees from the Continent for training in this
country'. This was, he added, provided that they would eventually
find a place of permanent settlement elsewhere after training.[113]

CONSERVATIVE SUPPORT FOR JEWISH REFUGEES

Although the Conservative leadership had expressed its concerns
that a pro-Jewish refugee policy would be opposed by many of its
own supporters and much of the general public, there had been a
surge in support for central European Jewry following the
Kristallnacht in Nazi Germany. A public meeting was held at the
Albert Hall. Amery, whose pro-Jewish views were well
established, was asked to represent the Conservative Party by
Central Office, at Chamberlain's suggestion. It was, according to
his diary, in the nature of a united national protest against racial
and religious persecution in Germany.[114]

On 6 December 1938 the Parliamentary Refugee Committee was
formed. Cazalet was elected chairman with Salter as one of the two
vice-chairmen. There were 20 MPs on the executive, of which ten
were supporters of the National Government, and seven took the
Conservative whip.[115]

There were also individual actions taken by pro-Jewish
Conservatives. Churchill had used his journalism to attack the

Nazi persecution of Viennese Jewry in his article of July 1938 entitled 'The Rape of Austria'.[116] Following Munich, another future Conservative prime minister, Macmillan, gave refuge to about 40, mainly Jewish, refugees in his Sussex home,[117] whilst a former prime minister launched a fund to aid refugees.

It was on 8 December 1938 that Lord Baldwin broadcast on the BBC to ask his listeners to 'come to the aid of the victims ... of an explosion of man's inhumanity to man'. He said that he spoke not as a party politician but as 'an ordinary Englishman who is shocked and distressed by the plight of those despised and rejected people and their innocent children'. He said that it was the task of the various international governments to see what they could accomplish to settle 'these unhappy people'.[118] This intervention by the former prime minister, although couched in non-political terms, would undoubtedly have had an effect upon the opinions of some Party members towards Jewish refugees.

The Baldwin Fund followed the Lord Mayor of London's Czech Refugee Fund which had been inaugurated in September 1938. The Lord Mayor's appeal closed in July 1939 and raised some £528,510,[119] whilst the Baldwin Fund which closed in September 1939 raised a further £522,651.[120] These public appeals must be regarded as significant fund-raising undertakings; the donations came largely from non-Jewish sources. The Jewish organisation, the Council for German Jewry, had itself raised some £500,000 by December 1938.[121]

GOVERNMENT FINANCIAL SUPPORT FOR REFUGEES

Whilst the government still maintained that the care and support of refugees was a matter for the Jewish community and private charitable support, by January 1939 *The Times* acknowledged that the problem had by then become too large for private effort alone.[122] However, the cabinet did not concede the necessity to provide government funds until that July.

Chamberlain believed that if public money was to be made available it was essential that the co-operation of the United States was secured in order to assist in meeting the anticipated attacks from critics.[123] However, it was a deputation from the now 200-strong Parliamentary Refugee Committee which on 17 July proposed that government assistance, either by loan or grant, should be made available.[124] The issue did not present itself, other than in the press, for general debate following Chamberlain's announcement in the Commons on 19 July that they were 'examining the question of Government participation in defraying the cost of emigration of refugees'.[125] It was a matter, therefore, that Chamberlain's pre-war government did not have to face, and it was thus able substantially to avoid criticism from the opponents of immigration.[126]

8

The Conservatives and Palestine, 1930–39

The tensions between Jews and Arabs in Palestine erupted in August 1929, the catalyst being a dispute over access to the Western Wall in Jerusalem. The ensuing riots spread across the country. On 24 August 66 Jews were killed and 45 wounded in Hebron and on 29 August 45 were killed in Safed. The total death toll was 133 Jews killed and 339 wounded; 116 Arabs killed and 232 wounded, primarily by the security forces.

The response of the Labour government was to establish a commission of enquiry into the disturbances. It fell to Lord Passfield, the ennobled Sidney Webb, as colonial secretary to appoint Sir Walter Shaw, a former colonial chief justice as chairman with three members of Parliament as the other commission members; these were Sir Henry Betterton (Conservative), R. Hopkin Morris (Liberal) and Harry Snell (Labour). The commission reported the following March.[1] It concluded that, although the outbreak of violence was, from its inception, an attack by Arabs on Jews, this had not been premeditated. The commission further found no fault with the behaviour of either the Palestine Arab Executive or the Palestine government. It considered that the fundamental cause was Arab hostility to Jews, being the consequence of the failure to implement Arab political and national aspirations and their fear for their economic future.

The commission recommended a clearly defined policy to regulate and control Jewish immigration, with consultation with non-Jewish interests on the subject. It also recommended that legislation be introduced to prevent the eviction of Arab tenant farmers from land sold to the Jews. The British government was encouraged to define with greater clarity the safeguarding rights in the mandate for the non-Jewish population and to take into account the Arab disappointment in not obtaining self-government when recognition granted to the Jewish Agency gave special status to the Jews.

The cabinet decided that there should be an authoritative inquiry into immigration, development and agricultural settlement in Palestine which would consider the political aspects of these issues.[2] Sir John Hope Simpson, a former Liberal MP who had latterly served as deputy chairman of the League of Nations Commission for the settlement of Greek refugees, was appointed to this end. His report, which was published in October 1930,[3] concentrated on the agricultural absorptive capacity of Palestine without fully considering industrial development potential. He concluded that the potential cultivable land was only some 60 per cent of the estimate of the Palestine government's commissioner of lands and that there was insufficient land to support the Arab fellahin. The Zionist Organisation's policy of employing only Jewish agricultural workers was considered to be incompatible with the mandate and good government. He called for the reduction in, or if necessary the suspension of, Jewish immigration if it adversely affected Arab employment.

The government issued its policy statement, known as the Passfield White Paper, in October.[4] This endorsed Hope Simpson's recommendations and consequently was seen as a betrayal of the Jewish national home. Weizmann was later to write that it was considered 'by all Jewish friends of the National Home, Zionist and non-Zionist alike, and by a host of non-Jewish well-wishers, as rendering, and intending to render, our work in Palestine impossible'.[5] The suspension of Jewish immigration in May and the publication of the White Paper led to Weizmann's resignation from the Jewish Agency.

THE CONSERVATIVE RESPONSE

On 23 October a letter was published in *The Times* expressing deep concern about Weizmann's resignation. The letter was signed by Baldwin, Austen Chamberlain and Amery. They paid tribute to his 'unswerving loyalty' and co-operation with the British government during the 12 years of his leadership of the Zionist movement. They stated that their personal experience of Weizmann convinced them that 'he would have gone to any length, compatible with his duties to his people, to facilitate the task of His Majesty's Government in carrying out the Mandate'.

The former Conservative ministers wrote that they were profoundly conscious of the obligations to both Arabs and Jews embodied in the mandate which, they argued, had been the basis of British government policy. They regretted that the Labour government had appeared to abandon this policy and had refused the Zionists' offer of a round table conference. Nor had they allowed parliamentary debate before adopting 'a policy so definitely negative in character' that it appeared to conflict not only with the intention of the League of Nations mandate but also with 'the whole sprit of the Balfour Declaration and the statements made by successive Governments in the last twelve years'. The letter concluded that the White Paper would create a feeling of distrust in British good faith 'upon public opinion in American Jewry and elsewhere'.[6]

A letter to *The Times* was not the most usual forum for the Opposition leadership to express its views on government policy. Although no opportunity for debate had yet presented itself to discuss the White Paper Baldwin was able to address the issue in his response to the King's Speech some five days later.[7] It was perhaps the desire to reach immediately a wider audience that motivated the Conservative leaders to write the letter. According to Amery, Blanche 'Baffy' Dugdale, Balfour's niece and an ardent Zionist, thought that the Conservative leaders ought to dissociate themselves as quickly as possible from the Labour government's policy. At Amery's suggestion, she saw Baldwin and had a letter drafted which was revised and amended by Amery and Chamberlain.[8] Weizmann also considered that the speed at which the Conservatives responded was due to Dugdale.[9]

The Conservative concern at the reaction of world Jewry was specifically mentioned in the letter in the reference to the American Jewish community. Thus the Conservative leadership continued to consider that Jewish opinion could still have an influence on world affairs, a view which been a factor in the decision to issue the Balfour Declaration which has been examined in Chapter 3. This may have been reinforced by the item which appeared in the following day's edition of *The Times*, when it was reported from New York that their letter had been received by the Jews 'with much gratification', whilst definite plans for 'reprisals' were under discussion if the British government persisted in its present policy. Ten days later, a report appeared of the meeting held at Madison Square Garden in New York where some 35,000 Jews attended to celebrate the thirteenth anniversary of the Balfour Declaration and to condemn the Passfield White Paper. They were supported by the presence of the Mayor of New York City, the United States Senator for New York, who sat on the foreign relations committee, and the Lieutenant-Governor of New York. 'Long messages opposing British policy, which were read out aloud to the cheering crowds', were sent by the Republican candidate for Governor of New York, the president of the American Federation of Labor and the Governor of New York, Franklin D. Roosevelt. Similar meetings were reported to have taken place in other major American cities.[10]

In the meantime two further politicians had written to *The Times*, Lord Hailsham, the former Conservative Lord Chancellor, and Simon, the one-time Liberal home secretary. These lawyers wrote that the White Paper appeared to involve a departure from the obligations imposed by the mandate. They opined that Britain could not afford to allow any suspicion of its good faith to be questioned nor 'its determination to carry out to the full its international obligations'.[11]

In the House of Commons two Conservative pro-Zionists, Walter Elliot, member for Kelvingrove and the former under-secretary of state for Scotland, and Brendan Bracken, the member for Paddington North, were able to obtain the prime minister's assurances that until the White Paper was discussed in Parliament no implementation of its policies would take place.[12] The undertaking would be redeemed some five days later, on the 17 November, when the Commons held the debate on the Passfield White Paper.

THE DEBATE ON THE PASSFIELD WHITE PAPER

Amery was the official spokesman of the Conservative Party.[13] He said that in addition to the reasons relating to the furtherance of the First World War, the decision to issue the Balfour Declaration was the permanent strategic reason connected with the Suez Canal. He argued that the Churchill White Paper of 1922 expressed the desire for Jews and Arabs each to have the opportunity to develop their national home and to combine it with a common patriotism for the Palestinian State, 'just as the French and English-speaking Canadians have their national home in Canada and combine it with a common Canadian patriotism'. He accepted that this interpretation of the 'national home' was a disappointment to some Zionists but it was accepted by the Zionist Executive 'under Dr Weizmann's leadership, with unquestioning loyalty'.

Amery criticised the Passfield White Paper as a document of some peculiarity, comprising, in part one, certain extracts from the Churchill White Paper and, in part two, certain passages from the Hope Simpson report. What he considered significant was that it contained only negative passages and 'all the balancing passages are carefully omitted'. The impression that this gave, he argued, was that the whole operation of the mandate for an indefinite period of years was to be crystallised at its present standard of development. 'No wonder', he added, 'that there has been an outcry all over the world.'

Amery then attacked the Labour government's retraction that 'all this was premature' and the assurances given by the prime minister to Jan Smuts that 'everything is as it was before'. The *status quo ante* had not, however, been restored, as Moslem feeling world-wide was being mobilised against the mandate itself, not its detailed application, whilst 'Jewish feeling all over the world has been mobilised against this country'. The official Conservative policy was not one that would oppose precautions being taken in respect of immigration which would prevent the spread of unemployment in Palestine, but the difficulties that Arab farmers faced 'should not be made an excuse for going back upon a policy to which we are bound not only by our own pledges and our own reputation, but by solemn international obligations'.[14]

The international implications of British policy in Palestine was taken up later in the debate by Elliot. He argued that it was 'a world question. You are dealing with the vast East on the one side and the whole of the New World, passing right across to the Pacific, on the other.' He said that they were 'dealing with the good will of a people widely spread over the earth'. He also maintained that the British should 'keep faith' with the Moslems as well as the Jews. He considered that the whole world had a responsibility to the Jews and the government had a greater responsibility than they appeared to have acknowledged. Ormsby-Gore, the former under-secretary of state for the colonies, simply told the Labour government that they 'have insulted the Jews'.[15]

However, the condemnation of the Passfield White Paper was not unanimous on the Conservative benches. Colonel Charles Howard-Bury spoke in support of the government. Howard-Bury was the Conservative member for Chelmsford, a seat that he won in a by-election in November 1926. He had previously sat for the Bilston division of Wolverhampton from 1922 until he was defeated in October 1924, and during this period had been Walter Guinness's parliamentary private secretary. He opined that the government had acted 'very courageously and impartially' in producing their White Paper. Howard-Bury said that in the policy adopted by previous governments over the previous eight years the Arabs had felt that the scales were weighted against them. They did not have the propaganda that the 'Jewish organisation' had in putting forward their case and thus riot and insurrection occurred. 'How would Hon. Members like', he asked, '100,000 Polish, Rumanian, or Russian people to be settled suddenly on their best farm land?'

He regretted that the Conservative leadership had written their letter to *The Times* as it 'put Palestine in the future at the mercy of political parties'. Howard-Bury stated that he feared that 'in Palestine we are to be committed to a Zionist policy, and it will mean that, whenever our party comes into office, pressure will be put upon us by Jewish organisations throughout the world to carry out a policy favourable to them'.[16]

THE ANTI-ZIONIST CONSERVATIVES

The intervention by Howard-Bury illustrated that the Conservative Party was not united in its views on Palestine. The Conservative chairmen of committees had not, in fact, wanted a debate on Palestine as they feared it would show divisions within the parliamentary Party. Amery therefore decided to ask the Liberal leader, Archibald Sinclair, to try to get a day themselves for a debate.[17]

This split in opinion had re-emerged noticeably in the autumn of 1929. Former Conservative ministers had spoken publicly of their policy towards the national home for the Jews. Churchill, speaking in Vancouver in early September, said that the Jews had as good a title as the Arabs to make their homes in Palestine and the Jews had brought great wealth and civilisation there. 'No British political party would', he continued, 'repudiate the War-time undertaking to the Zionist movement.'[18] This speech may have been considered to be too pro-Zionist and was redressed by a speech made the following month by Amery in Montreal. He stated that there had never been any intention of making Palestine 'solely the homeland of the Jews' and the Balfour Declaration had made it incumbent on the British to give equal opportunity to both Arab and Jew.[19]

In a letter to the editor of *The Times* Earl Winterton, the Conservative member for Horsham and Worthing and the former under-secretary of state for India, considered that his experience of being attached to the Arab forces in the First World War and his ministerial position led him to believe that there was difficulty in assessing the blame for any particular outbreak of fanaticism between religious communities in Palestine.[20]

In the Commons Howard-Bury went further by asking the extent and nature of the damage done to Moslem holy places by the Jews.[21] He implied that Jews were treated in a preferential way by the mandatory judiciary[22] and that Arab rights were under threat at the Western Wall.[23] He also implied that Palestine was included in the 'pledge' given to the Arabs by McMahon in 1915, although in this he was countered by Ormsby-Gore, who called on the government to publish the correspondence as he asserted that it would be clear that Palestine was excluded.[24] Howard-Bury, in the Supply debate in February 1930, again questioned the policy of supporting the Jews in Palestine. 'Is it', he posed, 'more important to protect a foreign minority in Palestine than it is in Iraq, in Egypt, or in India?'[25] It is possible that his continuing attacks led another Conservative MP, Austin Hudson, who represented Hackney North, to support the Conservative leadership, declaring that he was not a Jew but was 'a supporter of the Zionist Organisation and the Balfour Declaration'.[26] The activities of Howard-Bury caused such concern that the editor of the *Jewish Chronicle* found it necessary to write a leading article which criticised his contribution to the Supply debate.[27]

The pro-Arab parliamentarians met with the Palestinian Arab delegation at the House of Commons on 10 April. A resolution was passed which called on the government to 'go fully into Arab grievances in the hope of finding a solution which would meet the Arab claims and bring peace to Palestine'. The meeting was chaired by Lord Brentford, as Joynson-Hicks had become, and the resolution was moved by Howard-Bury and seconded by the Conservative peer, the Earl of Denbigh.[28] The Arab delegation had been met on its arrival by Lord Templemore, former parliamentary private secretary to the Earl of Onslow, and Howard-Bury.[29]

THE PRO-ZIONIST CONSERVATIVES

The pro-Zionists had again organised themselves into the Palestine Parliamentary Group in November 1929. Amery and Ormsby-Gore were among the members who attended that first meeting.[30] The *Jewish Chronicle* reported a further meeting of the group on 9 April 1930 at which John Buchan, the Conservative member for the Scottish Universities, was present; their purpose was apparently to press for a parliamentary debate on the Shaw Commission's report.[31]

At the same time *The Times* was used as an extra-parliamentary forum by MPs to further their arguments on the issue of the mandate. On 2 April John Buchan co-signed a letter with Lord [Robert] Cecil, now a cross-bencher, Malcolm MacDonald, the son of Ramsay MacDonald who was to become the National Labour colonial secretary in June 1935,[32] and Sir Archibald Sinclair, who became the Liberal secretary of state for Scotland in November 1931 and leader of the Liberal Party in November 1935,[33] which urged the government to reaffirm the adherence of Britain to both 'the letter and spirit of the Mandate'. In the same edition Boothby wrote that political conflicts should not be allowed to overshadow the 'great economic and social progress' in Palestine. He considered that 'Jewish energy and British guidance' had made roads and railways and had built hospitals and schools.[34]

The following day Winterton wrote that he deprecated active political support for either Arabs or Jews. 'It is surely beneath the dignity of British legislators to participate in such a struggle as active partisans.'[35] Six days later a letter from John Wardlaw-Milne, the Conservative member for Kidderminster, supported this opinion.[36] It is possible that those opposed to the Zionist cause sought this method to neutralise its supporters. However, the subsequent retraction of Labour policy set out in the MacDonald letter to Weizmann of 13 February 1931[37] would indicate that those who supported the Jewish national home, albeit in its modified definition, were of sufficient strength in Parliament in general and in the Conservative Party in particular.

This pro-Zionist viewpoint can be illustrated by the resolution which was passed at the conference of the Conservative Party's youth wing, the Junior Imperial League, in May 1931. It was proposed by the vice-president of the Stratford Divisional Council, Norman Aarons, and seconded by G. E. Rush, the chairman of the Plaistow Divisional Council, both East London constituencies. The motion declared the conference's adhesion to the policy laid down by Balfour in 1917 providing for the establishment of the Jewish national home in Palestine. It called on the Labour government to carry out the policy in accordance with the mandate and further 'records its wish that the next Conservative Government will continue to carry out the solemn obligations of the Palestine Mandate'.[38]

THE WHITECHAPEL BY-ELECTION

The issue of Palestine was at the fore in the by-election which was held in Whitechapel and St George's in the East End of London at the time of the publication of the Passfield White Paper. The Jewish proportion of the electorate has been estimated to have been between 32.5 and 40 per cent.[39] In 1929 the Labour candidate, Harry Gosling, had been elected with a majority of 9,180 over the Liberals, who achieved a vote of 4,521, with Loel Guinness, the Conservative, obtaining 3,417 votes. At the by-election all three main party candidates declared support for the Jewish national home. The Labour candidate, James Hall, pledged that he would vote against the government if it proposed to implement the White Paper.[40] The Liberal candidate was the Jewish Zionist solicitor Barnett Janner, whilst Loel Guinness again stood in the Conservative interest.

In his election address Guinness pledged to 'uphold, in the letter and the spirit, the undertaking given to the Jews in the Balfour Declaration'. He appealed to the Jewish electorate 'as a member of the only Party in the House of Commons which has the will and the power to resist the Government's attack on the Jewish people'.[41] Henry Mond, Lord Melchett's son, and Amery spoke at meetings in support of Guinness.[42] However, the Conservatives did not receive the support they needed. The intervention of a Communist candidate no doubt took Labour votes, whilst the Liberals received almost all the other votes from those electors who deserted Labour. Hall was returned for Labour with a vote of 8,544. His majority over Janner, who received 7,445 votes, was 899. Guinness obtained 3,735 votes, an increase of only 318.[43] It was no doubt clear to the Conservatives that, notwithstanding the spirited attack by its front bench and others on the White Paper, working-class Jews would not vote for them in these circumstances.

THE NATIONAL GOVERNMENT AND THE 1931 GENERAL ELECTION

In August 1931 the Conservatives and the Liberals joined with the rump of the Labour Party to form a National Government under the nominal leadership of Ramsay MacDonald. In the general election held in October the National Government won 554 seats, with Labour retaining only 52 seats, the Lloyd George Liberal bloc four seats and others five seats. The Conservatives dominated, with 473 MPs returned. There were 35 Liberal Nationals (Simonite), 33 Liberals (Samuelite) and only 13 National Labour; nevertheless MacDonald was retained as prime minister. However, the Colonial Office was given to Philip Cunliffe-Lister, who replaced National Labour's James Thomas.[44]

The cabinet did not consider policy for Palestine until April 1932. It then reconfirmed that Jewish immigration should be strictly governed by the principle of absorptive capacity. The government wished to encourage co-operation between the Palestine government and the Jewish Agency with regard to immigration.[45] It also decided that no pronouncement should be made regarding the establishment of a Legislative Council.[46] The Zionists did not wish to see any measure of self-government which would have given the Arab population a greater number of seats on any legislative or other governmental body and the failure to make substantial progress towards self-government could, therefore, be interpreted as a pro-Zionist policy.

The Palestine Parliamentary Committee was formed in November 1931 'in order to watch over the interests of the Jewish National Home in Palestine'.[47] According to Janner, who became its honorary secretary, 'its members made Zionism one of their Parliamentary duties'.[48] No member of the government could belong to it. Janner named 18 parliamentarians whom he felt worthy of specific mention, of whom half were Conservatives.[49]

One of those mentioned by Janner was Buchan, who was the chairman of the committee and an active lobbyist of the Jewish cause in Palestine until his appointment as governor-general of Canada in March 1935. At a dinner given in March 1932 by the Anglo-Palestinian Club in his honour, he explained his understanding of Zionism. He considered that it meant that there was 'an obligation of honour upon Britain' and he regarded it as a policy of extreme importance for the British Empire.[50] He made the same remarks in the Colonial Office Supply debate the following month. Britain's obligation was to prepare and 'make possible a National Home for such Jews as desire to return'. Buchan accepted that there should be a restriction on immigration but only by reference to the absorptive capacity of the land. He warned that if there was any suspicion in the minds of world Jewry that the government were not fulfilling their obligations the financial contributions could fall off and 'you may find up and down the globe the most serious distrust of the honesty and good will of the country'.[51]

In January 1933 Hitler became chancellor of Germany. As has been discussed previously, this marked an increase in the rise of continental anti-Semitism which was ultimately to have devastating results for European Jewry. The Zionists became increasingly aware of the importance of maintaining a broadly favourable approach towards the Jewish national home in British political circles. Early in March the British section of the Jewish Agency gave a dinner at the Savoy Hotel in honour of the 'Friends of Palestine in Parliament'. Weizmann presided while Melchett proposed the toast to the evening and was seconded by Samuel. Elliot responded for the guests while Labour's Clement

Attlee proposed, and Buchan seconded, the toast to the Jewish national home.

There were 88 MPs present of whom 58 were Conservatives.[52] This represented 14.3 per cent of all MPs. Over 20 per cent of the non-Conservative MPs attended the dinner whilst 12.3 per cent of the Conservative MPs were present. However, some notable pro-Zionist supporters from the Conservative ranks were absent, including Amery, Austen Chamberlain, Churchill and Cazalet. The only Conservative MPs who were also ministers that were present were Elliot, Ormsby-Gore and Sir Frederick Penny.[53] However, the quantitative result indicates that a reasonably large proportion of the Party was well disposed to the concept of the Jewish national home.

JEWISH IMMIGRATION

The Conservative champion of the Arab cause in Parliament, Howard-Bury, had retired at the previous election, apparently owing to the 'pressure of private affairs'.[54] It was not until November 1933 that the matter of immigration was raised effectively by two Conservatives, Captain Peter MacDonald, the member for the Isle of Wight, and Major-General Sir Alfred Knox, who represented Wycombe, Buckinghamshire. MacDonald wanted to know what action would be taken to prevent 'illicit immigration of Jews into Palestine',[55] whilst Knox questioned the substantial growth of immigration during 1933 and blamed it for the 'Arab revolt'.[56]

The government allowed the high commissioner in Palestine to limit the number of immigration certificates issued to the Jews and in April 1934 endorsed the policy that immigration had to be governed by the absorptive capacity of the country.[57] However, the Anglo-Jewish community was becoming increasingly concerned with the potential fate of European Jewry and the Board of Deputies took up the issue of immigration into Palestine with Cunliffe-Lister in June 1934, when a deputation met him. Sir Isadore Salmon, the Jewish Conservative MP for Harrow, was one of the delegation. Although he was the treasurer of the United Synagogue from 1925 to 1934, Salmon had not been a member of the Palestine Parliamentary Committee.[58] His inclusion within the delegation indicated the anxiousness felt for the fate of Jews in an increasingly hostile Continental environment. Cunliffe-Lister, although 'very glad to have had this full and practical discussion', would not advocate any change to the existing policy which allowed the high commissioner to decide upon the number of Jews who could enter Palestine.[59]

The issue of immigration was debated in the columns of *The Times*. In response to a letter from Sir Robert Waley Cohen,[60] William McLean, the Conservative MP for Glasgow Tradeston, argued that the problem of Jewish refugees from Europe should not be confused with the economic development of Palestine. He considered that 'in the uncertain world economic conditions today it would probably be a disaster for all concerned'. The British taxpayer, McLean argued, would ultimately have to meet the cost of all such crises in the dependencies.[61] The question of Jewish immigration would increasingly become the central issue around which other matters would be considered.

THE LEGISLATIVE COUNCIL PROPOSALS

In November 1935 the National government called a general election and was returned, albeit with a reduced majority. The Conservatives now had 387 MPs, National Labour was reduced to eight MPs, whilst the Liberal Nationals returned 33 members. Baldwin had become prime minister in June 1935 and, as a result, Malcolm MacDonald, the former prime minister's son, became colonial secretary. However, in November James Thomas, another National Labour minister, took over that office. His abilities were questioned by Dugdale, who wrote to her cousin in February 1936 that she would 'not rest until Billy Gore [William Ormsby-Gore] reigns in J. H. Thomas' stead. It is not fit that the future of Zion should be in the hands of a drunken ex-engine driver.'[62] Thomas was to resign in May 1936 as a result of a budget leak scandal.

The revival of the plan to implement the proposed Legislative Council was allowed by Thomas to be presented by Sir Arthur Wauchope, the high commissioner, in December 1935. The scheme has been described by one historian of the mandate as somewhat late-Tudor in character, in that the council could debate but could not assume a parliamentary right to govern.[63] The council was to have an Arab majority, consisting of 12 elected members (eight Moslem, three Jewish, and one Christian), nine members nominated by the high commissioner (three Moslem, four Jewish, and two Christian), two members representing 'commercial interests', and five officials.[64]

The pro-Zionist Conservatives opposed the creation of the proposed Legislative Council and the restriction on Jewish immigration. Amery wrote to *The Times* that to go back on, or weaken, the policy of the Jewish national home by deliberately creating difficulties in its fulfilment would be 'a stultification of ourselves and a betrayal of those who have placed their faith in us'. He saw that Palestine was the 'one door of escape' to sheer existence for German Jews.[65] Amery was to have another opportunity to express his views when the issue was debated in the Commons on the 24 March, although he did not catch the Speaker's eye until late in the debate.

The first Conservative to speak in this debate was Anthony Crossley, the member for Stretford (Lancs), who prefaced his remarks by stating that he was not an anti-Semite and that he had many Jewish friends. He said that, although supporting the position of the Arab population, he did not consider that Britain could evade its responsibilities under the mandate. However, he believed that the Jews had taken away the fertile areas of the country from the Arabs and these were now under Jewish cultivation. He thought that the Jews went to Palestine because they 'were more likely to get rich there' under British protection. Yet Crossley did not plead for the immediate implementation of the Legislative Council proposals, but rather wished for a solution to the problems between the communities by the establishment of a system of cantonisation.[66]

The only unqualified support for the government's proposals came from Colonel Douglas Clifton-Brown, the Conservative member for the Hexham division of Northumberland. He stated that while everyone was ' sorry for the Jews and their suffering', Palestine was only a small country and part of a big continent where there were millions of Arabs. The Arab countries were the key to Britain's communications to the East. The Arabs realised, he said, that 'as far as the Western world goes, the Jew is able to pull the strings in this Parliament, and at Geneva or elsewhere more than they can ever hope to do'.[67] Thus in these two speeches the stereotype of the Jew as the mercenary exploiter of the poor and manipulator of the Gentile was evoked.

Churchill led the pro-Zionist Conservative attack on the government. He argued that the Arabs had not been generally capable of dealing with municipal government and therefore to attempt to introduce a national quasi-democratic structure was premature. Thomas had somewhat lamely said that the high commissioner believed a legislative assembly would be in the best interests of both Jews and Arabs and it was 'on this ground that the Government feel compelled to endorse this policy'.[68] Churchill strongly rounded on this by stating that it was Parliament's responsibility and Parliament was not prepared to say that a colonial governor's viewpoint must necessarily be enforced on it.

He considered that notwithstanding the assurances that had been given that the Balfour Declaration and the mandate were safe, 'I personally feel great doubts about it'. Churchill said that at that time 'the Jewish race in a great country is being subjected to most horrible, cold, scientific persecution, brutal persecution'. He felt, therefore, that the House of Commons would not, using the same metaphor that Amery had employed two months earlier, allow the 'one door that is open, the one door which allows some relief, some escape from these conditions, to be summarily closed'.[69]

Cazalet considered that the government were contemplating a very rash and dangerous step. He argued that those who now deplored that Britain had accepted the mandate had to face the current position and that there was no use in furthering such arguments. He considered that the Arabs were only in favour of the Legislative Council because they believed it to be the best means of defeating the objectives of the Balfour Declaration. Cazalet said that the greatest religious persecution that had been known for hundreds of years was taking place and that Palestine was the hope of the persecuted Jews. If the government was to undertake any action which could be interpreted as revising Britain's policy this would be a blow 'as cruel to them as, in the long run, it will be against the best interests both of Palestine and this country'.[70]

Amery stated that there was no inconsistency between the fulfilment of Britain's mandatory obligation of setting up and encouraging a Jewish home in Palestine and the obligation to look after the welfare of the Arab population. Anything which would make it possible for the Arabs to prevent Jews going to Palestine was as intolerable from the point of view of the mandate as anything which would make it possible for the Jews to expel the Arabs. He considered that the policy of the mandate had brought 'happiness, comfort, wealth, and education' to the Arabs of Palestine. Amery stressed the strategic importance of the country as the effective air centre of the imperial system and for oil supplies to the Mediterranean under British control. He also mentioned what he described as 'the appalling suffering of the hapless Jewish people in Germany'.[71] These were almost classic restatements of what had been established Conservative policy towards the Jewish national home.

One of the eight Jewish Conservative MPs spoke in the debate; this was Marcus Samuel, the member for Putney. He evoked the picture of the Jewish immigrants as young people who were inspired by a determination to build up 'a thriving homeland by the sweat of their brows, and not animated by the commercial spirit which we see today in many places'. He stated that the difficulties in India had been dealt with by a round table conference prior to the changes enacted to the Indian constitution. He suggested this course of action for Palestine, 'speaking as an Englishman and a man of peace'.[72]

The last speaker in the debate was Major Henry Proctor, the Conservative member for Accrington. He also considered that in view of the unprecedented persecution of the Jews the proposal would be regarded as a blow against Jewish interests. Proctor believed that it was a mistake to regard Arab opinion as of greater value to the Empire. The Jews had taken the desert and 'life has burst forth in myriad forms'. He advocated delay for up to ten years by which time he envisaged that there would be a more balanced population and a more educated Arab population which would be more appreciative of the value of the Jews in Palestine.[73]

Amery confided in his diary that although Thomas' proposals had been badly battered by the debate he supposed he could or would not give way.[74] Both Churchill and Bracken, however, thought that if the Opposition parties pursued the matter the issue would be dead. Boothby was of a similar opinion.[75] These Conservative backbenchers were proved correct but without the need for further concerted parliamentary action. Although Thomas attempted to obtain the final endorsement of the proposals at the cabinet meeting on 1 April, he was not successful; the matter was delayed.

It was agreed to invite an Arab delegation to London to discuss the matter and Thomas was instructed to consider seeing, in private, government supporters who had opposed the measure. It was proposed to discuss with them confidential matters such as the pledges made to the Arabs, including those made by the high commissioner in 1935, and the possibility of Arab riots which if they arose could possibly retard the development of Zionism for years.[76] However, the issue was to be overtaken by events in Palestine after the Arab rebellion commenced that month.

THE ARAB REVOLT

The murder of two Jews by Arab highwaymen was followed by the killing of two Arabs near the scene of the crime the next night. On 16 April two more Jews were killed and their funeral on 19 April was turned into a riot when 20 more Jews were killed. In another incident nurses and patients in a Jewish clinic were butchered. At the same time the Arab Higher Committee declared a six-month general strike. Armed bands were formed, the most notorious under Fawzi al Kawakji.[77]

The situation continued to deteriorate and violence increased, requiring the security forces to be substantially reinforced. On 19 June a Supply debate on Palestine took place. Ormsby-Gore, who had become colonial secretary on 28 May, opened the debate.[78] He reminded the House that on 18 May the government had announced that upon the restoration of law and order a Royal Commission would be established which would investigate the causes of the unrest and any alleged grievances but would not bring into question the fundamental terms of the mandate. Ormsby-Gore stated that it was the government's intention to find a solution which was consistent with their obligations to the Jews and the Arabs and that these 'fundamental dual obligations' were obligations of honour.

There was an intervention from Vice-Admiral Ernest Taylor, the Conservative member for Paddington South, who asked what action had been taken in respect of the Arab grievances which had already been articulated. Ormsby-Gore responded that their demands could not possibly be conceded. The Arabs had called for the complete stoppage of Jewish immigration and the sale of land to Jews, together with the transfer of the government of Palestine to what they called a National Government responsible to an elected democratic assembly. However, the government's determination to resist the demands of the Arabs was not necessarily as strong as had been stated. Ormsby-Gore had conceded privately that almost his only support in cabinet was from Elliot.[79] This marks a shift in the Conservative leadership's position which was progressively to weaken its resolve to adhere to its established policy for Palestine.

At the same time the pro-Arab Conservatives were now becoming more vocal, as this debate was to demonstrate. Winterton proposed that a neutral course be adopted and he suggested that those MPs who 'so earnestly take up the Jewish cause' would have an opportunity when the report of the Commission was available.[80] Clifton-Brown considered that Britain's strategic interests required that it had the goodwill of the Arabs and should only carry out actions in Palestine that enjoyed this goodwill. He considered that the reversal of the policy of the Passfield White Paper 'gave rise to the idea that the British Government and the British House of Commons were entirely in the pocket of the Jews – that Dr Weizmann had only to crack the whip, and the British Government would respond'.[81]

Ormsby-Gore was subject to pressure to change policy following the Commons debate. This pressure appeared to Amery to have emanated from both inside and outside of the cabinet.[82] Notwithstanding that the lawlessness had not ended, the resolution of the government to oppose Arab demands appears to have weakened as the Royal Commission was appointed on 29 July under the chairmanship of Lord Peel, a former Conservative secretary of state for India.[83]

The following day a letter appeared in *The Times*,[84] in which it was proposed that the Commission should immediately proceed with its work. The signatories believed that it was necessary to 'allay the fears' of the Arabs that any recommendations made by the Royal Commission in their favour would not be carried out 'owing to the Zionist influence in Parliament and the Press'. The writers stated that they were prepared to take action in the House of Commons to safeguard the Arabs' interests. The letter was signed by 20 MPs, all but one of whom were Conservatives; these included Winterton, Crossley, Major-General Alfred Knox, Henry Page Croft, both Douglas and Howard Clifton-Brown, and Sir Arnold Wilson. It also was signed, somewhat surprisingly in view of her previous involvement with the Palestine Parliamentary Committee, by the Duchess of Atholl.[85] Wilson wrote a further letter to *The Times* five days later in which he said that Tel Aviv was 'the chosen focus and recognised ganglion of Communistic propaganda in the Near and Middle East'.[86]

At the meeting of the cabinet on 2 September Ormsby-Gore, who had previously been one of the leading Conservative pro-Zionists, was ready to accept a decision that Jewish immigration into Palestine should cease, although he thought it important not to appear to be surrendering to disorder. However, other ministers such as Duff Cooper, the minister of war, considered that Britain could not surrender to violence. This view prevailed and the cabinet agreed that intensive measures should be taken to crush the Arab rebellion and that no decision should be made at that time to suspend permanent immigration.[87] However, although the Arab rebellion was put down in the autumn, Ormsby-Gore announced that he had asked the high commissioner 'to take a conservative view of the economic absorptive capacity of the country' and the total number of certificates was fixed for 1936 at 6,300, compared with 11,250 for 1935.[88]

THE PEEL COMMISSION REPORT

After the examination of some 66 witnesses the government published the Royal Commission's report on 7 July 1937, which was accompanied by a statement of policy. The report recommended that Jews should be prevented from acquiring land in certain parts of Palestine and that Jewish immigration should be restricted to 12,000 per year for the next five years. The Commission further concluded that the mandate was not workable and that the country should be partitioned between the Arabs and the Jews with Britain retaining certain areas of control.[89] The government statement expressed general agreement with the arguments and findings in the report. The matter was debated in the House of Lords on 20 July. Dugdale, who observed the proceedings, considered that Peel made a pro-Arab speech, Dufferin, the under-secretary of state for the colonies, a very tactless one, while Melchett made a 'very fine' pro-Zionist speech.[90]

The debate in the Commons took place the following day. Ormsby-Gore argued that, notwithstanding the material benefits that the Jews had brought to the Arabs of Palestine, the latter increasingly opposed Jewish immigration and the Jewish national home because of Arab nationalism. He said that the increasing persecution of the Jews had increased the desire to find a refuge for them in Palestine. He considered that the government could not go on as before and that partition was the only resolution of the problem.[91] Amery supported the government's position as he believed nothing would induce the Arabs to accept Jewish equality of rights in the same territory as them. He considered that the Arabs were to get at least, if not more than, total fulfilment of the pledges made to them, whilst the Jews 'have seen what they believed to be promised to them whittled down step after step'.[92]

Support for the government also came from the pro-Arab Conservatives, who had agreed at a caucus meeting the previous week that this was the only possibility of a permanent solution.[93] Wilson considered that Zionism had been a 'cult of a shrine' but had been transformed by the persecution of Jews who were 'being extruded from Poland and elsewhere'.[94] Clifton-Brown supported the proposal not because he liked it but because he could see no other alternative at that time.[95]

Crossley, who considered that he was a 'very trusted friend of the Arabs' considered that the two Jewish MPs who had spoken in the debate, Daniel Frankel, the Labour member for Mile End, and James de Rothschild, who sat in the Liberal interest for Ely, were 'direct spokesmen' of Zionism. He also considered that the Jews had been granted too much under the tentative proposal.[96] Winterton, who was speaking for the government,[97] appeared to be indignant that Jews (but not, he said, Frankel) had actually criticised the attitude of Britain to world Jewry, maintaining that the British Empire had broken faith with the Jews.[98]

Churchill spoke against partition; the principle, he argued, could not be judged fairly apart from the detail by which it is expressed. He was concerned with security and the obligations which would inevitably fall to Britain to stand between the two proposed states. He said that he would have preferred the government to have continued to pursue the previously existing policy, 'hard and heavy though it might be, with all its inconveniences'.[99] Churchill proposed that the government's policy should not be approved by the House but that it should be referred to the League of Nations with a view to enabling them to make further enquiries and thereafter present a definite scheme to Parliament. The government conceded without resistance and accepted this proposal, which was designed to delay any decision.[100]

There was irony in this debate and its results. Amery advocated partition only as a second best because he believed that the right policy of firmly carrying out the mandate had failed.[101] He was not supported by other pro-Zionists despite the acceptance of the policy by a majority of Jews.[102] Indeed, at a dinner party given by Sinclair, which was attended by Weizmann, Amery and Cazalet together with Josiah Wedgwood, Rothschild and Attlee, Churchill, in a drunken but eloquent manner, fulminated against partition and attacked the Zionist leaders' stand on the matter.[103] The pro-Arab Conservatives supported partition but the Palestinian Arab delegation declared that the Arabs were 'irrevocably opposed to the scheme'.[104]

THE RETREAT FROM THE PEEL COMMISSION REPORT

Early in September Churchill wrote an article 'Why I am Against Partition' which appeared in the *Jewish Chronicle*. The argument was centred on the almost inevitable armed conflict which would result. He considered that the Jews would not be content with the area assigned to them and that the establishment of a Jewish army would be seen by the Arabs as a provocation.[105] He had previously written in the *Evening Standard* that the government's proposals were 'a counsel of despair' and he questioned its assumption that 'the difficulties of carrying out the Zionist scheme are so great as they are portrayed'.[106]

At the League of Nations Council on 14 September Anthony Eden, now the foreign secretary, stated that the Palestine Mandate was unworkable. The inherent conflict between Arab and Jewish nationalism had been intensified by the growth of European anti-Semitism and the growth of Arab nationalism.[107] However, some eight weeks later Eden launched an attack on the partition proposal in the form of a Foreign Office paper to the cabinet under his signature. The paper drew attention to the opposition to the government's proposals from the independent Arab states and stated that partition could only be imposed by force.[108]

Dugdale was informed of the paper by Elliot, her confidant, four days later. She considered that its contents could have been taken 'straight out of any Arab Nationalist paper'. Ormsby-Gore told Elliot that the real author was not Eden but George Rendel, the head of the Eastern Department of the Foreign Office. According to Elliot, Eden was a very tired man who was obsessed with the notion of Britain's weakness and who was 'unable to endure the thought of a disturbed Middle East on top of everything else'.[109] Ormsby-Gore responded with a paper defending the partition proposal.[110]

It has been suggested that this struggle over policy was one conducted by the bureaucratic officials who were primarily concerned with their relative departmental influence over policymaking.[111] It is argued here that the proposition that policy on Palestine was left to officials is not sustainable even if the political heads of the ministries concerned were either a tired man or a 'broken reed'.[112] The intense interest both inside Parliament and elsewhere would not enable the political issues to be ignored by the cabinet. Whilst the high commissioner in Palestine, like other colonial administrators, had a large measure of freedom of action, the policy was decided by the politicians. In fact the Zionists had complained from the time of the military administration following Allenby's conquest of Palestine that the officials were mainly opposed to the Balfour Declaration. This antagonism was perceived as extending beyond the colonial administration in Palestine to the bureaucracy in Whitehall.[113] Yet, until the changes that were initiated towards the end of 1937, when partition to provide a Jewish national home was no longer favoured, the Conservative leadership supported the Jewish national home. It was the inexperienced Labour government of Ramsay MacDonald that had accepted the officials' advice and abandoned the established pro-Zionist policies of the previous administrations. This reversal of policy was vigorously attacked by the Conservative leadership, as has been examined previously, and the *status quo ante* was then restored.

However, there was, in fact, an acute division of political opinion over fundamental policy at this time. Ormsby-Gore felt that the only support he received was from Elliot and MacDonald[114] but it is probable that Hore-Belisha, the Jewish Liberal National minister of war, was at least a tacit ally.[115] In any event the cabinet decided that they could not currently reverse their stated policy but announced the establishment of a 'technical commission' to advise on the future boundaries and practicalities of the Peel Commission report.[116]

THE WOODHEAD COMMISSION AND THE END OF THE PARTITION PROPOSALS

The technical commission was appointed at the end of February 1938 under the chairmanship of Sir John Woodhead, a former civil administrator in India. He was assisted by Percival Waterfield and Thomas Reid, who were also Indian civil servants, together with a lawyer, Sir Alison Russell. They visited Palestine in April, returning to London in July; their report was published in November – almost a year after the decision to set up the Commission.

During this period a number of the leading figures had changed. Wauchope, the high commissioner in Palestine, was replaced in February 1938 by Sir Harold MacMichael. He applied severe coercion on the Arabs who had instigated widespread violence since the previous October. Eden had resigned from the government in February over appeasing fascist Italy, which he considered to be 'another surrender to the dictators'.[117] He was replaced by Halifax, who as Lord Irwin, had been Viceroy of India from 1926 to 1931. Ormsby-Gore, who succeeded his father to become the fourth Lord Harlech in May, resigned from the cabinet and was replaced as colonial secretary by MacDonald.

The situation of European Jewry substantially deteriorated during this period, particularly following the German annexation of Austria in March. This was followed by the Munich agreement in September, which sanctioned the German annexation of the Sudetenland, and *Kristallnacht*, the nation-wide pogrom in Germany in November.

The plight of European Jewry featured in the Supply debate which took place in early March 1938. Amery considered that the fate of the 'great experiment', the Jewish national home, would depend upon the findings of the Woodhead Commission and the government's decision on it. If the policy which emerged was to continue with the aims of those who initiated the Balfour Declaration, he considered that 'it will enable us to do something substantial to mitigate the suffering of a race which in wide areas of Europe today is undergoing a measure of oppression, humiliation and degradation such as few of us would have thought conceivable only a few years ago'.[118] Vyvyan Adams, the Conservative member for Leeds West, argued that an increase in Jewish immigration would allow a reduction in the cost to the British taxpayer for the defence of the country.[119] There was also concern expressed over the delay in completing the further investigations required by the government. Cazalet considered that it indicated procrastination.[120]

The government continued to avoid any decisive expression of policy. In June, when questioned about the forthcoming Evian Conference, which had to deal primarily with the issue of Jewish refugees, MacDonald stated that it was considered premature to make any announcement as to the government's policy in connection with Jewish immigration into Palestine.[121]

The government's position was outlined one month later at the Evian Conference when Winterton, who had been appointed Chancellor of the Duchy of Lancaster in March and was the cabinet minister charged with refugee affairs, said the problem of Jewish refugees could not be solved by unrestricted immigration into Palestine. 'Such a proposition', he maintained, 'was wholly untenable.' Palestine was a not a large country and also there were special conditions arising out of the mandate and the local situation which, he said, were impossible to ignore.[122] This was a clear indication that Jewish immigration into Palestine was to be severely limited.

The Woodhead Commission effectively reported that partition was not practicable and concluded by recommending a basis for a settlement by negotiation. This enabled the government to call a conference of the Arab states, Jews and Palestinian Arabs. The issues were subject to a debate in the Commons on 24 November. MacDonald repeated what was now the clear position of the government, that the problem of European Jewish refugees could not be settled in Palestine. He stated that the Woodhead Commission report considered that partition, as envisaged by the Peel Commission, was impractical as only the Jewish state (which was only 400 square miles in area) would be economically viable. The government had therefore proposed that separate discussions should take place in London between itself and Arab representatives and Jewish representatives respectively.[123]

Churchill attacked the government's position. He said that its fault was not being able to make up its mind and considered that this was another example of a government with an overwhelming majority which was addicted to the 'vice of infirmity of purpose'. Churchill believed that previously the immigration quota had been allowed to rise too suddenly and rapidly, and now proposed that for a period of ten years Jewish immigration should be fixed at a level which would not decisively alter the balance between the Arab and Jewish populations.[124]

Cazalet also criticised the government's position, which he considered to be one without policy. He warned them that Britain would not get out of its difficulties by trying to whittle down the promises made to the Jews in order 'to please and placate temporarily someone else at the expense of the Jews'. He considered that the restraint and self-discipline shown by the Jews could not be assumed to continue. He supported Churchill's immigration proposals and proffered a further proposition in respect of land purchase. Cazalet suggested that the mandatary government should purchase land and then lease it on advice from a joint board of Jews and Arabs.[125]

The pro-Arab Conservatives supported the government statement. Pickthorn wanted the forthcoming conference to deal with the 'management of Palestine, and not the relief of the Jews'. He considered that the 'quantity and quality' of anti-Semitism had been affected by political Zionism; anti-Semitism was the fault of the Jews themselves.[126] Ralph Beaumont, the Conservative Member for Portsmouth Central, repeated that Palestine should not be regarded as primarily a place of refuge for Jews. He welcomed the invitation to the Arab states to attend the London talks but deprecated the exclusion of the Mufti of Jerusalem from the discussions.[127] Major Sir Ralph Glyn, who sat for the Abingdon division of Berkshire, considered that the raising of 'the flood gates and allowing so many Jews into the country' was a mistake that should not be repeated. He considered that, in the long run, it would not be wise to allow Jews into Palestine. He said that Britain, although Christian, was the greatest Moslem power and 'if we can prove by our acts that Christians and Moslems can live together, then surely the Jews can settle down happily with both us and the Arabs'.[128]

Winterton replied for the government and said that it was not possible to consider the case of Palestine in isolation as it touched 'world causes, world Jewry, and the position of Islam'. Although a clear public statement of policy would not emerge until 1939, the government had already made its choice. Two months earlier, at the time of Munich, MacDonald had told Weizmann and Ben-Gurion that, like the Czechs, the government was 'going to sell the Jews also – give up Partition, for fear of the Arabs and the Germans and the Italians'.[129] This capitulation included the refusal of the cabinet to sanction the admission to Palestine of 10,000 Jewish children who would have been placed with existing families. MacDonald now considered that this humanitarian gesture could prejudice the London discussions and that therefore nothing should be done other than to consult with the high commissioner[130] and let the matter be discussed at the London Conference.[131] The stage was set to enact the policy of appeasing the Arabs and abandoning the Balfour Declaration.

THE LONDON CONFERENCE AND THE 1939 WHITE PAPER

The Conference was held at St James's Palace and was attended by representatives of Egypt, Saudi Arabia, Transjordan, Iraq and Yemen as well as Palestinian Arabs and the Jewish Agency. Chamberlain opened the Conference on 7 February 1939, giving two separate but similar speeches to the two sides as the Arabs would not sit in the same room as the Jews. The discussions lasted until 15 March; there was no agreement between the parties.

MacDonald had circulated to a cabinet committee a paper which proposed that there should be no Jewish state and no Arab state. There was to be no stoppage of Jewish immigration but there would, however, be a ten-year proviso that the Jewish population of Palestine should not exceed 40 per cent at most, and that there should be some restriction on land sales.[132] In fact, there were two suggested immigration proposals, which would have allowed the Jewish population to be at either 35 per cent or 40 per cent, both with an Arab veto on further immigration.

However, by 8 March MacDonald told his cabinet colleagues that the best that he could achieve with the Arabs was for Jewish immigration of between 75,000 and 100,000 over five years with an Arab veto thereafter, instead of 150,000–300,000 over ten years. He acknowledged that these proposals would provoke the opposition of world Jewry. He said, possibly as some form of self-justification, that the Jews had made no attempt to co-operate with the Arabs for 20 years but now they would have to do so.

Chamberlain said that he 'would have liked, if possible, to have done rather more for the Jews, who might be considered to have been rather roughly treated if the various expectations held out to them in previous years were taken into account'. He was satisfied, however, that it was impossible to obtain a better settlement for them. He also considered that Palestine could only accommodate 'a fraction of the Jews who wished to leave the countries in which they are living' and that taking the Jewish refugee problem as a whole a difference of between 80,000 and 100,000 Jewish immigrants into Palestine over a five-year period 'was not very material'.

Elliot had difficulty in accepting this view of immigration and was afraid that Britain might encounter serious trouble if Jewish immigration was dramatically reduced. He considered that the only hope for a solution to the problems in Palestine lay in a cantonal arrangement with each side having clear majorities in their own cantons. He believed that on this basis, and subject to special provisions, Jewish immigration could continue on a limited scale into the Jewish cantons after the five-year period.

The question of Britain's pledges to the Jews were dismissed by Lord Maugham, the Lord Chancellor, who advised the cabinet of his 'careful study of the pledges and undertakings given at various dates'. He advised that, with reference to the statement made to the Sherif of Mecca by Commander Hogarth in respect of the Balfour Declaration in particular, he was satisfied that 'the honour of this country demanded some such limitation of Jewish immigration as the Colonial Secretary proposed'.[133]

The Palestine Parliamentary Committee sent a delegation headed by Amery[134] to see the prime minister. It presented him with a memorandum setting out British declarations of policy in respect of the future of Palestine. They asked that these be incorporated in the settlement; Chamberlain was non-committal.[135]

On 12 March Duff Cooper, who had resigned from the government the previous October in protest at the Munich agreement, spoke at the dinner of the Anglo-Palestinian Club: 'It should be made abundantly clear, if anybody now is beginning to doubt it, that our word is our bond and that we will carry out what we have promised ... They must realise that the claim of the Jews upon them was far stronger today than when any promise was made twenty years ago or at any moment in their history.'[136] Two days later, on the same day that the government presented its final proposals to the Jewish delegation, German troops marched into what was left of Czechoslovakia.

The cabinet postponed the issuing of the White Paper which set out the government's future policy for Palestine for a number of reasons. One of those reasons was the attempt to get the Arab states to endorse the proposals. This proved unachievable but delay continued because of the fear of Jewish violence in Palestine and anti-British agitation which would be mounted, particularly by American Jews. It was also considered that the White Paper would arouse considerable criticism in the Commons. It was felt that whilst the issues cut across party lines most of the Labour and Liberal Opposition would oppose the scheme and 'there would be strong opponents among the Conservative Party'.[137] On 20 March 23 MPs who supported the government, but who were sympathisers for a Jewish national home, met to consider their 'great anxiety' about the government's policy. They were inclined to demand that the whip be removed in the forthcoming debate on the White Paper to allow a free vote.[138] The whips were not prepared to recommend this course and instead advised the government to delay.

The cabinet decided that, in partial mitigation of their policy, they should offer the Jews the potential of immigration to British Guiana. They considered, however, that the appropriate course would be to await the results of a commission of enquiry which had been established to investigate the matter.[139] It was later agreed to issue a statement on British Guiana six days before the publication of the White Paper.[140]

Elliot was the only member of the cabinet who continued to support the Jewish position. He submitted a memorandum to the cabinet at the beginning of May. This suggested that it was not possible to proceed at that time with far-reaching constitutional changes and advocated the strengthening of British forces in Palestine. Elliot also proposed that the government should work towards a federal solution whilst taking no administrative steps leading to government by either one race or the other. The cabinet rejected these proposals and agreed not to change its policy.[141]

When issued the White Paper was a restatement of the government's proposals which had been made on 15 March. It proposed that an independent Palestinian state, in treaty relations with Britain, be established after a transitory period of ten years. The constitution would be determined by a national assembly and would have to include safeguards for the national home and British interests. A total of 75,000 Jewish immigrants would be allowed but this still required the Jews to make a satisfactory case on absorptive capacity; thereafter immigration could be completely vetoed by the Arabs. Land sales to Jews were to be entirely excluded in some areas and restricted in other areas.[142]

THE COMMONS DEBATE ON THE WHITE PAPER, MAY 1939

On 22 May MacDonald opened a two-day debate on the White Paper. He told the House that although the government did not accept that the Arabs were promised Palestine in the McMahon correspondence, the Hogarth assurance to the Sherif of Mecca meant that a Jewish national home in Palestine would not mean a Jewish state in Palestine against the wishes of the Arab population. He maintained that even when Arab opposition to Jewish immigration took violent form, Britain was prepared to sacrifice the lives of its own men to fulfil the promise made to the Jews. The government believed Palestine could and should make a further contribution towards relieving the tragedy of the Jewish refugees in central Europe and therefore Jewish immigration would continue for a further five years. The government could not foresee what type of state the proposed independent Palestine would be after the transitionary period but confirmed that Britain had 'certain vital strategic requirements' which would be maintained in a future treaty arrangement.[143]

Crossley, in the course of a speech which, he admitted, was to deploy the Arab case, inferred that the Jews controlled the newspapers in Britain, large amounts of City finance and advertising. He also maintained that Ashkenazi Jews were the descendants of Tartars and other tribes of Asia Minor who were converted to Judaism in the eight and ninth centuries.[144] In his support of the government's position, Lt-Col. Edward Wickham, the Conservative member for Taunton, said that the Jews would have to be satisfied with the undertakings given to them in the White Paper. He reminded the House that 100,000,000 Moslems were subjects of the Crown and their hostility and that of the remainder of the Moslem world would be aroused if the Jews were allowed to achieve majority status in Palestine.[145]

Beaumont considered that it was a source of satisfaction that the government had 'at last' accepted the Arab claims in spite of 'the immense power, the propaganda, and the influence of the Zionists'.[146] On the second day of the debate Glyn said that the House should not be 'carried away by any spasm of sentimentalism' for the Jews, who did not appreciate what had been done for them by Britain.[147]

Amery spoke towards the end of the first day's debate and, according to Dugdale, was 'absolutely magnificent'.[148] He considered that the White Paper was a repudiation of the pledges on the strength of which the mandate had been granted to Britain.

Amery restated his view that Palestine was of unique strategic importance and it was the Jews who could bring Western civilisation to the East. He said that the Churchill White Paper of 1922 was a drastic scaling-down of Jewish hopes but it was the final settlement. He considered that the present White Paper was a direct invitation to the Arabs to make trouble and broke all the promises and pledges to the Jews; that was to be their reward for loyalty. He warned the House that Palestinian Jewry were not like their co-religionists in Germany. They were a 'formidable body of people' who had undergone military training and who were quite capable of defending themselves.

Amery considered that the government had adopted a policy of appeasement of the Arabs, 'appease them at all costs. Appease them by abandoning the declared policy of every Government for 20 years past. Appease them by breaking faith with the Jews. Appease them at the cost of sacrificing all the prestige which we might have gained from either Jews or Arabs by consistency, by firmness, by justice to both sides.' He considered that the reasons for this were the lack of purpose, the lack of belief in the mandate and the lack of faith in British ability. He said that in the absence of any alternative acceptable to the whole House being proposed he would vote with the Opposition. 'I should be ashamed', he said, 'to take any other course.'[149]

The Rev. Dr James Little, the Conservative member for County Down, had made his maiden speech on the second day of the debate. He said that he had concluded that the White Paper had been drawn up 'with an eye on the terrorists' in Palestine and, 'just as the arrangement in Ireland had not brought peace but a sword', so, he thought, the same would happen in Palestine. Little considered that the immigration proposals would not only stop the incoming of Jews but that it would become impossible for them to live in the land. He said that he held no brief for the Jews but wished to say that 'there is no country on the face of the earth that has dealt hardly with the Jews but has suffered for it … Today Germany, by her treatment of the Jews, is laying up for herself wrath against the day of wrath.' He did not wish anyone ever to have the remotest ground for saying that Britain had even once dealt hardly with the Jews for, 'despite all their defects, God still has a deep interest in the Jews'.[150]

Churchill, in his speech, did not invoke God but rather the comments made by Chamberlain in October 1918. He had written in October 1918 that 'the sympathy of the British Government with Zionist aspirations does not date from yesterday … My father was anxious to find such a territory within the limits of the British Constitution ... Today the opportunity has come. I have no hesitation in saying that were my father alive today he would be among the first to welcome it and to give his hearty support.' Churchill said that Zionists were entitled to look to the prime minister to 'stand by them in the days of his power'.

Churchill considered that the Balfour Declaration and the mandate had been 'violated' by the government's proposals; their action was a breach and a repudiation of the Balfour Declaration. The pledge of a Jewish national home was a pledge of a home of refuge and asylum, made not to the Palestinian Jews but to the Jews of the Diaspora, 'to that vast, unhappy mass of scattered, persecuted, wandering Jews'.

He asked if Britain's state was so poor that in weakness her pledges must be sacrificed. Churchill thought that Britain's enemies would consider that she was 'on the run again. This is another Munich.' He went on to say: 'I warn the Conservative Party ... that by committing themselves to this lamentable act of default, they will cast our country, and all that it stands for, one more step downward in its fortunes.'[151]

There were two votes at the end of the debate. The first was on a motion to exclude the Labour Party amendment. The government, on a three-line whip, obtained 281 votes, with 181 against: a majority of 100. There were 19 National Government supporters who defied the whip, of which 16 were Conservatives. These included both Amery and Churchill, who had declared in their speeches that they would vote against the government; the rebels also included Macmillan. On the substantive motion, the vote to approve the White Paper, the government received 268 votes, with 179 against.[152] Curiously, in this vote Churchill and Richard Denman, the National Labour Member for Leeds West, both abstained.

The issue of abstention is not without some significance in view of the whipping arrangements. There were 13 abstentions by those Conservatives who had supported the government in its defeat of the Labour amendment. These included Eden and two government ministers, Winterton, who had previously been an advocate for the Arab cause, and Geoffrey Shakespeare, the Liberal National parliamentary and financial secretary of the Admiralty. There were, of course, other abstentions such as Little, who took part in the debate and who had said that he did not wish to embarrass the government, and Captain Strickland, the member for Coventry, who had declared his support for the Jewish national home.[153] Elliot and Hore-Belisha were also absent from the government lobby.[154] Amery noted that despite the three-line whip a great many government supporters had abstained.[155] Dugdale considered that Churchill's speech 'must have accounted for a good many of the enormous number of abstentions'; she wrote that 'we had not hoped for anything so good'.[156]

There were eight Jewish Conservative MPs at the date of this debate, including the Independent Conservative Daniel Lipson. Lipson was the only Jewish Conservative to vote against the government. This may be compared with the two future Conservative prime ministers who went into the opposition lobby. Sir Isadore Salmon and Louis Gluckstein voted with the government; the remaining five did not vote. It is possible that Sir Philip Sassoon's absence may have been connected with his health, as he was to die less than two weeks later.

It has been suggested that the vote on the White Paper, when the government, with an overall majority of 225, had its majority reduced to 89, could be compared with that in the debate on the Norwegian campaign in May 1940.[157] When the House divided on the latter occasion the government's majority was reduced to 81 and the Chamberlain government felt obliged to resign.[158] On that occasion there were 38 government supporters who voted with the opposition, compared with 18 on the substantive motion in the Palestine debate. Furthermore, at a time of war, party loyalty can be expected to be greater to the government party than in peacetime, albeit a peace which was rapidly vanishing.

These votes may also be compared with the division on the Government of India Bill in June 1935. On that occasion, 75 Conservatives voted against the government; this represented some 13.7 per cent of the parliamentary party. If the National Labour and Liberal National dissenters are added to the Conservative rebels, then the May 1940 division had 9 per cent of the government party voting against it. In the vote on the White Paper, the figure is 4.3 per cent. It should be noted that this analysis does not take account of the abstentions. There were the fewest MPs absent from the India Bill division (107). Those absent from the lobbies in May 1939 numbered 168, whilst the number in May 1940 was 136. This indicates that the greater number of abstainers, the lower the percentage of actual positive revolt.

Therefore, it can be suggested that although the numbers of Conservatives who actively opposed government policy was lower than in those of the two other divisions considered, the significance of the revolt should not be understated. Three future

Conservative prime ministers either voted against or abstained from supporting Chamberlain. It led to the request by Sir Joseph Ball for a meeting with Weizmann. Ball considered that the Palestine issue would have an adverse affect on the Party in the forthcoming general election. He hoped that by talking with the head of the Zionist Organisation he could 'find some constructive way out of the difficulty'.[159] The Palestine White Paper, as Churchill put it in the debate, was another manifestation of the policy of appeasement which seemed to have become the overriding principle of Chamberlain's government. The Conservative rebels and the Labour opposition even stigmatised the White Paper as a 'Middle Eastern Munich'.[160]

PALESTINE AND THE MOSLEMS

When Baldwin, Austen Chamberlain and Amery wrote to *The Times* in opposition to the Passfield White Paper they had restated two major reasons for Conservative support of the Jewish national home. One was the requirement, as they saw it, to maintain and uphold the pledges, promises and undertakings that had been made by previous British governments (all of which had been dominated by the Conservatives). The other was the fear of provoking the hostility of world Jewry, particularly those Jews who lived in the United States. At that time the Conservative pro-Zionist views prevailed and the British government policy was to return to that which had been settled by the Conservatives in the 1920s.

However, with the outbreak of the Arab Revolt the conflict between Arab and Jew became more significant internationally than hitherto. Whilst the issue of the Jewish national home had never been a British 'domestic' affair, 1936 saw an increasing concern about events in Palestine expressed by Moslems in India. The Indian Assembly saw discussion of the problem in September 1936 and that same month the Viceroy agreed to receive a Moslem delegation which wished to express its views on the attitude of Indian Moslems to the situation in Palestine.[161] The secretary of state for India, Zetland, had earlier that year warned the cabinet of the repercussions in the Moslem world, and particularly in India, of British policy in Palestine. He believed that it was important to remove any impression that the policy was 'run by the Jews'.[162] He warned the cabinet in the following months that Moslem reactions to the ostensibly pro-Zionist policies of the government could potentially become serious.[163] Zetland urged that a settlement be reached with the Arabs, as there was increasing concern for the possible repercussions in India.[164]

The concern of the India Office intensified in 1937. In November Zetland warned his colleagues that Moslem opinion in India was becoming rather aggressive against the partition proposals.[165] In December he advised that the president of the All-India League had made a statement that 'unless the difficulties in Palestine were fairly and squarely met it would be the turning point in the future of the British Empire'.[166] At the meeting of the cabinet which considered issuing the White Paper in 1939, Zetland said that unless the government could substantially meet the Arab claims, 'we should have serious trouble with Indian Moslems. We have already enough trouble on our hands with the Hindus.'[167]

The controversy over India within the Conservative Party had caused bitter divisions in the 1930s both in the parliamentary party and in the National Union. The Conservative government would not have wished Palestine to disrupt Britain's already difficult position in the sub-continent which could potentially lead to the reopening of splits in the Party. It may also be significant that most of those appointed to the Palestine commissions of enquiry had a background of service in India. It is possible that a government which espoused appeasement found it relatively easy to sacrifice the commitments to the Jews when faced with potential conflict with Moslems in the Empire.

THE ROLE OF WORLD JEWRY

The position of European Jewry had deteriorated in the 1920s with governments in Poland and Romania, in particular, ignoring the rights of their Jewish minorities which were supposed to be protected by the Minorities Treaty – a treaty which the successor states were obliged to sign, to protect ethnic and religious minorities within their territories, as a condition of allowing their statehood following the Versailles peace conference. The rise to power in 1933 of the Nazis in Germany, however, elevated anti-Semitism to a new plane. As the decade progressed the condition of the Jews worsened. Although some of the pro-Arab Conservatives invoked the image of the Jews as the all-powerful manipulators of society, the actuality of Jewish suffering revealed that the Jews were substantially powerless.

American Jewry, which provided much of the funding to the Jewish national home did, however, appear to have some influence. It was able to mobilise political support against the

Passfield White Paper. It could obtain comforting letters from President Roosevelt for the fund-raising work of the United Palestine Appeal[168] and encourage the American Christian Conference to lobby the British government in favour of the Jewish national home.[169] The State Department issued a statement in October 1938 which opened with the assertion of the interest of the American people in the establishment of a Jewish national home.[170]

The reaction of world Jewry was discussed by the cabinet when it was considering the issuing of the White Paper of 1939. It was considered at the meetings held on 8 and 22 March.[171] On 26 April MacDonald told his colleagues that the Jews exercised 'a certain influence in the United States' and that they would use the occasion of the publication of the White Paper to stir up trouble. The American Ambassador, Joseph Kennedy, told the British that although the Jews would not be able to invoke a strong pro-Jewish agitation they might be able to work up an anti-British one. He thought that this could last only for some two or three months. It was a period of time, however, that could be vital to the British government in attempting to obtain the support of American public opinion.[172] Kennedy was an anti-Semite, who, according to a dispatch of the German ambassador to Britain written shortly after *Kristallnacht* in November 1938, said that very strong anti-Semitic tendencies existed in the United States and 'that a large portion of the population had an understanding of the German attitude toward the Jews'. Herbert von Dirksen considered that 'from his whole personality I believe he would get on well with the Fuhrer'.[173] Kennedy subsequently told MacDonald that the publication of the White Paper would not make any difference to an already difficult situation and made the same claim as that which he had conveyed to the German ambassador, that '[t]he Jews, in his opinion, were unpopular in America' and the results of the Jewish agitation would not be long-lasting.[174] It is possible that Kennedy was able to minimise the role of the Jews as a people with power and influence in the one country where previously it had been considered by the British government that their goodwill was required.[175]

One of the original considerations for the Conservatives which led to support for the Jewish national home was to prevent the immigration into Britain of eastern European Jewry. The Jewish refugees who were now requiring help came primarily from central Europe. Furthermore, Jewish immigration into Palestine was probably the most acute problem which the British government had to consider. It would appear that by 1938, and certainly in 1939, the government considered more favourably the immigration of Jews into Britain than into Palestine.

'NATIONAL' OR CONSERVATIVE GOVERNMENT

Although the government continued to use the term 'National', it is the view of this study that certainly after the Samuelite Liberals left the administration in September 1932, the Conservatives had overriding influence in determining policy, and had control due to their parliamentary strength compared with Ramsay MacDonald's National Labour and Sir John Simon's Liberal Nationals. Cuthbert Headlam, the Conservative member for the Barnard Castle division of Northumberland, questioned whether there was any difference, other than the name, between the Conservatives and the Nationalists.[176] Sir Joseph Nall, the die-hard Conservative MP for Hulme, Manchester, considered that Ramsay MacDonald was, in many respects, 'a better Tory than Baldwin'.[177]

Harold Nicolson allowed his name to be put forward for the Conservative candidature in the by-election in Sevenoaks in July 1935, but actually stood as a National Labour candidate in the general election in that year for Leicester West. His candidature was effectively confirmed by the local Conservative Association in the constituency.[178]

Whilst it has been argued that Baldwin wished to have a 'national' government in order to neutralise his right wing,[179] the policies pursued generally from 1931 onwards were essentially Conservative. The conduct of the affairs of Palestine, even when entrusted to National Labour ministers, cannot be separated from the Conservatives who, in any event, would control both cabinet and the Commons through their sheer weight of numbers.

Therefore, it is considered here that it is correct to dismiss any attempt to imply that the decisions made by the British government in respect of Palestine during the period under review were not taken or sanctioned by the Conservative leadership. The Conservatives actually took their decisions at an 'inner-cabinet' and only spoke to their National colleagues subsequently.[180] The retreat from pro-Zionist policies also occurred primarily after Chamberlain became prime minister, when Conservatives occupied more government posts.

However, during the nine years of the National government the Colonial Office was occupied by a National Labour secretary of state for 38 and a half months. It is not clear whether, on Ormsby-Gore's resignation in May 1938, MacDonald was appointed as another potential 'sop' to the Jews as he, like Ormsby-Gore before him, had in the past been a passionate Zionist. Nevertheless, he was to 'preside' over the dismemberment of the pro-Zionist policies of the government.

THE CONSERVATIVE PRESS

Unlike the period in the 1920s when Palestine became a major battle ground in the press, the 1930s saw no sustained campaigns against the Jewish national home. *The Times* followed the general policy which had been advocated by the Conservative Party. Thus in May 1930 it called for the admission of Jews into Palestine in accordance with the criterion of absorptive capacity which should not be interpreted so strictly 'as to be almost equivalent to prohibition'.[181] In March 1936 it advocated 'making haste slowly' with the proposed Legislative Council in Palestine.[182]

In May its leader stated that at a time when international pledges were being broken and 'Jews driven in desperation from one country [it] seems hardly the time when the British Government should allow any doubts to arise as to their determination to carry out the promise of 1917'.[183] *The Times*, along with most of the rest of the Conservative press, accepted the proposals of the Peel Commission. However, the *Daily Express* stated that the government 'should hand back the country to the people who have chiefly inhabited it, the Arabs, and turn their efforts to the better government and development of the Empire'.[184]

In March 1938, after the Supply debate on Palestine, *The Times* urged the government to implement the preliminaries of partition without any unnecessary loss of time.[185] It did not entirely abandon this position after the White Paper was issued in May 1939. *The Times* called for the establishment of a federal constitution, under British supervision, which would allow each community, in its own autonomous territory, to control immigration and land sales.[186]

9

The Conservatives and the Jews during the Second World War

As the initial period of the war proceeded, Chamberlain's Conservative administration was increasingly regarded as ineffective not only by Labour and the Liberals but also by the government's own backbenchers. It was increasingly criticised for having failed adequately to rearm and for its policy of appeasement which was now considered to have contributed to the outbreak of hostilities; Chamberlain himself believed that the outbreak of war demonstrated a personal failure.[1] In May 1940 Chamberlain's resignation as prime minister, but not as Party leader, allowed Churchill to form a coalition government which was, at least as far as Churchill himself was concerned, non-party in composition. The Labour and Liberal parties were over-represented in relation to their parliamentary strength and non-party politicians played a greater role than had been the case in the administrations formed during the First World War. Churchill, even after his elevation to the leadership of the Conservative Party, did not regard himself, at this time, as a party man. This was no doubt in part because of his isolation and partial ostracism in the 1930s and his role as a leading member of the Liberal Party during the period of the First World War. Furthermore, whilst the Labour Party was largely politically cohesive during the wartime period, the Conservative Party became increasingly moribund, with the suspension of party conferences and the effective disintegration of some local party associations. Therefore, an examination of this wartime period must focus on individual Conservatives, particularly those holding office, as most of the senior ministers dealing with the Jews were Conservatives.[2]

Churchill saw his personal role as that of winning the war. The priority of concentrating on the hostilities led to the suspension of any new initiatives or changes to the existing policies the Coalition had inherited from the Chamberlain administration.

Thus the policy towards Palestine remained fundamentally that which had been adopted by Chamberlain's government in the 1939 White Paper. Although Churchill had opposed the White Paper (as he reminded his colleagues), he did little effectively to overturn it, notwithstanding the influence that he undoubtedly had as prime minister. Although Palestine was considered by a cabinet committee during the war years, no change in policy was to be adopted.

THE EXTERMINATION OF THE JEWS

According to Channon there was 'a sublime extraordinary assembly' in Parliament on 17 December 1942.[3] Eden read to the House a declaration (which was also being made public in Moscow and Washington) which revealed that the German authorities were carrying out the extermination of the Jews of Europe.[4] However, when asked by the Jewish Labour politician Sidney Silverman what counter-measures were being taken by the Allies, Eden replied that what could be done at that stage 'must be inevitably slight'. In response to a further question in which it was presumed that those escaping from the Germans would be welcome and given every assistance by the Allies, Eden replied that '[t]here are, obviously, certain security formalities which have to be considered'. The Commons then stood in silence as a protest against the German actions.[5] Whilst this gesture was possibly unique in parliamentary history, it can be seen from Eden's comments that there would be little or no practical help for Germany's victims.

Six months later a delegation to the Foreign Office, which included the Conservative MP Quintin Hogg, complained that practically nothing had been done. The Foreign Office note of the meeting related that 'Lord Samuel raised with some bitterness the question of admission to the United Kingdom, and the guarantee of visas for people who were still in enemy occupied territory'. Samuel also complained that 'since the Declaration of December 17th last practically nothing had been done'.[6] Hogg was also part of another parliamentary delegation to the Foreign Office in January 1944. According to Nicolson, who was a member of the delegation, Eden received them with great cordiality and for an hour they discussed what could be done to rescue more Jews from Germany. 'One goes away thinking', he wrote, 'how reasonable, how agreeable and how helpful he has been, and then discovers that in fact he has promised nothing at all.'[7]

THE SUPPLY DEBATE ON REFUGEES

In the May 1943 debate, Osbert Peake, the Conservative under-secretary of state for home affairs, seemed to play down the particular nature of Jewish suffering at the hands of the Nazis. He stated that the policies 'of labour conscription, of deportation and of extermination have been applied, not only to the Jews but to other large sections of European peoples'.[8] He also stated the government was not prepared to divert shipping in an attempt to rescue refugees since this could slacken the war effort.[9]

Colonel Sir Albert Lambert Ward, the Conservative member for North West Hull,[10] considered that there were great difficulties in admitting large numbers of refugees to Britain as a considerable proportion of the population did not want them and this could easily fan 'the smouldering fires of anti-Semitism which exist here into a flame'.[11] He stated that, particularly in the East End of London, the black market was blamed on the Jews and that when a terrible disaster took place at an air raid shelter at the beginning of the year a rumour was put about that it was caused by panic on the part of foreign Jews, which, he stated, was quite untrue.[12] Ward's proposed solution to the problem was to allow Jewish immigration to the North African territories liberated by the Allies rather than admit them to Palestine. This view was supported by Sir Austin Hudson, the Conservative Member for Hackney North.[13]

Another Conservative, William Colegate, the member for The Wrekin, declared that he was repelled by 'the propaganda' and 'over zealousness' of those friends of the Jews which, he said, 'puts me absolutely against the Jews'. He cited the refusal of Jewish farm workers to milk cows on the Jewish Sabbath as a cause of anti-Semitic feeling and was unmoved by the intervention of Locker-Lampson who reminded the House that Scottish farmers would not milk on Sunday. Colegate also considered that the admission of a large number of Jews into Palestine would be 'a gross violation of the pledges of this country and would mean grave injury to a very friendly race who have proved considerable support in this war'.[14]

Eden rejected suggestions that the government did not care about the Jewish refugees problem, stating that there was a cabinet committee which had been dealing with the matter and that it included three members of the war cabinet.[15] However, this committee had produced no tangible results which would assist Jewish immigration into Palestine or elsewhere. Whilst it is obvious that the British government had no control over the policy of the

Axis powers, it was not prepared itself to make any substantial gesture which could have resulted in resources being diverted towards assisting Jewish escape from occupied Europe. When pressed, for example, by the Americans to assist Jews threatened with extermination in south-eastern Europe in March 1943, Eden pointed out that if 'we do that, then the Jews of the world will be wanting us to make similar offers in Poland and Germany. Hitler might well take us up on any such offer, and there simply are not enough ships and means of transportation in the world to handle them.'[16]

There has also been some debate among historians regarding the requests made to Britain and the United States to bomb Auschwitz-Birkenau, to interrupt the mass killings being carried out by the Germans. In 1944, bombers could have reached the target from Foggia in Italy, albeit the distance was such as to be near the limit of their range.[17] Wasserstein, in his study, concludes that politicians were in favour of mounting such raids but were thwarted by civil servants.[18] However, as has been demonstrated earlier in this work in respect of immigration policy into Britain during the 1930s, if there is real political will the elected politicians can overrule official objections and manoeuvring.

During the Supply debate Cazalet stated that he considered that anti-Semitism was increasing in Britain and that this was 'a measure of the victory of Goebbels'.[19] One example of British wartime anti-Semitism can be seen in the treatment by Chamberlain of his secretary of state for war.

LESLIE HORE-BELISHA

An early wartime example of anti-Semitism was the treatment of Hore-Belisha, who was dismissed as secretary of state for war by Chamberlain in January 1940. Hore-Belisha's reforms of the army and his style of behaviour had led to substantial opposition to him by senior military figures and he was loathed by George VI. Chamberlain succumbed to the pressure from these quarters and removed him from office.[20] However, the prime minister had intended to retain Hore-Belisha in the cabinet as minister of information. Almost at the point when he was to make the appointment, Chamberlain was dissuaded by Halifax, who stated that it would have a bad effect on neutrals both because Hore-Belisha was a Jew and because his methods would let down British prestige.[21] Hore-Belisha refused the offer of the Board of Trade and effectively ended his ministerial career.

Chamberlain would not tell Hore-Belisha the full extent of the prejudice against him and made no mention of anti-Semitism on the two occasions when they met to discuss the matter.[22] Ball's *Truth*, in its issues of 12 and 19 January, carried articles consisting of allegations about Hore-Belisha's previous financial dealings and business failures which were 'tinged with a liberal sprinkling of anti-Semitism'.[23] The issue of 12 January had been sent by Ball to every member of both Houses of Parliament. Hore-Belisha himself recognised that the root cause of hostility towards him was the offence he had given to the military and the high social castes who resented his appointment to the War Office as 'a Jew and an ordinary person not of their own caste'.[24] The father of the then president of the Board of Deputies, Nathan Laski, himself a prominent member of the Manchester Jewish community, was glad that Hore-Belisha had been dismissed, not from the national but from the Jewish point of view. 'It was all right as long as things were going well', he considered, 'but if things began to go wrong with the army Hore-Belisha would have been blamed and the Jews would have been made the scapegoat.'[25]

SYMBOLIC GESTURES

After May 1943, there were no further major parliamentary discussions regarding the fate of European Jewry. The government was to take no action to assist the refugees, not even that of a symbolic kind as suggested by Squadron Leader Edward Fleming, the Conservative Member for Manchester Withington.[26] He proposed that British nationality should be granted to the remaining Jews in Nazi-occupied territories on similar terms to the offer of common nationality made to the French in 1940, in order, he said, 'to maintain their morale and to help them in their struggle for freedom from destruction'.[27]

Chief Rabbi Hertz had appealed to Churchill in May 1944 in a similar manner, calling for a declaration that all Jews in enemy territories be granted the status of British-protected persons.[28] This was rejected by the war cabinet in June after Eden had stated that the Foreign Office considered that the difficulties in the proposals were insuperable and that there was no reason to think that 'its acceptance would in any way improve the position of the Jews'.[29]

HUNGARIAN JEWRY

In April 1944, Horthy's government in Hungary acceded to Hitler's request and allowed the start of deportations of Hungary's one million Jews to the death camps. In July, Churchill wrote to Eden this was 'probably the greatest and most horrible crime ever committed in the whole history of the world ... It is quite clear that all concerned with this crime who may fall into our hands, including people who only obeyed orders by carrying out the butcheries, should be put to death after their associations with the murders has been proved.'[30] On 8 July, as a result of demands by the Allies and neutrals, the deportations were stopped by the Hungarian regent. However, by this time some 437,000 Hungarian Jews had already been deported.[31] The Hungarian government told Swiss diplomats that all Jews possessing entry permits for other countries, including Palestine, would be permitted to leave Hungary and that the German authorities would provide transit permits to cross Axis-occupied territory.[32]

Although Eden accepted that the Hungarian offer appeared to be genuine and that it should be accepted with the least possible delay, he objected to the American proposal that Britain and the United States should issue a declaration that they would 'undertake to care for all Jews who are permitted to leave Hungary'. In addition to transportation difficulties, he stated that the Colonial Office were already much disturbed by the numbers of Jews that had been arriving in Palestine. He suggested that there should be agreement to a joint declaration, but Britain's capacity to receive refugees had become limited.[33] This view was supported by the colonial secretary, Stanley, and also by the cabinet when it considered the matter on 9 August.[34] In the event, the Germans would not agree to the emigration of Hungary's Jews and by mid-October Horthy had been replaced by a German puppet regime. It would be the advance of the Red Army that would save the remnant of Hungary's Jewish community.

ARMING THE YISHUV

From the beginning of his premiership Churchill wanted troops which were garrisoned in Palestine to be freed for active service against the enemy and to arm the Jewish community for their own self-defence. Initially Churchill did not want such forces to serve outside of Palestine, notwithstanding the desire of the Zionist leadership to have a large contingent of Jews fighting on the Allied side.[35] The retention of some 20,000 troops in Palestine was, according to Churchill, the price Britain had to pay for 'the anti-Jewish policy which has been persisted in for some years'.[36] There was opposition to Churchill's desire to arm the Jews of

Palestine and he later wrote that he encountered every kind of resistance to his proposals.[37] He maintained that troops were wasted in Palestine, but found that by September he was being advised that troop reductions had been made and that Palestine was a location for reserves who could be despatched to the Egyptian delta or the desert.[38]

The principle of a Jewish fighting force was accepted, however, at the end of 1940 but no positive action followed.[39] A year later Weizmann wrote to Lord Moyne, the then colonial secretary, complaining that Moyne had misled the Lords by suggesting that agreement had not been reached and the failure lay at the door of the Zionists.[40] However, this still did not produce any success and Weizmann, amongst others, pressed Conservative politicians to attempt to influence Churchill to take action.[41] What the Zionists did not know was that in October 1941 the cabinet had decided against a scheme for the recruitment of Jewish units and instead suggested that 5,000–10,000 Jews be encouraged to join the military or Palestine Police.[42]

It was not until the summer of 1944 that positive action took place to form what would be called the Jewish Brigade, which was to fight in Italy rather than be used in the defence of a Palestine no longer under threat from the Germans.[43] Churchill wrote that he liked the idea of the Jews trying to get at the murderers of their fellow-countrymen in central Europe.[44] The Jewish Brigade was formed in September 1944, four years after it had been proposed by the Zionists and despite the apparent support and enthusiasm of Churchill for the project. The delay in its establishment meant that it could play no part in the defence of the Yishuv in the dark days when Rommel's troops threatened the heart of Egypt and the liquidation of Jewish settlement in Palestine appeared to be a real possibility. The delay also meant that the opportunities open to a Jewish fighting force were restricted and that the political effect of its existence would be limited.

CABINET CONSIDERATIONS

The cabinet dealt with Palestine intermittently during the war period. In November 1940 it was faced with the problem of the illegal immigrant survivors of the *Patria*, a ship which had been sabotaged by the Haganah, the Jewish underground army, whilst in Haifa harbour. The high commissioner, Sir Harold MacMichael, had proclaimed that the refugees would never be allowed to enter Palestine. The cabinet was divided on the issue. Lloyd, as colonial secretary, supported the stance of the high commissioner. However, the cabinet decided that, as a special act of clemency, the *Patria* survivors would be allowed to remain in Palestine but, in future, all other illegal immigrants would be interned in Mauritius.[45]

In October 1941 the cabinet again discussed Palestine; Dugdale presumed this was because of the visit home of Oliver Lyttelton who was minister of state resident in the Middle East. Churchill was reported to have said that he had never accepted, and did not now accept, the 1939 White Paper and that the Jews 'must have territory'.[46] The official minutes of the meeting, however, record that the prime minister stated that, assuming an Allied victory, 'the creation of a great Jewish State in Palestine would inevitably be one of the matters to be discussed at the Peace Conference'.[47]

In December 1941 a ship called the *Struma* left Romania with over 750 Jewish refugees, half of them women and children. It was detained by the Turkish authorities, owing to the pressure exerted by Britain. The return of the passengers to Romania was seen by Oliver Harvey, Eden's private secretary, as a death sentence and he wrote a Foreign Office memo in February 1942 pleading: 'can nothing be done for these unfortunate refugees? Must HMG take such an inhuman decision. If they go back they will all be killed.' The response was that the passengers were illegal immigrants (who might have included Nazi agents) and that Moyne, the colonial secretary, took 'a strong line about them'.[48] However, Moyne had already conceded that the children on board could be admitted to Palestine, but the Turkish government would not allow overland travel. The British would not or could not provide a ship and, consequently, the children, along with their parents, were sent into the Black Sea on 24 February. Shortly after the Turkish tugboat had left the ship there was an explosion and the *Struma* sank very quickly, with only two survivors. Britain was held by the Jewish Agency and much Jewish public opinion to have been morally responsible for the deaths.

On 22 February Cranborne had replaced Moyne as colonial secretary and Dugdale recorded the hope that matters at the Colonial Office would 'take a turn for the better under him'. Weizmann had a satisfactory interview with Cranborne three days after his appointment.[49] On 5 March the cabinet had considered Cranborne's proposal to admit into Palestine refugees escaping from Europe but to deduct them from the legal annual quota. The cabinet decided not to endorse this policy but to await the next occasion when a refugee ship reached Istanbul.[50] On 11 March, Macmillan, on behalf of the government, told the Commons that Britain would do all she could to prevent a reoccurrence of the *Struma* affair.[51] On 15 May the cabinet agreed that illegal immigrants would initially be placed in a detention camp and released subject to the quota and security checks and the principle of economic absorptive capacity having been satisfied.[52] Cranborne told the Zionist leadership in Britain that this policy change had occurred after a great struggle with the war cabinet. As Dugdale recorded, this had modified the government's attitude towards illegal immigration but was a peculiarly British way of getting round a difficulty.[53] However, the practical results of this change were limited, for during 1942 the total number of both legal and illegal immigrants to Palestine was only 3,038. The fears of a mass exodus of Jews from Europe were not realised.[54] In July 1943, it was decided by the cabinet to accept the proposal by Stanley[55] to extend the period for the White Paper quota for Jewish immigration beyond the terminal date of 31 March 1944 until the 75,000 total had been reached.[56]

The cabinet also decided to set up a committee to consider future policy for Palestine. Dugdale recorded that Amery, who was a member of the committee, indicated that the two current options were either the establishment of an undivided Jewish state or a partitioned Palestine with the Arabs controlling Samaria.[57] However, the actual terms of reference instructed it to examine the Peel Commission's report and consider whether it, or a variation of it, could be implemented.[58]

Churchill had decided that the pro-Zionist Amery was to be included as a member of the committee. Churchill, playing on Eden's sensibilities, wrote to him of the appointment, stating that Amery had Churchill's 'way of [pro-Zionist] thinking on this point, which no doubt is to be deplored'.[59] Amery had recorded in his diary that the decision to reconsider the policy towards Palestine was extremely important for the Jews and that Churchill would be considered a real friend of the Jewish people.[60] Amery's exuberance was misplaced in view of subsequent events. Yet even when considering the establishment of the committee, Churchill was mindful of timing and did not consider that it was then appropriate to take action 'which would bring into prominence the Jew–Arab question'.[61] Eden insisted that the Foreign Office was represented as he considered that it was more intimately concerned 'with the ramifications of this unhappy subject' than the Colonial Office. Richard Law, the minister of state, was his nomination and he was subsequently to produce a minority report.[62]

The committee did not report to the cabinet until January 1944, when a partition plan was approved in principle.[63] The scheme was a further modification of the Peel Commission plan and it gave the Jews a minimal amount of territory.[64] Amery and the other pro-Zionist, Sinclair, accepted this on the basis that the proposal should be 'an irreducible minimum' and that it should be implemented without delay.[65] However, with Churchill's concerns regarding timing and with the opposition of Eden and others to a Jewish state, even in part of Palestine, being so strong, the matter was not reconsidered by the cabinet until the autumn of that year.[66] Somewhat modified recommendations were then put forward but no further decision was made at that time.[67]

THE ASSASSINATION OF LORD MOYNE

On 6 November 1944 Moyne, who was now minister resident in the Middle East, was assassinated by two members of the extreme nationalist group Lehi, otherwise known as the Stern Gang. Moyne was pro-Arab and opposed a Jewish homeland in Palestine. As David Ben-Gurion later recalled, 'he rejected Palestine for the Jews because the Arabs objected. But something would have to be done for the Jews after the war, so he looked at a map of Europe, marked a piece of Germany which would hold a few millions, and that's where he would put the Jews.'[68]

Dugdale, on hearing the news of the assassination, considered that it was a dreadful disaster for the Zionist cause and spoiled the relationship with the British government.[69] Churchill advocated caution in Britain's reaction to the murder. He wrote to Cranborne that the suspension of immigration, or even the threat of it, would play into the hands of the extremists in Palestine. He favoured greater enforcement of penalties against those in possession of weapons and action against the nominally respectable leaders of extremist parties.[70] Churchill was, however, appalled by the loss of a close friend. When he spoke in the Commons that same day Churchill appeared publicly to distance himself from the Zionist cause. 'If our dreams for Zionism', he said, 'are to end in the smoke of assassins' pistols and our labours for its future to produce only a new set of gangsters worthy of Nazi Germany, many like myself will have to reconsider the position we have maintained so consistently and so long in the past.'[71]

THE CONSERVATIVE PRESS

There was little comment on Jewish affairs made by the leader writers of the national Conservative press during the wartime period. However, the declaration regarding the extermination of the Jews did prompt commentary. The *Daily Express* considered that until the Nazis had been punished 'we are not clean men' and that it degraded 'our whole generation'.[72] The *Daily Mail* wrote that it was a monstrous crime against the Jewish people and that it would be 'a crime on our part to forget it'.[73] The *Times* leader, published ahead of the Commons statement, believed that, whenever and wherever it was possible to assist Jews, 'the allied Governments must give their aid ungrudgingly'. It also considered that where emigration was still possible from occupied Europe 'it must be encouraged and promoted'.[74] The *Daily Telegraph*, however, wrote that such assistance, as Eden had stated, would only be a slight alleviation of the agony.[75]

The murder of Moyne produced a headline in the *Daily Mail* 'Gunmen Murder Lord Moyne, Jew Terrorists'.[76] However, it is probable that the use of 'Jew' was not meant to be derogatory and was merely to save space, as the subsequent leader stated that it would be 'illogical to blame the Jews as a whole for these outrages'.[77] The *Daily Telegraph* opined that the murderers were 'hardly less dangerous enemies of their race than Hitler'.[78] The *Times* believed that complete co-operation with the authorities would be forthcoming, not only from the Jewish Agency, but from 'all other responsible groups in Palestine' and that the government should look for unconditional Jewish aid and leadership in order to eradicate the terrorist groups.[79]

CHURCHILL AND THE ZIONISTS

Many historians have seen the assassination as a watershed in Churchill's relationship with the Jews and his attitude to Zionism.[80] He never again met with Weizmann and Churchill's inaction allowed the anti-Zionist forces in the government to kill the partition plan. Yet this explanation does not appear to recognise the failure to progress pro-Zionist policies prior to Moyne's death. Churchill and the other pro-Zionist politicians did not take any meaningful steps to reverse the policies enshrined in the 1939 White Paper. It is true that Churchill stated to Cranborne that the White Paper was not 'the firmly established policy of His Majesty's present Government' but was a 'gross breach of faith committed by the Chamberlain Government'. He wrote that the position was merely that, owing to the exigencies of war, the policy adopted by Chamberlain's administration had been carried on for the time being and that his own position had remained strictly as he had set it out during the Commons debates on the White Paper in 1939.[81]

It had taken until the middle of 1943 before a cabinet committee was established to consider the policy towards Palestine. This committee reached its conclusions at the end of 1943 and its findings were considered by cabinet in January 1944, but no action was taken. Indeed, when Weizmann met with Churchill on 4 November the prime minister told him that no active steps would be taken until the war with Germany was over, although Churchill had said that he was in favour of a partition that would include the Negev in the Jewish territory. Whilst Weizmann was greatly encouraged by the meeting, this may have been, in reality, merely yet another occasion when Jewish hopes were raised that, eventually, progress would be made.[82] In fact, in May 1945 Stanley wrote that for various reasons there had 'as yet been no decisions even on main lines of policy'.[83] In June 1945 Churchill wrote curtly to Weizmann to say that he proposed to leave the future of Palestine to the peace conference which would be convened.[84] As has already been noted, Churchill had been of this view as early as October 1941,[85] and he repeated this opinion in cabinet in March 1942[86] and again in July 1943.[87] Churchill, however, was no longer prime minister when the war was finally concluded, and Palestine's fate was not to be decided by any peace conference.

— 10 —

The Conservatives and Palestine, 1945–48

In July 1945, the Conservative Party went into opposition for the first time since 1931. Unlike the Labour Party, it had not made any encouraging remarks of a pro-Zionist nature at the general election. Churchill was to criticise Labour for their 'most strenuous pro-Zionist speeches and declarations'[1] and the 'lavish promises' which excited 'passionate expectations' throughout the Jewish world which, he said, 'were no sooner made than they were disregarded'.[2] The Labour government's policy was directed by the foreign secretary, Ernest Bevin.

On 13 November 1945 it was announced in the House that the 1939 White Paper policy would continue but that an Anglo-American Committee of Enquiry would be established to report within four months. In April 1946 the committee announced its findings, which included the abolition of the 1939 White Paper, the immediate immigration of 100,000 Jews and the removal of land purchase restrictions. However, it rejected the claim for a Jewish state and recommended the mandate be transformed into a trusteeship. The Labour government made implementation conditional upon the disarming of the Yishuv, which the Jews were not prepared to contemplate.[3]

The Haganah moved against the mandatory government in October 1945 when it brought about the release of 200 immigrants detained at the Athlit detention camp and on 1 November attacks were organised on some 150 rail and water installations. The failure of successive British governments to reverse the White Paper policy for Palestine had now led to the breakdown of relationships between the Yishuv and Britain, and not just with the extremist minority.

In June 1946 two members of the Irgun were sentenced to death by a British military court. In retaliation, the Palmach blew up the bridges connecting Palestine with its neighbouring countries, while the Irgun took six British officers hostage. As a result the mandatory authorities arrested some 3,000 Jews, including Jewish Agency leaders. The violence continued to escalate and, on 22 July, the Irgun blew up the King David Hotel which housed the chief secretariat of the British administration. Despite a warning, nearly 100 Britons, Arabs and Jews were killed and many more were injured.

The Attlee administration again attempted to secure American support for its Palestine policy by establishing another bi-national committee to considered the technical aspects of the Anglo-American report. The result was the Morrison–Brady Plan which proposed cantonisation under British trusteeship but which was unacceptable to both Arabs and Jews. Early in 1947 Bevin met separately with the parties and offered an alternative proposal. This provided for British trusteeship with local autonomy and 100,000 immigrants to be admitted over two years which would be followed by a bi-national unitary state after five years; this, too, was rejected by both parties. The Labour government thereafter announced that the problem would be referred to the United Nations, which in May 1947 set up a special committee on Palestine to investigate and report. The committee recommended partition, which was accepted by the general assembly in November 1947. The British government announced that it would relinquish the mandate on 15 May 1948, withdrawing its personnel from Palestine by August.

In Palestine, the relationship between the British and the Jewish community continued to deteriorate. British naval vessels intercepted illegal immigrant ships, with their occupants being placed in detention camps in Cyprus or, in the case of the *Exodus 1947* in July 1947, being sent back to Germany. Following the attack on Acre gaol in May 1947 when 41 prisoners escaped, three of those involved who had been captured were executed by the British in July. In retaliation, two days later the Irgun executed two British army sergeants and booby-trapped the ground underneath their bodies. In Palestine several Jews were murdered by British troops as a counter-reprisal whilst in Britain anti-Semitic riots occurred in parts of Liverpool, Manchester, Glasgow and London. In September 12 British members of the Palestine police were killed by either the Irgun or the Stern Gang. After the United Nations vote for partition in November 1947 the Arabs in Palestine, with aid from the neighbouring Arab countries, renewed their acts of terrorism against the Jewish community. There were also attacks on Jews in Aden, Egypt, Syria, Lebanon and Tripolitania. The bloodshed was to continue until 15 May, when the Arab states invaded Jewish Palestine.[4]

THE CONSERVATIVES IN OPPOSITION

Stanley was the principal Conservative spokesman dealing with Palestine. He considered that Palestine was a running sore which had caused the death of thousands, the unhappiness of millions and a perpetual poisoning of international relationships. He stated that there would be no long-term solution unless the two sides themselves got together and agreed.[5] The acts of terrorism perpetrated by the Jewish community were condemned and the Labour government urged to take all necessary action to prevent its repetition. However, such action should not prejudice the long-term policy to be employed.[6] Labour was urged to take firm action against those committing outrages. The Conservatives believed that, prior to any solution to the problems in Palestine, law and order had to be restored.[7] Thereafter, any solution which might be found would be, of necessity, a compromise. Stanley had agreed to the White Paper in 1939 but accepted that the hopes of those who had supported it were now incapable of fulfilment. Whilst colonial secretary, he had devoted time to exploring schemes for partition. The difficulty that he saw with the Labour proposal for cantonisation was its lack of finality.[8]

Churchill had not accepted the White Paper and in his speeches took a somewhat more sympathetic view of the Jewish cause than did his other front bench colleagues. According to Macmillan, on at least one occasion his remarks were not 'altogether to the taste of his followers'.[9] Churchill considered that Labour's plans represented a failure to fulfil the obligations Britain had accepted and was a negation of Zionist policy, which was an 'integral and indispensable condition' of the mandate. He also considered that the 'procrastination and indecision' of the Labour government was no excuse for the actions of the extremists in Palestine who had resorted to terrorism and that this, if protracted, would release Britain from its obligations to Zionism. Churchill also believed that it was an unfair burden for Britain to have to bear the whole weight of Zionist policy and the antipathy of the Moslem world, whilst the United States and other countries 'sat on the sidelines' and criticised British actions. He felt that, from the time that Britain was unable to carry out properly and honestly 'the Zionist policy as we have all these years defined it and accepted it', Britain's duty was to offer to relinquish the mandate. He said that at the end of the

Second World War Britain should have surrendered the mandate to the United Nations and fixed a date for the withdrawal of troops unless the United States had been prepared to share the burden.[10] However, the Conservatives now wished that any proposal meet with the approval and agreement of the United States, but did not oppose the general thrust of Labour government policy. Churchill considered that it was not a party issue.[11]

Stanley criticised the Attlee administration for the failure to prevent the continuation of terrorist activity. He found the 'tit for tat' punishment of British personnel by Palestinian Jews humiliating and that unless the government could prevent it he would prefer that Britain withdraw from Palestine. He considered that by January 1947 the position in Palestine was grave for British personnel and had dealt blows to British prestige.[12] Churchill raised the issue of the large financial cost of maintaining troops in Palestine; money which he considered could be better employed in Britain. He believed that there was no longer any British interest which required the country to remain in Palestine and felt that the responsibility for stopping what he described as the civil war between Jews and Arabs ought to be borne by the United Nations.[13] The Conservatives, in March 1947, therefore accepted that the referral to the United Nations was a necessary step to disentangle Britain from its obligations. Owing to the continuing humiliation, as they saw it, of the military in Palestine, they urged that the matter was placed before the United Nations as quickly as possible.[14]

Churchill now believed that the Labour government wanted to continue to fight in Palestine 'at all costs' and considered that Britain was now fighting the Jews to give the country to the Arabs, which he could not accept. He further felt that the practical effect on Britain was harmful in that it was an immense source of expense and it was bringing a great deal of disapprobation from many countries upon Britain.[15]

The Conservatives accepted the partition plan which the General Assembly of the United Nations approved in November 1947, although its details did not necessarily find favour with the leadership. The matter was considered to be out of the hands of the British and the Conservatives wished only for the earliest evacuation and surrender of the mandate that was possible. This course of action gave them neither happiness nor pride as it was a humiliating end to what they considered to have been the 'honourable role' that Britain had played in Palestine. Instead of leaving with the gratitude and affection of Jews and Arabs, Britain would quit as the target for the hostility of both sides and with all that had been done forgotten. Furthermore, the decision to leave had not been part of a solution but merely a transfer of responsibilities to the United Nations.[16]

In March 1948 the Conservatives supported the Palestine Bill, which ended the mandate, but with regret and concern that there was no agreed handover of responsibility to the United Nations to attempt to implement the partition plan or provide security.[17] The frustration of the Conservative Party at the way in which the mandate was to end prompted a group of Conservative MPs to set down a motion at the end of April 1948 which criticised in detail the government's conduct of affairs in Palestine. It sought to censure the administration for the inadequate provision of troops, the restrictions placed upon them to suppress armed revolt and punish the murderers of British servicemen; for the damage to trading and other commercial interests; for the failure to negotiate with the United States, France and other members of the United Nations for the peaceful and orderly transfer of the mandate; for the 'grave risk' of desecration of the holy places; and, 'in general, for their abdication of the high and honourable duty of government prior to the transfer of the Mandate in a country which is the cradle of civilisation and the centre of a world religion'.[18]

THE ANTI-ZIONIST CONSERVATIVES

If official Conservative Party policy was quasi-neutral as between Jew and Arab, the back-benches continued to supply a number of speakers who were decisively anti-Zionist and arguably anti-Semitic. Some of those who were active in the late 1930s were either no longer alive, such as Crossley and Wilson, or had been defeated in July 1945, such as Beaumont. Others, such as Glyn and Clifton-Brown did not contribute to the debates in the House. However, Pickthorn,[19] who had vociferously attacked Zionism in the pre-war period, renewed his attacks from the opposition benches. He considered that Zionism was one of the great mistakes of human history[20] and that he was himself 'an almost pre-natal anti-political Zionist'.[21] His use of language could display the strength of his feeling against the Jews in Palestine. He considered that the Arabs in Palestine were being 'swamped by these people being brought in'[22] and that Britain was to exercise military force to permit immigration without having any control of its 'quantity and quality'.[23]

Another MP who opposed Jewish immigration into Palestine

was Major E. A. Harry Legge-Bourke, who had been elected in July 1945 to represent the Isle of Ely. He considered that Jews should never have been allowed to settle in Palestine and that Britain should never have accepted the mandate.[24] He admitted that his views were fairly extreme because, he said, 'I believe that Zionism is a menace to world peace'.[25]

Legge-Bourke was supportive of the action taken by Lieutenant-General Evelyn Barker, who was the General Officer Commanding (GOC) in Palestine in July 1946. Following the bombing of the King David Hotel Barker wrote a general order to his troops putting all Jewish establishments out of bounds. This measure, he wrote, 'will be punishing the Jews in a way the race dislikes as much as any, by striking at their pockets and showing our contempt for them'.[26] Legge-Bourke questioned whether this incident required investigation by the Chief of the General Staff and considered that it was a definite obligation of the government to back Barker in the meantime.[27]

Another supporter of Barker was Major Tufton Beamish, who succeeded his father, Rear-Admiral Tufton Beamish, as the member for Lewes. Beamish believed that the activities of Jewish 'terrorists' would have been absolutely impossible without the support of a very large majority of the Jewish population. He, therefore, urged that the House gave their 'whole hearted support' to the actions of Barker.[28] Although Tufton Beamish was widely regarded as a right-wing maverick, his view in this matter was not divergent from that of the Party's front bench, as support for Barker also came from that quarter. Stanley, in an apologetic speech, considered that the strain that the conditions in Palestine brought on 'may well be held to excuse a certain bitterness in words'.[29] Whilst Conservative support did not, however, save Barker, who shortly after was removed from Palestine, it does indicate, by their acceptance of what was a racist action taken by the Palestine GOC, the Conservatives' increasing antipathy towards Jews.

The evidence for anti-Semitic attitudes on the Conservative benches may be illustrated by the re-emergence of the accusation that the Jews were involved in spreading communism. Sir Peter Macdonald, who had been an MP from October 1924 and who had represented the Isle of Wight since 1929,[30] alleged that 'young, fit men, and young women, many of them pregnant', who were well clothed and many with large sums of money, were entering Palestine at the behest of the Russian government. He stated that they were 'prepared to undertake any kind of atrocity'. Macdonald had, before making these assertions, advised the House that he certainly had no racial prejudice but that certain events had made him 'very angry indeed'.[31] He returned to this theme during the debate on the Palestine Bill in March 1948. He again alleged that several thousand Jews had been brought to Palestine from Russia. They were, he said, 'all trained Communist soldiers ... That is the Fifth Column waiting today for our departure from Palestine.'[32]

The communist conspiracy theory led Reginald Manningham-Buller, the member for Daventry,[33] to state that the Irgun was an extreme left-wing movement.[34] There would appear to be no excuse for him to have made this error for he had served as a member of the Anglo-American Commission of Enquiry on Palestine in 1946, and consequently should not have been unaware of the political views of the military wing of the Zionist Revisionist Organisation. The Revisionists, who wished to see a Jewish state on both banks of the River Jordan and who opposed the socialism of the Palestine labour movement, were often accused of fascism by their political opponents and the accusation that the Irgun was left wing was absurd.

Legge-Bourke considered that the inspiration of political Zionism was 'similar to that which lay behind Bolshevism in 1918'. He further believed that the aim of the people who financed the Zionists was to get control of the economic resources of Palestine 'which have been deliberately kept out of the public eye'. He hoped it would be realised, he said, 'that there is a far bigger issue in this than a mere war between Arabs and Jews. It is an economic war, and power politics of the very worst sort.'[35] Sir Waldron Smithers, the member for Orpington,[36] told the House that during 1948 Palestine would provide a harvest for 'atheistic and materialistic Soviet Communist propaganda' which was threatening to engulf the world.[37] The Jews were therefore seen by at least some Conservatives as communists or otherwise engaged in a conspiracy which would result in their domination of others. In view of the terrible suffering and mass killings of European Jewry by the Nazis and their allies it is ironical that accusations not dissimilar to those which appeared at the time of the Russian revolution should have re-emerged.

One Conservative MP, Col. Douglas Dodds-Parker,[38] warned that there was a long-standing fear that the Zionists' claim was not limited to Palestine and he likened them to Hitler's *Volkdeutsche* movement, alluding to the possibility that the Jews would claim Baghdad as it had a sizeable Jewish population.[39] Another member, McNeill Cooper-Key,[40] considered that there had been sordid lobbying which led to the vote at the United Nations in favour of partition. He said that the decision had been described as 'illegal and unjust' and said that this had been backed by a Jewish population of between 10 and 20 million compared to a Moslem world of 200 million people. It would appear that Cooper-Key considered that the Jews exercised some diabolical influence in order to achieve the creation of a Jewish state.[41]

THE PRO-ZIONIST CONSERVATIVES

The ranks of the pro-Zionist Conservatives were depleted by the loss of their parliamentary seats by MPs such as Amery[42] and Adams, while Cazalet, who Channon considered had Jews as his hobby,[43] had died on active service while travelling with General Sikorski. Others, such as Elliot and Macmillan, did not participate publicly as sympathisers of the Zionist cause.

The only Conservative backbencher openly to support Zionism in the post-war period of the mandate was William Teeling,[44] during 1946. He stated that he had been genuinely keen on Zionism for 25 years. His first reason was the defence and protection of the Empire because he believed that the Jews in Palestine were of more use to Britain than was anyone else. The second reason was his sympathy for the Jews in their troubles and problems, and the desire to find them a home. He considered that Chamberlain's policy of appeasement of the Arabs before the war was unsuccessful then and that it would not work currently. He considered that the Arabs were somewhat backward and the modernising Jews would better serve British interests, and the Arabs would be better off and happier under Jewish and British control.[45] In addition, he refused to believe that the terrorist atrocities that had been committed were the responsibility of all of Palestinian Jewry. 'I maintain', he said, 'that if the Jews had been properly backed by the British Government, and if the British Government's policies had been carried out, there would have been none of this whatsoever.'[46]

The only other sympathetic voice towards Zionism came from Churchill, whose contributions on the future of Palestine have been discussed above. Churchill considered himself, and was widely regarded by contemporaries, as pro-Zionist. As discussed elsewhere in this study he was one of those Conservatives who saw the advantage of a Jewish state as part of Britain's imperial presence and had considered that Jews, if they had not turned to Zionism, would expound communism. Churchill also considered that the Arabs were not a suitable alternative. On one occasion he berated Malcolm MacDonald in the lobby of the Commons, telling him that he was crazy to help the Arabs 'because they were a backward people who ate nothing but camel dung'.[47]

Yet, when in office as prime minister, Churchill did nothing effectively to progress the cause of Zionism. As early as September 1940 Ben-Gurion told Lloyd that he considered that Churchill, although a Zionist, did not at that time act like one.[48] Churchill avoided meetings with Weizmann, possibly because of a bad conscience about failing to progress Zionist interests rather than the pressure of other business.[49] He also did not reply to letters which Weizmann sent him.[50] In July 1945 Dugdale recorded that Weizmann felt very bitter at Churchill's 'do-nothing policy'[51] and Churchill refused to see Weizmann ever again. Whether this was a lingering result of Moyne's assassination, or the terrorism of the Irgun, or the embarrassment of a man who had failed those who had relied upon him, is not entirely clear. However, Churchill's explanation to Boothby that it was because he found Weizmann so fascinating that he would spend too much of his time talking to him seems somewhat incredible.[52]

Although he spoke at Party conferences and meetings and in the House on the issue of Palestine whilst leader of the Opposition, much of his focus was on the failure of the Labour government to act expeditiously in surrendering the mandate and their betrayal of the Zionist cause which they had expounded until the election campaign in 1945.[53] In July 1948, although sending Weizmann his warmest personal regards, he conveyed through Elliot his view that 'the Palestine position now, as concerns Great Britain, is simply such a hell-disaster that I cannot take it up again or renew my efforts of twenty years. It is a situation which I cannot help in, and must, as far as I can, put it out of my mind.'[54]

THE CONSERVATIVE PRESS

It was the terrorist acts in Palestine which produced the main commentaries from the Conservative press in the post-war period, although there was support for the Anglo-American Commission of Enquiry.[55] When the King David Hotel was bombed the *Daily Mail* stated that responsible Jewish spokesmen had repudiated the action.[56] The *Daily Telegraph* considered that this sort of action was doing the Jewish cause much harm, but it did absolve 'the responsible Jewish leadership of all complicity'.[57] The *Daily Express* compared the action to Nazism but stated that repression was no substitute for policy. This was a theme which was echoed in the *Daily Mail* and *The Times*.[58]

The hanging of the two British sergeants 12 months later led to a renewal of the comparison with Nazism by the *Daily Mail* and *The Times*. The *Daily Mail* implied that if the British withdrew from Palestine the Jews would be much worse off, whilst *The Times* opined that, notwithstanding the repudiation of the murders by members of the Jewish community world-wide, great harm had been done to Jewish aspirations in Palestine.[59] The *Daily Express* called on the Jews actively to oppose the terrorists and considered that 'assuredly British Jewry will give the lead'. It considered that, in this way, 'an unnatural feud' between Britain and the Zionists would be prevented. The leader further called for Britain's departure from Palestine, echoing its campaign in the early 1920s, 'she should get out, bag and baggage, quickly!'.[60] The *Daily Telegraph*, although acknowledging that Jews as a body should not be considered a party to the crime, did imply that the Jews should have done more to eradicate terrorist action.[61]

The United Nations resolution to partition Palestine was reluctantly supported by the Conservative press. The *Daily Telegraph* predicted war as the United Nations had no troops to maintain the peace.[62] *The Times* considered that Britain had, in any event, fulfilled its objectives under the mandate, whilst the *Daily Express* believed that Britain had only one obligation in Palestine and that was to get out.[63] At the termination of the mandate *The Times* wrote that the British people shared deeply in the sorrow and regret at the failure of what it called a 'great mission'.[64] The *Daily Telegraph* believed that nobody came well out of the matter except the British officials, police and military in Palestine.[65] The *Daily Express*, perhaps somewhat ironically in view of the attitude it had previously displayed, remained more positive in its leader. It wrote of Britain's proud achievements of 'justice and toleration' and concluded 'Good luck to Palestine!'.[66]

The Conservative press, like the Party, had become increasingly intolerant of the actions of the Jews, particularly when some resorted to violence. The failure of the Labour government to both suppress this violence and formulate a policy leading to withdrawal was criticised by Conservative papers. The mood of the press was increasingly anti-Jewish. Esmond Rothermere confided in Nicolson in May 1948 that he had great difficulty in getting his *Daily Mail* staff to write an article in support of the Jews, or rather in criticism of British backing of the Arabs. 'They saw it would harm the paper', Nicolson recorded, 'because of the strength of anti-Semitism in the country.'[67]

Conclusion

The first part of this chapter summarises the practice of Conservative attitudes to the Jews, which has been examined here through studies of episodes and themes, whilst the second is an attempt to encapsulate this through examples of Conservative culture and the language used. It has been demonstrated in the preceding chapters that Jews were regarded by Conservatives as different from 'Englishmen' and that there was prejudice exhibited against them at all levels in the Party throughout the entire period under review. However, it has also been shown that the perception of this difference varied according to the type of Jew under consideration and the nature of the Conservative holding the view.

The Conservative Party in the decades following the turn of the century were to regard aliens as an undesirable element within British society. Jews had been particularly identified because not only did they represent such a large proportion of the alien population but increasingly were regarded as a sinister force bent on the destruction of the Empire.

Although it was the Liberal radicals who had embarked on an anti-Semitic attack on Jews in South Africa as the cause of the Boer War, it is not inconceivable that the thesis that the Jews were attempting to manipulate the Crown found sympathy in the Unionist ranks. Jews were identified not only with capitalism as exploiters of British labour but as revolutionary socialists who would corrupt the British worker. Jews were seen by many as an insidious force which had exerted undue influence on King Edward VII. They figured, according to political polemicists such as Leo Maxse, too prominently in the upper ranks of the Liberal Party.[1] They were seen as the power behind pro-German influences before and during the First World War and the controllers of revolution in Russia and elsewhere after 1917.[2]

The phase of overt anti-Semitic behaviour, which included

prominent participation by members of the Unionist Party and the Conservative press, has been described by a leading historian of anti-Semitism as occupying the period 1917–22.[3] In the view of this study, that opinion does not give sufficient consideration to the agitation for restriction nor the structural changes which were made through the enactment and implementation of legislation. The legislation was aimed primarily against Jews wishing to enter Britain to live, work and obtain citizenship. It included not only the activities of the Conservative central government but also those of the local authorities, most notably, the London County Council, which denied housing, employment and academic scholarships to aliens and their children.

This study argues that the development of radical Unionism, primarily through the adoption of tariff reform, resulted in an increased predisposition to anti-alienism and anti-Semitism. By 1913, the changes which were in progress within the Unionist Party no longer required the issue of tariff reform to be at the forefront of Conservative policy to affect the move towards a more radical party. Indeed, when the issue of tariff reform re-emerged in 1923 the rhetoric adopted by the tariff reformers was more muted than it had been in the 1900s. However, the rhetoric of anti-alienism had not undergone any similar modification, in fact it was the reverse.

The belief that Jews were conspiring to overthrow European Christian civilisation in general, and the British Empire in particular, was a continuing undercurrent in Conservative thought in the period. It was manifested in increasing demands for restrictions on immigrants who were primarily Jewish. These demands were substantially satisfied by Conservative and Unionist ministers in the governments in which they served and dominated throughout much of the period under consideration.

The notion that Jews were loyal to a third party held increasingly greater sway amongst Conservatives in the first decades of the century. The attitude that Jews had a loyalty to Germany was the predominant view in the period until the Bolshevik revolution. Thereafter Jews were seen as loyal to a German–Soviet alliance and thereafter to communism in general and/or some Jewish–communist conspiracy to dominate the world. The perceived power of the Jews affected the thinking not only of the die-hard right wing of the Party but also the Conservative press and, more significantly, the leadership who exercised governmental control for much of the period.

One of the responses to the attitudes that eastern European Jews, in particular, were undesirable as British citizens and that Jewish power should be harnessed to British imperial interests was the promotion of Jewish territorial ambitions.[4] Initially, this was focused on British colonial territory in East Africa, thereafter in Palestine, and ultimately in a Central American British colony.

While the anti-alien legislation of the Unionists, which had been strengthened by wartime measures, had resulted in the erection of a barrier against immigrants, there was the prospect that eastern European Jewry, which had been badly treated, particularly by the Russian government in the war zone, would wish to migrate westwards. The agreement to dismember the Ottoman Empire, after an Allied victory, focused the minds of the Unionist leadership on the future of Turkish holdings in the Middle East and the competing claims of Britain's allies to the spoils.

It is the view of this study that the Unionists' continued desire to protect the route to India and to maintain hegemony in Egypt and the Sudan made it convenient to support Zionism for British imperial purposes. Yet it was the perception of Jewish power and the wish not to see further numbers of an unassimilable 'international' race in Britain which, in the critical wartime atmosphere that existed in 1917, resulted in the issuing of the Balfour Declaration. This policy was not subject to any general debate in the Party; a decision which would cause increasing dissension over the next two decades within the Party.

The period 1914–20 witnessed dramatic and devastating upheavals which affected and changed European society. The emergence of a Bolshevik Russia caused great anxiety long after the Germans had signed the Armistice with the Allied powers in November 1918. Traditional values and a stable British society were seen as being under threat from insidious foreign alien ideas. The anti-Semitic attitudes that had become increasingly manifest in the first decade of the twentieth century became more pronounced after 1914. The Conservatives' fear of Jewish influence and power became more overt within the Conservative Press and amongst Unionist politicians. The feeling that Jews were a potentially dangerous and un-English element within British society would impact upon Conservative policies and attitudes to the Jewish community in the inter-war period.

An anti-Zionist campaign was effectively waged from 1920 until 1923 and produced substantial modifications in government policy towards the Jewish national home. It had attracted a large number of Conservative MPs and peers, together with most of the Conservative press. However, the Conservative cabinet would not abandon the mandate for strategic reasons and also the potentially damaging diplomatic effect of abandoning an international commitment.

The primary reasons for the issuing of the Balfour Declaration in 1917 had far less relevance as the 1920s progressed. Those who continued to believe in 'Jewish power' saw it fundamentally as an anti-Christian world conspiracy linked to Bolshevism. Yet this alleged power of the Jews did little to prevent the pogroms which occurred in Poland and elsewhere in 1919 and 1920. Nor did it prevent the continued subjugation of civil rights in the successor states in eastern Europe despite the Minorities Treaty that had emerged from the Versailles Peace Conference.

The formation of a Bolshevik government in Russia had effectively closed off the opportunity for Russian Jewry to migrate westward while the problems of economic development in Palestine restricted practically (as well as legislatively) the absorptive capacity of the country. Furthermore, the hostility of the Palestinian Arabs to Jewish immigration created fresh problems for Britain rather than solving the issue of Jewish migration from central and eastern Europe.

The strategic role of Britain in Palestine remained and arguably grew in importance when Britain's role in Egypt changed after 1922. This consideration did not, however, require support for Zionism. There were increasingly fewer Conservatives who supported the Balfour Declaration, even as modified, as a method of implementing its Middle Eastern policy.

Although there appeared to be a growth in anti-Semitism during the 1930s this was not reflected in a more stridently hostile attitude towards Jews in the Party generally. Hardly any Conservatives adopted the fascist model and the type of anti-Semitism exhibited by Edward Doran and Archibald Ramsay was regarded as un-English behaviour. German atrocities against Jews were condemned openly by many Conservatives and privately by others such as Neville Chamberlain, who wrote that he was horrified by the German behaviour to the Jews following *Kristallnacht*.[5]

The role of the British government in its admission of Jews into Britain in the 1930s has been the subject of recent critical historiography. It has been alleged that the plight of Jews was perceived as a problem of immigration rather than a duty to rescue persecuted refugees.[6] It has also been maintained that the British government was happier to appease those who were hostile to Jews rather than attack anti-Semitism itself, or indeed appease any anti-Semitic sentiment in Britain.[7] An earlier view of British government policy (which has not been revised in the recent edition of the work) considers that, in the context of the pre-war period, it was comparatively compassionate, even generous.[8]

Although accurate figures for the admission of Jewish and other refugees from the Reich are unlikely ever to be known, it is possible that the numbers admitted were in the order of 70,000 people.[9] This compares with the admissions to the United States during the period from the Reich and Spain of 136,000. This is a lower number than the quota for Germany alone for the period (20,000 per annum). Also in the pre-war period some 40,000 refugees were admitted to France, 25,000 to Belgium, 23,000 to Holland and 10,000 to Switzerland.[10] These countries each have a common border with Germany.

As this study has shown, notwithstanding the inherent anti-Semitism in, at least, an element of the Conservative Party, which included members of its leadership, the extreme fascist form of anti-Semitism was rejected by all but a few Conservatives. There was also a significant number of pro-Jewish Conservatives who fought for the admission of Jewish refugees. It has also been demonstrated that a relatively large number of Jews were admitted to Britain in the period under examination. In the earlier part of the 1930s the effective ban on Jews allowed into Britain was removed and the numbers grew dramatically following the German occupation of Austria, *Kristallnacht* and the invasion of Czechoslovakia. The policy to admit these Jews to Britain was taken at cabinet level. Even if the issue of immigration in this period was left primarily to the officials to administer, as has been maintained in a recent study of immigration control procedures, the civil servants were carrying out Conservative policies which had been initially instituted in 1906. Furthermore, that historian has accepted that the changes which occurred in admissions were as a result of political decisions taken at the highest level.[11]

The type of Jew from central Europe, who presented himself as an alien immigrant, was probably more acceptable to Conservative opinion than the eastern European Jews who had entered Britain during the period of the mass migrations. The desire to avoid increasing immigration into Palestine may have also had some bearing on the decision-making process. Furthermore, it is argued here that the Conservative leaders were moved, at least in part, by humanitarian considerations and also by the potential benefit to Britain of the entry of many gifted individuals.[12] However, this policy was, at least partially, concealed in order to mislead those, particularly within the Party, whose anti-Semitism had led to vigorous opposition to Jewish immigration. The relatively large admission of Jews to Britain in 1938 and 1939 can be contrasted with the restrictionist policies adopted in respect of Jewish immigration into Palestine at the same time. The Unionist policy for dealing with Jewish immigration had been turned on its head.

The anti-Zionist campaign waged in the Commons throughout the 1930s was primarily that of Conservative MPs. However, the outbreak of sustained Arab violence in 1936 marked the beginning of the adoption of policies by the government which were to become increasingly hostile to Zionism.

The Conservative leadership, particularly under Chamberlain, was to reach the view that the mandate was unworkable and abandoned the Balfour Declaration, as modified by the Churchill White Paper of 1922, as the basis of its policy in Palestine. The goodwill of the Jews for Britain was no longer regarded as necessary whilst the goodwill of the Moslems, particularly in India, was seen as increasingly important. The Chamberlain government sought to appease the Arabs as it had done the Italians and the Germans, but ultimately without success.

Nevertheless, support for the Jewish cause remained relatively strong in the Conservative Party, partly owing to the increasing suffering of Continental Jewry at the hands of the Nazis and their sympathisers and partly because of the actions of the Chamberlain administration. Duff Cooper, for example, considered that, owing to the policies of appeasement, Britain bore a share of the responsibility for the 'ghastly, hideous and shocking persecution that has befallen the Jewish race'.[13] This view ultimately resulted in the defiance of the Party whip by a not inconsequential number of government supporters in May 1939. Whilst the numbers concerned were less than those who had rebelled over the India Act, it was a precursor to the revolt in May 1940 which brought down the Chamberlain government.

The Nazi persecution of the Jews during the Second World War did not result in any increase in sympathetic attitudes towards Jews by Conservatives. The Jews received extremely limited assistance from those Conservative politicians who controlled the ministries which affected their fate. The solution to the Jewish refugee problem was reduced effectively to their admission to Palestine but the Chamberlainite White Paper policy was continued, notwithstanding Churchill's premiership and Lord Lloyd's assertion that all the cabinet were Zionists.[14] Indeed, the fear of upsetting Arab and Moslem opinion, coupled with the relegation of Jewish matters to an often undefined future date, prevented even Churchill, one of the most pro-Zionist Conservatives, at least until the death of Walter Moyne, from changing the policy adopted by Neville Chamberlain. It has been demonstrated that Churchill took no effective action to change a policy which he often stated that he found unacceptable. The wartime period demonstrates the decline in Conservative sympathy for the Jews who were seen by the Conservatives as increasingly ungrateful and ever demanding.

Churchill, even though his enthusiasm for Zionism had waned after the death of Moyne, was resented in the Party for having pro-Zionist leanings.[15] This probably says much more regarding the general feeling in the Party towards Jews and Zionism in the 1940s than about Churchill's own commitment. Although another front-bench Conservative, Cranborne, favoured a Jewish State, it was one to be located in Africa. He wrote to Eden in May 1943 that he believed this would silence the wealthy American Jewish supporters of Zionism and 'only thus will we be able to get some of the Jews out of this country [Britain], in which there are now far too many'.[16]

Eden had admitted in a private note to Harvey in September 1941 that if it was necessary to have preferences he would prefer the Arabs to the Jews.[17] This view was shared by many in the Conservative Party. Macmillan was later to write that he considered that from the 1930s pro-Arab sentiments had predominated in the Conservative Party. He considered that by the end of the mandate the Party was unhappy and divided with the majority of the Opposition not sympathetic to the approach Churchill had adopted.[18] Jewish terrorist action, which intensified after 1945, resulted in increased hostility to the Jews by the Party. Jews were again described in familiar terms as communist agents bent on the destruction of British interests. It is suggested that the persistent accusations that Jews were communists, anti-British and trouble-makers in Palestine deepened the attitude that Jews were un-English.

It is probable that the level of anti-Semitism in the Conservative Party had risen as it had done generally in the country, and some of the speeches in the House by Conservative MPs, which have previously been noted, would appear to support this supposition. Yet the Party leadership took steps to avoid any open recognition of anti-Semitism, as for example at the Party conference in October 1947. A proposed anti-Semitic amendment to a motion on Imperial policy, which the press considered would have been supported by an overwhelming majority of delegates, was forestalled by the intervention of two MPs, Quintin Hogg and Sir Ian Fraser.[19] Nevertheless it is possible that by the end of the mandate the relationship between the Jews and the Conservative Party had reached its nadir.

Although it is not possible to discern a single Conservative attitude, there is an ambivalence throughout the period. Jews may have been considered to be outsiders but this did not mean, however, that they were necessarily excluded. When Lt-Col. A. H. Lane publicly attacked Jews working for the Conservative and Unionist Central Office, Baldwin's parliamentary private secretary received a response from Central Office, which praised the work that Percy Cohen and Albert Clavering had rendered to the Party and dismissed Lane as 'an anti-Semitic lunatic'.[20]

The apparent contradictions also extended to personal relationships. Neville Chamberlain had a personal as well as a professional relationship with Sir Joseph Ball, as has been mentioned above. Ball's financial and editorial control of *Truth* demonstrates blatant anti-Semitism. Yet the former Jewish Conservative MP and government minister, Arthur Michael Samuel, who had been ennobled as Lord Mancroft, wrote to Chamberlain that 'our mutual personal friendship ever since we both entered the House of Commons together has given me intense pleasure & has been a source of pride to me'.[21]

There were 28 Jewish Members of Parliament who were elected and sat in the Conservative interest in the period under review.[22] Only Walter Rothschild, Lionel de Rothschild and Isadore Salmon held senior positions in leading Jewish institutions, whilst Samuel Finburgh was a leading advocate of Jewish interests in Parliament, even against the actions of a Conservative government.[23] Advocacy of Jewish interests was, however, rare. Indeed, involvement in the affairs of the Anglo-Jewish community was restricted to only half of the 28 MPs.[24]

Sir Philip Sassoon had, according to 'Chips' Channon, an 'Oriental mind with all its vanities'.[25] However, he considered Sassoon 'though hated Jews'.[26] Thus, even if there was a desire not to identify with other Jews, those Jewish MPs who did not participate in communal affairs could still be identified by others in the Party with the Anglo-Jewish community.

Only two of the 28 Jewish Conservatives obtained ministerial rank. Perhaps it was significant that neither of them played any part in communal affairs. Sir Arthur Samuel began his government career as the parliamentary secretary for overseas trade in the Board of Trade in November 1924. In November 1927, he became financial secretary to the Treasury. He was not re-appointed to a government position in the National Government of August 1931. Cuthbert Headlam considered that the job of financial secretary was too much for Samuel.[27]

Sir Philip Sassoon had served as Lloyd George's parliamentary private secretary from 1920 to 1922. In November 1924, he was appointed by Baldwin as the under-secretary of state for air; a position he held until the fall of the Conservative administration in June 1929. He was re-appointed to that position in September 1931. He remained in that post until he was promoted to ministerial rank as First Commissioner of Works in May 1937. He died in office in June 1939.

The positions held by both Samuel and Sassoon were junior and even the latter's promotion was to the least senior of the ministerial posts. In comparison, several Jewish Liberal Party members obtained cabinet rank. Herbert Samuel was chancellor of the Duchy of Lancaster (1909–10), postmaster-general (1910–14), president of the Local Government Board (1914–15), and home secretary (January–December 1916 and 1931–32). Rufus Isaacs, created Lord Reading, was attorney-general (1912–13) and foreign secretary (August–November 1931). Edwin Montagu was chancellor of the Duchy of Lancaster (February–May 1915 and January–July 1916), minister of munitions (July–December 1916) and secretary of state for India (1917–22). Sir Alfred Mond was minister of health (1921–22). The other Liberal to achieve cabinet rank was Leslie Hore-Belisha, who sat as a Liberal National from 1931. (He and the other 'National' MPs were supported by the Conservatives in the 1935 general election.) He became a cabinet member as minister of transport (1936–37) and secretary of state for war (1937–40). He was dismissed by Chamberlain, owing to anti-Semitic pressure, as examined in Chapter 9.[28]

The 'achievement' of Jewish Conservatives in government does not compare with that achieved by Liberals. Indeed, even when the strength of the Liberal Party had been diminished it fell to two Jews to represent it in the principal offices of state in the National Government in 1931.

It is not possible to identify any one reason for the disparity between the political parties and the number of Jews who were selected as candidates, elected as MPs or who held government office. However, it is possible to conclude that Jewish Conservatives generally performed less well than Jewish Liberals and latterly Jewish Socialists.

Jewish Conservatives did not exactly replicate the profile of the parliamentary Conservative Party. However, this group did reflect, in part, the type and character of many of the parliamentary Party's members. Jewish Conservative MPs did not play a major role in the governance of Britain during the period under review, nor generally made major contributions in those policy areas affecting Jews either domestically or abroad.

The lower numbers and percentages of Conservative Jewish candidates and relatively lower number of Conservative Jewish MPs, when compared with the Liberal Party and latterly the Labour Party, may have been, in part, as a result of anti-Semitism, either in the Party or as perceived in Conservative supporters. In the period following both world wars anti-Semitism was at a relative high level in Britain, and not restricted only to the fascist right. In 1921 Sir Robert Sanders, then a junior minister, considered the Conservative defeat in the by-election at St George's Westminster; he wrote that 'a number of people would not vote for Jessel [the Conservative candidate] because he is a Jew'.[29]

The *Jewish Chronicle* commented in August 1945 that anti-Semitism on the part of Party supporters had led many local political associations not to select Jewish candidates. It extended this view to include the Liberal Party as well as the Conservatives. The Liberals responded by a letter to the editor denying the charge and indeed the number of Jewish Liberal candidates do clearly refute this assumption.[30] There was, however, no refutation by any Conservative to the charge.

In the period 1914–39 the most interesting thing about the religious affiliations of members of the Conservative Party, wrote one analyst of its Members of Parliament, was that only about one-sixth belonged to denominations other than the Church of England, and of that group many were members of the Church of Scotland.[31] Even if the identification with the established Church diminished in the period under review,[32] the Party saw Jews generally as outsiders. The identification of Jews with Bolshevism and socialism, and as 'trouble makers' in Palestine, no doubt further encouraged anti-Semitism in the Party. One result may have been the limited number of Jewish MPs and their limited role in the Conservative Party during this period.

The only Jewish Conservative to sit in the House after the 1945 general election was the independent Conservative Daniel Lipson, who had first been elected for Cheltenham at a by-election in June 1937.[33] Lipson was originally a Liberal and at that time he had served as mayor for five years and on the county council for 12, but the constituency selection committee had rejected his nomination in favour of a Lt-Col. R. Tisham Harper. Although not openly stated at the time, it is the view of this study that the fact that Lipson was a Jew played a not insignificant part in their decision.

The formal minutes of the Cheltenham Conservative Association Selection Committee meeting held on 18 December 1936 read as follows: 'The chairman mentioned that Mr D. L. Lipson had approached him officially & had asked that his name be submitted to the committee for consideration. A short discussion ensued and on a vote taken, it was unanimously decided not to recommend Mr Lipson.' However, the contemporaneous note taken at the meeting was somewhat more dramatic and indicative of virulent feelings in that it read 'Lipson *unanimously not approved*'.[34] Lipson, therefore, stood as an independent and pledged to take the National Government whip.

The refusal of the Cheltenham Conservative Association to adopt Lipson was not entirely popular with leading Conservatives in the constituency or elsewhere. It led to the resignation/ retirement of the chairmen of two of the Conservative ward associations whilst Lipson's victory at the polls was followed by a letter of congratulations from Colonel James Baldwin-Webb, the Conservative MP for The Wrekin.[35]

Yet, although Lipson was acceptable to at least some Conservatives, his Jewish status would mean that he, like other Jews, would be viewed as not quite English. This did not mean that the Conservatives would necessarily exclude Jews, for Austen Chamberlain wrote to a correspondent from Birmingham that '[w]e have had a Jew as Lord Chief Justice of this country, as Viceroy of India and in Disraeli's person as Prime Minister. We have Jewish judges and Jewish professors, Jewish lawyers, and Jewish doctors, and nobody would think of proscribing them.'[36] Yet some years before he had described Benjamin Disraeli to his sister: 'tho' an English patriot [he] was not an Englishman'.[37] These views, expressed by the only leader of the Party in the period not to have become prime minister, perhaps encapsulate the ambivalence that the Conservative Party had exhibited towards Jews, both individually and as a group, during the period under examination.

Notes

1: Introduction

1. Oxford, 1983.
2. London, 1989.
3. See Chapter 5 and Chapter 9.
4. There is, however, a possible exception in that Professor William Rubinstein has recently shown that Leo Amery, who plays a prominent role in this narrative, had Jewish roots which were concealed. See W. D. Rubinstein, 'The Secret of Leopold Amery', *History Today*, Vol. 49 (February 1999), pp.17–23.
5. This study has not examined the role of the national parties, as the focus of this work is not institutional and this is a further field of examination which may be undertaken.
6. See Chapter 4.
7. See Chapter 8.
8. See E. H. H. Green, *The Crisis of Conservatism: The Politics, Economics and Ideology of the British Conservative Party 1880–1914* (London, 1995), pp. 7–11.
9. See Chapter 2.
10. See David Dutton, *'His Majesty's Loyal Opposition': The Unionist Party in Opposition 1905–1915* (Liverpool, 1992), in which he argues that the 'debate over tariff reform thus highlights a fundamental struggle which went on inside the Unionist ranks in the years before the First World War to determine what sort of party it was going to be and how successfully it could cope with the challenges of a new era', p. 258.
11. See Chapter 9.
12. *Encyclopaedia Judaica*, Vol. 3 (Jerusalem, 1972), Col. 87.
13. Ibid. Vol. 16, Col. 1032.
14. See Robert S. Wistrich, *Between Redemption and Perdition* (London, 1990), Ch. 19, pp. 214–24.
15. See Chapter 8.
16. See Chapter 4.
17. See Chapter 6.
18. Isidore Harris (ed.), *Jewish Year Book* (London, 1901), p. 181.
19. Albert M. Hyamson (ed.), *Jewish Year Book* (London, 1947), pp. 297–9. These figures are based upon estimates produced in 1940 and 1946.
20. Cited in David Butler and Gareth Butler, *British Political Facts 1900–1985* (6th edn, 1986), p. 323, from the *Annual Reports of the Registrar-General for England and Wales, Scotland and Northern Ireland*.
21. Tom Clarke, *My Northcliffe Diary* (London, 1931), p. 125.

22. PRO HO 213/44 E 409. Letter to Neville Chamberlain, 21 February 1940, cited by Tony Kushner, 'British Anti-Semitism 1918–1945', in David Cesarani (ed.), *The Making of Modern Anglo-Jewry* (London, 1990), p. 200.
23. The Marconi affair had involved the awarding of a government contract, on a non-competitive basis, by Jewish Postmaster-General Herbert Samuel to a company whose managing director was the brother of the Jewish Attorney-General Sir Rufus Isaacs. Furthermore there were associated subsequent share dealings by ministers, including Isaacs, in a Marconi company. Another 'scandal' arose at this time with Jews as the dominant players; the Indian Silver affair. In March 1912 the firm of Samuel Montagu & Co. commenced acting for the government of India in the purchase of silver. Herbert Samuel was involved through family connections. His brother, Sir Stuart Samuel, was a partner in the firm of Samuel Montagu & Co., whilst his cousin Edwin Montagu was the son of the founder of the firm, and was under-secretary of state for India. The India Office instructed brokers to purchase silver on its behalf but this had led to a ring being created, which resulted in the price of silver being forced up. The Bank of England was replaced secretly and without competition by Samuel Montagu & Co. to break the ring. Thus both 'affairs' had Jewish businessmen entering into secret and/or non-competitive contracts with the Liberal administration in areas where Jewish politicians may have been involved and which were highly sensitive politically.
24. *National Review*, Vol. LX (December 1912), pp. 552–3.
25. Ibid., March 1913, p. 6.
26. *Commons Debates*, 4th Series, Vol. 149, Col. 155, 10 July 1905.
27. Austen Chamberlain to Ida Chamberlain, 11 July 1920, AC5/1/168, in R. C. Self (ed.), *The Austen Chamberlain Diary Letters* (Cambridge, 1995), p. 137.
28. See Chaim Bermant, *The Cousinhood* (London, 1971).
29. See V. D. Lipman, *Social History of the Jews in England 1850–1950* (London, 1954), and *A History of the Jews in Britain since 1858* (London, 1990); Albert M. Hyamson, *The Sephardim of England* (London, 1951); Geoffrey Alderman, *Modern British Jewry* (Oxford, 1992); W. D. Rubinstein, *A History of the Jews in the English Speaking World* (London, 1996), and also Harold Pollins, *Economic History of the Jews in England* (London, 1982), and Eugene C. Black, *The Social Politics of Anglo-Jewry 1880–1920* (Oxford, 1988).
30. See William J. Fishman, *East End Jewish Radicals 1875–1914* (London, 1975) and Henry Felix Srebrnik, *London Jews and British Communism 1935–1945* (London, 1995).
31. H. Channon, *'Chips', The Diaries of Sir Henry Channon*, Robert Rhodes James (ed.), 2nd edn (London, 1993), 4 April 1938, p. 153.
32. See A. J. P. Taylor, *Essays in English History* (London, 1977), p. 18 and Anthony Seldon 'The Tory Party in Power 1783–1996', in Anthony Seldon (ed.), *How Tory Governments Fall: The Tory Party in Power since 1783* (London, 1996), p. 18.
33. Lord Butler (ed.), *The Conservatives* (London, 1977), p. 17.
34. Lord Hugh Cecil, *Conservatism* (London, 1912), p. 244.
35. Quintin Hogg, *The Case for Conservatism* (London, 1947), p. 15.
36. Baldwin appears to be silent in speeches or correspondence regarding his own attitude towards Jews. However, he did sponsor the Baldwin Fund in 1938, appealing for support for the victims of Nazism.
37. Stanley Baldwin, *Our Inheritance* (London, 1928), p. 30.
38. Ibid., p. 224.
39. Kenneth O. Morgan, *Consensus and Disunity: The Lloyd George Coalition Government 1918–1922* (Oxford, 1979), p. 33.

40. Srebrnik, *London Jews and British Communism 1935–1945*, p. 151.
41. Tony Kushner, *The Persistence of Prejudice: Antisemitism in British Society During the Second World War* (Manchester, 1989), p. 83. Kushner appears to have followed W. D. Rubinstein in 'Jews Among Top British Wealth Holders', *Jewish Social Studies*, XXIV (1972), pp. 80–1.
42. Stuart Ball, 'Local Conservatism and Party Organization', in Anthony Seldon and Stuart Ball (eds), *Conservative Century: The Conservative Party Since 1900* (Oxford, 1994), p. 265.
43. Rubinstein, *History*, p. 116.
44. Published in Cardiff.
45. Seldon and Ball, *Conservative Century*, p. 556.
46. Ibid., pp. 650–1, and 656–7.
47. A. J. Davies, *We the Nation*, pp. 156–9.
48. Oxford (1990), p. 96.
49. Oxford (1971).
50. London (1989).
51. Irish immigration is considered to constitute 'internal' immigration owing to the citizenship and nationality rights which are enjoyed by the Irish.
52. The most comprehensive study of Jewish immigration into Britain remains Lloyd Gartner, *The Jewish Immigrant in England 1870–1914* (2nd edn, London, 1973). The more recent study by David Feldman, *Englishmen and Jews: Social Relations and Political Culture 1840–1914* (London, 1994), examines the relationship between English society and the Jewish community. The Aliens Act 1905 is examined in John H. Garrard, *The English and Immigration 1880–1910* (London, 1971) and Bernard Gainer, *The Alien Invasion* (New York, 1972).
53. James Margach, *The Abuse of Power: The War between Downing Street and the Media from Lloyd George to Callaghan* (London, 1978), p. 53, records that Neville Chamberlain, in a private meeting with select journalists before the final outbreak of the Second World War, in answering any question about reports of the persecution of the Jews, Hitler's broken pledges or Mussolini's ambitions, a journalist 'would receive a response on well-established lines: he was surprised that such an experienced journalist was susceptible to Jewish–Communist propaganda'.
54. See Peter and Leni Gillman, *Collar the Lot: How Britain Interned And Expelled Its Wartime Refugees* (London, 1980) and David Cesarani and Tony Kushner (eds), *The Internment of Aliens in Twentieth Century Britain* (London, 1993), *passim*.
55. Bernard Wasserstein, *Britain and the Jews of Europe 1939–1945* (Oxford, 2nd edn, 1988).

2: The Conservatives and Alien Jewish Immigration, 1900–18

1. Jose Harris, *Private Life, Public Spirit: A Social History of Britain 1870–1914*, (Oxford, 1993), pp. 41–5.
2. Lipman, *A History*, p. 49.
3. Gainer, *Alien Invasion*, p. 175.
4. For the impact on party politics in the last decade of the nineteenth century see I. Finestein, 'Jewish Immigration in British Party Politics in the 1890s', in Aubrey Newman (ed.), *Migration and Settlement* (London, 1971).
5. Cited in Milton Shain, *The Roots of Anti-Semitism in South Africa* (Charlottesville, VA, 1994), pp. 42–3.
6. *Westminster Gazette*, 17 September 1900, cited in Colin Holmes, *Anti-Semitism in British Society 1876–1939* (London, 1979), p. 68.

7. *East London Observer*, 22 September 1900, p. 5.
8. Holmes, *Anti-Semitism*, p. 67.
9. *Commons Debates*, Fourth Series, Vol. 101, Col. 1269, 29 January 1902.
10. Ibid., Col. 1284.
11. Norman was of Jewish descent, but not recognised as a part of the Anglo-Jewish elite (he does not feature in the contemporary Jewish Year Books). G. Alderman does not, however, make a distinction between Norman and other Jewish MPs. See Alderman, *The Jewish Community*, p. 69. Norman, in common with some Jewish Unionist MPs, was in favour of restricting further Jewish immigration. This attitude may have arisen from the fear that the existing Jewish community would be subject to anti-Semitism if 'alien' Jews were permitted to settle. This view was held by some in Jewish welfare organisations such as the Jewish Board of Guardians which had policies of repatriation and emigration for 'alien' Jews. See Feldman, *Englishmen and Jews*, pp. 302–5.
12. *Commons Debates*, Fourth Series, Vol. 109, Col. 96, 9 June 1902; Col. 839, 17 June 1902; Vol. 115, Col. 622, 27 November 1902.
13. Ibid., Vol. 132, Col. 987 *passim*, 29 March 1904.
14. Ibid., Vol. 133, Col. 1103, 25 April 1904.
15. Ibid., Vol. 137, Col. 1220, 11 July 1904.
16. Ibid., Vol. 139, Col. 566, 2 August 1904.
17. Ibid., Col. 571.
18. Gainer, *Alien Invasion*, p. 185.
19. Alan Sykes, *Tariff Reform in British Politics 1903–1913* (Oxford, 1979), p. 81.
20. *Commons Debates*, Fourth Series, Vol. 133, Col. 1116, 25 April 1904.
21. This has been estimated at over 8 per cent. See Alderman, *Jewish Community*, p. 186.
22. *Jewish Chronicle*, 13 January 1905, p. 10.
23. *Commons Debates*, Fourth Series, Vol. 145, Col. 464, 18 April 1905.
24. Ibid., Col. 706, 2 May 1905.
25. Ibid., Vol. 149, Col. 155, 10 July 1905.
26. Ibid., Col. 952, 17 July 1905.
27. Ibid., Vol. 133, Col. 1137, 25 April 1904.
28. The immigrant population in Leeds increased the Jewish community from about 2,500 in 1881 to 20,000 in 1907. See Lipman, *A History*, p. 50.
29. See Harris, *Private Lives*, p. 44; Lipman, *A History*, p. 45 and *passim*; Feldman, *Englishmen and Jews*, p. 157. For contemporary estimates see *Jewish Year Book 1901* and commentary on same by Lipman, *A History*, p. 89.
30. J. A. Froude, *England's War* (London, 1871), cited in G. R. Searle, *The Quest For National Efficiency* (Oxford, 1971), p. 10.
31. Data cited in Paul Kennedy, *The Rise and Fall of the Great Powers* (London, 1988), p. 199.
32. Ibid., p. 202.
33. *Contemporary Review*, Vol. 81, January 1902. Cited in Samuel Hynes, *The Edwardian Turn of Mind* (London, 1968), p. 22.
34. Ibid., p. 26.
35. A. J. A. Morris, *The Scaremongers: The Advocacy of War and Rearmament 1896–1914* (London, 1984), p. 64.
36. Bryan Cheyette, 'Jewish Stereotyping and English Literature 1875–1920: Towards a Political Analysis', in Tony Kushner and Kenneth Lunn (eds), *Traditions of Intolerance: Historical Perspectives on Fascism and Race Discourse in Britain* (Manchester, 1989), pp. 12–32.
37. He was adopted as the Conservative candidate for the Liberal-held seat of

Peebles and Selkirk in 1911. However, he did not obtain a seat in the Commons until 1927.

38. John Buchan, *A Lodge in the Wilderness* (London, 1906), p. 23.
39. John Buchan, *The Thirty-Nine Steps* (London, 1930 omnibus edition entitled *The Four Adventures of Richard Hannay*), p. 7.
40. Henry Wickham Steed, *Through Thirty Years 1892–1922: A Personal Narrative*, Vol. I (London, 1924), p. 163.
41. See *Report of the Royal Commission on Alien Immigration*, Cmd. 1742 (London, 1903).
42. Wickham Steed, *Through Thirty Years*, p. 95.
43. Michael Howard, 'Empire, Race and War in pre-1914 Britain', in H. Lloyd-Jones *et al.* (eds), *History and Imagination: Essays in Honour of H. R. Trevor-Roper* (London, 1981), p. 345.
44. Searle, *National Efficiency*, p. 54.
45. Frans Coetzee, *For Party or Country–Nationalism and the Dilemmas of Popular Conservatism in Edwardian England* (Oxford, 1990), argues that tariff reform was one of a number of Unionist pressure groups which arose, the Navy League being another, albeit less prominent, example. However, Matthew Fforde, *Conservatism and Collectivism 1886–1914* (Edinburgh, 1990), considers that tariff reform was a Unionist reaction to the collectivist policies of both the Liberal and Labour parties.
46. Cited in L. S. Amery, *My Political Life*, Vol. 1: *England Before The Storm 1896–1914* (London, 1953), pp. 261–2.
47. *The Times*, 23 November 1887, p. 3.
48. Sykes, *Tariff Reform*, p. 7.
49. Ibid., p. 63.
50. See Amery, *My Political Life*, Vol. 1, p. 274, and Sykes, *Tariff Reform*, p. 83 *passim*.
51. Cited in Blanche E. C. Dugdale, *Arthur James Balfour*, Vol. 1 (London, 1936), p. 354.
52. A. K. Russell, *Liberal Landslide: The General Election of 1906* (Newton Abbot, 1973), p. 83.
53. It is considered that Garrard does not take adequate account of the changing nature of the Unionist Party as a dynamic towards legislation.
54. *Jewish Chronicle*, 28 September 1900, p. 5.
55. *The Times*, 12 July 1904, p. 10.
56. Henry Pelling, *Social Geography of British Elections 1885–1910* (London, 1967), p. 37.
57. *Commons Debates*, Fourth Series, Vol. 133, Col. 1091, 25 April 1904.
58. Ibid., Vol. 145, Col. 767, 2 May 1905.
59. See remarks made by Vincent, *Commons Debates*, Fourth Series, Vol. 89, Col. 117, 14 February 1901 and Evans-Gordon, *Commons Debates*, Fourth Series, Vol. 101, Col. 1279, 29 January 1902.
60. See Feldman, *Englishmen and Jews*, pp. 302–6 and V. D. Lipman, *A Century of Social Service 1859–1959: The Jewish Board of Guardians* (London, 1959), pp. 89–102 for the activities of the Board in this respect.
61. *Commons Debates*, Fourth Series, Vol. 133, Col. 1119, 25 April 1904.
62. Ibid., Vol. 149, Col. 155, 10 July 1905.
63. Sykes, *Tariff Reform*, p. 80.
64. Blake, *Conservative Party*, pp. 180–1.
65. Russell, *Liberal Landslide*, p. 83.
66. *East London Observer*, 6 January 1906, p. 2.
67. Ibid., p. 7.
68. Ibid., 13 January 1906, p. 9.

69. Recent historians have questioned the extent of the tariff reformers ascendancy, reducing their number to about 80. See Sykes, *Tariff Reform*, p. 100.
70. Russell, *Liberal Landslide*, p. 182.
71. It has been suggested that, in the case of Claude Hay, this may, at least in part, have been owing to the distribution of between £200–300 worth of Christmas presents in the form of 3s 6d food parcels. See Sykes, *Tariff Reform*, p.133.
72. As defined by Pelling.
73. *Regulations made by the Home Secretary under the Aliens Act*, Cmd. 2879 (1906).
74. *Commons Debates*, Fourth Series, Vol. 153, Col. 141, 5 March 1906, and Col. 1312, 14 March 1906.
75. Ibid., Vol. 164, Col. 1058, 12 November 1906.
76. *Jewish Chronicle*, 13 July 1906, p. 8.
77. *Commons Debates*, Fourth Series, Vol. 157, Col. 612, 17 May 1906.
78. The Hon. Lionel Walter Rothschild was the Liberal Unionist member for Aylesbury (1899–1910). He succeeded to the peerage as the second Baron Rothschild in 1915 and was the formal recipient of the Balfour Declaration in November 1917.
79. *Jewish Chronicle*, 23 March 1906, p. 9.
80. *Commons Debates*, Fourth Series, Vol. 159, Col. 768, 26 June 1906.
81. *The Times*, 22 June 1906, p. 4.
82. Chaim Weizmann in *Trial and Error* (London, 1949), pp. 118–20, writes sympathetically about Evans-Gordon upon whom, Weizmann believed, the Jews had rendered too hard a verdict.
83. Sir Howard Vincent died the following year, thus depriving the anti-alienists of two of its most vigorous politicians.
84. *East London Observer*, 4 May 1907, pp. 5 and 10.
85. The Liberals and Lib/Lab candidates were to hold six seats but, in addition to the loss of Brigg to the Unionists, lost two seats to Labour/Independent Labour.
86. *The Times*, 27 July 1907, p. 12 and 29 July 1907, p. 9.
87. See below for discussion of some aspects of this by-election where Winston Churchill was defeated by William Joynson-Hicks.
88. *Commons Debates*, Fifth Series, Vol. 1, Col. 961, 25 February 1909.
89. *Commons Debates*, Fourth Series, Vol. 173, Col. 534, 29 April 1907.
90. Ibid., Vol. 186, Col. 1696, 26 March 1908.
91. *Commons Debates*, Fourth Series, Vol. 172, Col. 1147, 18 April 1907.
92. Alderman, *Jewish Community*, pp. 82–3.
93. *Jewish Chronicle*, 18 June 1909, p. 28.
94. Cited in Feldman, *Englishmen and Jews*, p. 355.
95. Lipman, *Social History*, p. 143.
96. *East London Observer*, 15 January 1910, p. 7 and 26 November 1910, p. 5.
97. See Pelling, *Social Geography of British Elections*, p. 43.
98. *Commons Debates*, Fifth Series, Vol. 21, Col. 452, 9 February 1911.
99. Ibid., Vol. 24, Col. 2108, 29 April 1911.
100. Ibid., Vol. 24, Col. 623, 18 April 1911.
101. The Aliens (Prevention of Crime) Bill was formally withdrawn on 4 December 1911.
102. *Commons Debates*, Fifth Series, Vol. 65, Col. 1986, 5 August 1914.
103. Aliens Restriction Act 1914 (4 & 5 Geo. 5, Ch. 12), 1(1)(k).
104. See Panikos Panayi, 'An Intolerant Act by an Intolerant Society: The Internment of Germans in Britain During the First World War', in Cesarani

and Kushner (eds), *The Internment of Aliens in Twentieth Century Britain* (London, 1993).
105. *Commons Debates*, Fifth Series, Vol. 70, Col. 883, 3 March 1915.
106. Ibid., Vol. 71, Col. 1862, 13 May 1915.
107. Ibid., Vol. 81, Col. 1047, 29 June 1916.
108. Trevor Wilson, *The Myriad Faces of War* (Oxford, 1986), p. 413.
109. *The Times*, 18 October 1916, p. 5 and 6 January 1917, p. 3.
110. *The Times* supported these proposals in general and the proposed restrictions upon membership of Parliament and/or the Privy Council in particular, 6 January 1917, p. 9.
111. Wilson, *Myriad Faces of War*, pp. 396–401, and pp. 645–6.
112. Bernard Wasserstein, *Herbert Samuel: A Political Life* (Oxford, 1992), pp. 214–19. Julia Bush, *Behind The Lines: East London Labour 1914–1919* (London, 1984), Chapter 6, passim.
113. *The Times*, 28 February 1917, p. 3.
114. Ibid., 21 June 1918, p. 7.
115. The view of the executive of the Jewish National Labour Council of Great Britain was quoted in *The Times*, 18 June 1918, p. 2, that it noted 'with regret that many East London Borough Councils have from time to time passed anti-Alien resolutions'.
116. *The Times*, 9 July 1918, p. 7 and 10 July 1918, p. 3.
117. *Commons Debates*, Fifth Series, Vol. 108, Col. 522.
118. *The Times*, 31 July 1918, p. 3.
119. See Chapter 4.
120. *Morning Post*, 9 March 1918, p. 3.
121. *The Times*, 10 July 1918, p. 7.

3: The Unionists and Zionism, 1900–18

1. Barbara Tuchman, *Bible and Sword* (London, 1957), p. xiii.
2. Leonard Stein, *The Balfour Declaration* (London, 1961), p. 552.
3. Mayir Vereté, 'The Balfour Declaration and its Makers', *Middle Eastern Studies*, Vol. 6 (1970), p. 50.
4. David Vital, *Zionism: The Crucial Phase* (Oxford, 1987), p. 297.
5. M. Levene, 'The Balfour Declaration: A Case of Mistaken Identity', *English Historical Review*, Vol. CVII (January 1992), p. 76.
6. William Evans-Gordon, *The Alien Immigrant* (London, 1903), p. 7.
7. Ibid., p. 37.
8. Ibid., pp. 53–4.
9. Ibid., pp. 132–3.
10. Ibid., pp. 161–3.
11. Ibid., pp. 246–7.
12. Ibid., p. 295.
13. Marvin Lowenthal (ed.), Theodor Herzl, *Diaries* (New York, 1956), 23 October 1902, p. 375.
14. Alex Bein, *Theodor Herzl*, 2nd edn (Philadelphia, 1962), pp. 417–20.
15. Joseph Chamberlain Papers, 12/1/2/2, Theodore Herzl to Joseph Chamberlain, 20 January 1903.
16. The firm of solicitors of which David Lloyd George was a partner.
17. PRO FO 2/785.
18. Quoted in Bein, p. 447.
19. For a detailed examination of the 'Uganda' offer see Robert G. Weisbord, *African Zion* (Philadelphia, 1968).

20. Joseph Chamberlain Papers, 12/1/2/14, Chamberlain to Langermann, 11 November 1905.
21. See Michael Burns, *Dreyfus: A Family Affair 1789–1945* (London, 1992).
22. *The Times*, 16 December 1904, p. 8.
23. Weizmann, *Trial and Error*, pp. 118–20.
24. Cited in George Monger, *The End of Isolation* (London, 1963), p. 64.
25. The anti-Semitic attitudes of the British military during the Second Boer War are examined by Keith Surridge in ' "All you soldiers are what we call pro-Boer": The Military Critique of the South African War, 1899–1902', *History* 82, 268 (1997), pp. 583–600.
26. See Anthony Alfry, *Edward VII and his Jewish Court* (London, 1992).
27. Technically Smuts was a constant attendee rather than a formal member of the War Cabinet.
28. C. P. Scott, the editor of the *Manchester Guardian* and a close associate of the Prime Minister, recorded in his diary that he breakfasted with Lloyd George on 28 September 1917 and said that the war cabinet 'was far too Tory. The effective members of it were Curzon and Milner, who alone were able to give the work undivided and continuous attention, both very able and very industrious and essentially reactionary.' Trevor Wilson (ed.), *The Political Diaries of C. P. Scott 1911–1928* (London, 1970), p. 273.
29. The organisation of government is described by John Turner 'The Higher Direction of War', in Kathleen Burk (ed.), *War and the State* (London, 1982), pp. 57–83.
30. Cited in Nahum Sokolow, *History of Zionism: 1600–1918*, Vol. II (London, 1919), p. 111.
31. Questions were raised in the Commons after the publication of the Declaration. See *Commons Debates*, Fifth Series, Vol. 99, Col. 382, when Joseph King (Liberal, Somerset North) inquired as to the nature of the polity to be established for the Jewish national home. Balfour answered that it was not possible 'at this stage to forecast the future constitution of Palestine'.
32. Hankey did not even mention the Balfour Declaration in his diary.
33. Vereté, 'The Balfour Declaration', p. 66.
34. Lloyd George Papers, F/3/3/30, Lloyd George to Balfour, 27 August 1918, emphasis added.
35. Earl of Oxford and Asquith, *Memories and Reflections 1852–1927*, Vol. 2 (London, 1928), p. 65.
36. Cited in Viscount Samuel, *Memoirs* (London, 1945), Lord Reading to Herbert Samuel, 5 February 1915, p. 143.
37. David Lloyd George, *War Memoirs*, Vol. I (London, 1938), p. 349.
38. See Weizmann, *Trial and Error*, pp. 143–4 and Dugdale, Vol. 1, pp. 433–6.
39. Earl of Swindon, *Sixty Years of Power* (London, 1966), p. 27.
40. He wrote to Lady Desborough that a serious element of his time at Bad Gastein was keeping 'German Jews at a reasonable distance'. Desborough Papers, A. J. Balfour to Lady Desborough, 19 August 1910, cited in Max Egremont, *Balfour: A Life of Arthur James Balfour* (London, 1980), p. 225. The following year he wrote to Lady Elcho that he was 'rather bothered by the number and fidelity of my friends! – chiefly Jews!'. Jane Ridley and Clayre Percy (eds), *The Letters of Arthur Balfour and Lady Elcho 1885–1917* (London, 1992), A. J. Balfour to Lady Elcho, 15 August 1911, p. 271.
41. Leonard Stein (ed.), *The Letters and Papers of Chaim Weizmann, Vol. VII, August 1914–November 1917* (London, 1975), Chaim Weizmann to Ahad Ha'am, 15 December 1915, p. 81.
42. Sokolow, *History of Zionism*, Vol. I, pp. xxix–xxxiv.

43. Dugdale, *Arthur James Balfour*, Vol. II, p. 216.
44. R. Meinertzhagen, *Middle East Diary, 1917–1956* (London, 1959), pp. 24–5.
45. War Cabinet Eastern Committee, Minutes of 43rd meeting, 16 December 1918, cited in Michael Howard, *The Continental Commitment* (London, 1989 edn), p. 71.
46. Report of a speech by Smuts at a Zionist meeting, 30 April 1926. *Zionist Record*, cited in Stein, *Balfour*, p. 311.
47. Samuel, *Memoirs*, p. 145.
48. Stein, *Balfour*, pp. 314–16.
49. L. S. Amery, *My Political Life: Volume 2, War and Peace, 1914–1929* (London, 1953), p. 115.
50. Stein, *Balfour*, p. 317.
51. Weizmann, *Trial and Error*, p. 226.
52. C. Headlam (ed.), *The Milner Papers*, Vol. II (1933), Lord Milner to S. Goldreich, 11 July 1902, p. 378.
53. *South African Jewish Chronicle*, 7 August 1903, cited in Shain, *Roots of Anti-Semitism in South Africa* (Charlottesville, VA, 1994), p. 69.
54. Cited in Shain, ibid., p. 44.
55. Amery, *My Political Life*, Vol. II, p. 116.
56. This was a memorandum submitted to the Liberal cabinet in November 1914 by Herbert Samuel; see Samuel, *Memoirs*, p.141.
57. Gaster was the *Haham* (chief rabbi) of the Sephardi community of England, although he himself was an Ashkanazi Jew from Romania. Gaster was a controversial and outspoken figure who was constantly at odds with the Anglo-Jewish establishment. He was a vice-president of the English Zionist Federation and a man who had his talents utilised by the British government on occasion in connection with eastern European matters.
58. Sokolow, *History of Zionism*, Vol II, p. 106.
59. Weizmann was at that time employed as a research scientist at the ministry of munitions. He was a vice-president of the English Zionist Federation, and also a member of the Greater Actions Committee of the World Zionist Organisation. Sokolow, another Russian-born Jew was a member of the Zionist Executive Smaller Actions Committee. Cowen was the president of the English Zionist Federation. Sacher was a leading Manchester Zionist and a member of the Board of the *Manchester Guardian*. Bentwich was a founder of the English Zionist Federation and one of its vice-presidents.
60. Sokolow, *History of Zionism*, Vol. II, p. 52.
61. Stein, *Weizmann Letters*, C. Weizmann to Vladimir Jabotinsky, 8 February 1917. p. 328.
62. Weizmann, *Trial and Error*, p. 229.
63. Ibid., p. 230.
64. M. Sykes to A. Dowling, 24 June 1900, cited in Shane Leslie, *Mark Sykes: His Life and Letters* (London, 1923), p. 70.
65. M. Sykes to Miss E. Gorst, 1 July 1900, ibid., p. 72.
66. M. Sykes to Miss E. Gorst, 15 May 1901, ibid., p. 148.
67. Sledmere Papers, 4/136. Sykes to Simon, 6 January 1917, cited in Vital, *Zionism*, p. 104 .
68. Leslie, *Mark Sykes: His Life and Letters*, p. 291.
69. Amery, *My Political Life*, Vol. II, p. 115.
70. PRO FO 800/204/100. L. S. Amery to A. J. Balfour, 29 March 1917.
71. Weizmann, *Trial and Error*, p. 231.
72. PRO FO 371/3083/48. A. J. Balfour to Lord Rothschild 19 July 1917.
73. Ronald Storrs, *Orientations*, definitive edition (2) (London, 1945), p. 259.

74. N. Sokolow to Rothschild, 19 July 1917, cited in Stein, *Balfour*, p. 470.
75. PRO CAB 21/58. W. Ormsby-Gore to M. Hankey, 23 August 1917.
76. PRO CAB 23/3/WC227.
77. PRO FO 371/3083/82. E. Montagu to Lord R. Cecil, 14 September 1917.
78. PRO CAB 24/28. Memorandum dated 9 October 1917.
79. PRO CAB 24/27. E Montagu to Lord R. Cecil, 14 September 1917.
80. *Lloyd George Papers* F/39/3/30. E. Montagu to D. Lloyd George, 4 October 1917.
81. PRO FO 371/3083. The paper was compiled by 'R.McN' (possibly Robert McNeil MP).
82. PRO CAB 23/3 WC 245.
83. PRO CAB 24/24 GT1803. The original draft submitted by Rothschild to Balfour dated 18 July 1917 read: 'In reply to your letter of the July 18, I am glad to be in a position to inform you that His Majesty's Government accept the principle that Palestine should be reconstituted as the national home of the Jewish people. His Majesty's Government will use their best endeavours to secure the achievement of this object and will be ready to consider any suggestions on the subject which the Zionist Organisation may desire to lay before them.'
84. PRO CAB 23/3/WC 245.
85. PRO CAB 21/58/41.
86. PRO CAB 21/58/39.
87. Weizmann, *Trial and Error*, p. 255.
88. *The Times*, 29 May 1917, p. 7.
89. Ibid., 26 October 1917, p. 7.
90. *Pall Mall Gazette*, 9 November 1917, p. 6.
91. *Morning Post*, 11 December 1917, p. 6
92. *Observer*, 16 December 1917, p. 6.
93. *Zionist Review*, Vol. I, No. 8, December 1917, pp. 133–42.
94. There is no record in the war cabinet minutes or in Bonar Law's papers of his attitude towards the Declaration. In his diary C. P. Scott recorded on the 19 October 1917 that he had met with Weizmann stating that 'Bonar Law [was] the difficulty – not hostile but pleading for delay'. Cited by Stein in *Weizmann Letters*, Vol. VI, p. 532.
95. J. Barnes and D. Nicholson (eds), *The Leo Amery Diaries: Vol. I, 1896–1929*, (London, 1980), L. Amery to E. Carson, 4 September 1917, p. 170.
96. Sokolow, *History of Zionism*, Vol. I, pp. xxxi–xxxii.
97. *Zionist Review*, Vol. I, No. 8, December 1917, p. 138. Joynson-Hicks was, however, to become a rabid anti-Zionist by 1922.
98. Note of interview by Weizmann, 25 April 1917. Stein, *Weizmann Letters*, p. 375.
99. PRO CAB 21/77.
100. PRO CAB 21/77.
101. Stein, *Weizmann Letters*, C. Weizmann to A. Ha'am, 27 August 1917, p. 234.
102. Lloyd George Papers, F/38/2/6. Lord Milner to D. Lloyd George, 31 May 1917.
103. PRO FO 800/210.
104. Elie Kedourie, *Arabic Political Memoirs and Other Studies* (London, 1974), p. 244.
105. Vital, *Zionism*, pp. 115–16.
106. PRO CAB 23/3 WC 245.
107. PRO CAB 21/58/39.

4: Conservative Attitudes towards Jews in the
Great War and the Russian Civil War

1. *The Times*, 23 November 1917, p. 7.
2. *Morning Post*, 24 January 1918, p. 6.
3. *Jewish Chronicle*, 31 July 1914, p. 7, and 7 August 1914, p. 5.
4. This attack was rebutted in the *Jewish Chronicle* leader, 13 November 1914, p. 8.
5. Lord Reading, *Rufus Isaacs: First Marquess of Reading*, Vol. II (London, 1945), pp. 18–19.
6. H. Bolitho, *Alfred Mond* (London, 1933), p. 210.
7. *The Times*, 23 April 1915, p. 5.
8. *Jewish Chronicle*, 28 May 1915, p. 7.
9. Ibid., 4 June 1915, p. 17.
10. Bolitho, *Alfred Mond*, p. 193.
11. Israel Zangwill, *The War For The World* (London, 1916), p. 58.
12. *Jewish Chronicle*, 10 August 1917, p. 5.
13. See Julia Bush, *Behind the Lines – East London Labour 1914–1919* (London, 1984), Chapter 6 dealing with East End Jews and the First World War.
14. See Chapter 2 above which examines Jewish aliens and conscription.
15. *Morning Post*, 1 April 1918, p. 5.
16. Ibid., 10 July 1918, p. 4.
17. *The Times*, 6 February 1918, p. 5.
18. Ibid., 28 December 1918, p. 5.
19. Ibid., 26 January 1919, p. 11.
20. Ibid., 1 April 1919, p. 13.
21. Ibid., 21 January 1919, p. 4.
22. *Morning Post*, 20 January 1919, p. 4.
23. Ibid., 21 January 1919, p. 4.
24. Ibid., 20 March 1919, p. 6.
25. Ibid., 8 April 1919, p. 6.
26. Ibid.,5 August 1919, p. 6.
27. Ibid., 20 March 1919, p. 6.
28. Ibid., 8 April 1919, p. 6.
29. Ibid., 11 April 1919, p. 4.
30. Ibid., 30 August 1919, p. 6.
31. *The Times*, 22 May 1919, p. 13.
32. Ibid., 21 July 1919, p. 11.
33. *Morning Post*, 10 November 1919, p. 8.
34. Norman Cohn, *Warrant for Genocide*, Pelican edn (London, 1970), p. 126.
35. *The Times*, 8 May 1920, p. 15.
36. *Spectator*, 15 May 1920, p. 640.
37. Ibid., 5 June 1920, p. 750.
38. Ibid., 17 July 1920, p. 68
39. Ibid., 16 October 1920, p. 489.
40. Keith M. Wilson, *A Study in the History and Politics of the Morning Post 1905–1926* (London, 1990), pp. 170 and 172.
41. *Morning Post*, 15 December 1920, p. 3, and 18 December 1920, p. 6.
42. Reginald Pound and Geoffrey Harmsworth, *Northcliffe* (London, 1959), p. 447.
43. Wickham Steed, Vol. II, pp. 8–9.
44. Pound and Harmsworth, *Northcliffe*, pp. 462–3.
45. See Austen Chamberlain's account of this period in A. Chamberlain, *Down The Years* (London, 1935), Chapter VI.

46. Tom Clarke, *My Northcliffe Diary* (London, 1931), p. 237.
47. Ibid., p. 125.
48. Wickham Steed's anti-Semitism may have developed during his period as the *Times* correspondent in Vienna. See Sharman Kadish, *Bolsheviks and British Jews* (London, 1992), p. 28.
49. See Cohn, *Warrant for Genocide*, p. 166.
50. The exception was Lloyd George who was, in any event, estranged from his Party's organisational structure and its traditional leadership.
51. Keith Wilson (ed), *The Rasp Of War* (London, 1988), H. A. Gwynne to Lady Bathurst, 30 January 1918, p. 241.
52. Cohn, *Warrant for Genocide*, p. 169.
53. This examination of the Conservative press has been restricted to the 'quality' journals and consequently it has not considered either the Rothermere or the Beaverbrook press.
54. *Morning Post*, 10 November 1917, p. 3
55. Bruce Lincoln, *Red Victory: A History of the Russian Civil War*, Cardinal edn (London, 1990), p. 176.
56. Ibid., p. 220.
57. Ibid., p. 263.
58. Ibid., p. 288.
59. Kadish, *Bolsheviks and British Jews*, p. 12.
60. See Lincoln, *Red Victory*, p. 317 and Richard H. Ullman, *Britain and the Russian Civil War* (London, 1968), p. 218.
61. Lincoln, *Red Victory*, pp. 322–33.
62. *Commons Debates*, Fifth Series, Vol. 118, Col. 180, 15 July 1919.
63. Alfred Raper had been elected at the Coupon election. He had served in the RAF during the First World War and had been posted to Russia as part of the Russian Aviation Mission, for which he was awarded the Order of St Stanislas by the Tsarist government. He was part of the Special Mission to Finland in 1918 with whose White government he was connected in the 1920s. He did not serve in Parliament after 1922.
64. *Commons Debates*, Fifth Series, Vol. 119, Col. 515, 7 August 1919.
65. Ibid., Vol. 119, Col. 880, 11 August 1919.
66. Ibid., Vol. 119, Col. 1248, 12 August 1919.
67. Ibid., Vol. 121, Col. 733, 17 November 1919. Malone had visited Russia in 1919 to prepare a book entitled 'The Russian Republic'. He was soon to join the British Socialist Party, which merged with the British Communist Party in August 1920.
68. Ibid., Vol. 125, Col. 1414, 20 February 1920.
69. Ibid., Vol. 122, Col. 1606, 11 December 1919.
70. Ibid., Vol. 131, Col. 2570, 15 July 1920.
71. Ibid., Vol. 114, Col. 2801, 15 April 1919.
72. Board of Deputies of British Jews, *Annual Report 1926*, p. 41.
73. *Commons Debates*, Fifth Series, Vol. 120, Col. 1579, 5 November 1919.
74. Ibid., Vol. 120, Col. 1633, 5 November 1919.
75. *The Times*, 5 January 1920, p. 7.
76. Churchill Papers, CHAR 2/110/3, Churchill to H. A. L. Fisher, 25 January 1920.
77. *Illustrated Sunday Herald*, 8 February 1920, p. 5.
78. Churchill had visited Palestine in March 1921 for one week following the Cairo Conference.
79. *Popular View*, May 1921, p. 11.
80. Amery, *Diaries*, 21 March 1918, p. 210.

5: The Conservatives and Jewish Immigration, 1918–29

1. F. W. S. Craig, *British General Election Manifestos 1900–1974* (London, 1975) pp. 28–9.
2. J. D. Kiley, who had been elected unopposed to represent Whitechapel in the Liberal interest in the by-election in 1916 following the resignation of Sir Stuart Samuel, took the seat with a majority of 502 over Labour, with the Coalition Unionist, G. A. Cohen, placed third of four candidates.
3. The seats won by the Unionists were Mile End, Bow & Bromley, and Bethnal Green South West.
4. Sir Ernest Wild, the Unionist member for the Upton division of West Ham, made this allegation during the debate on the Second Reading of the Aliens Restriction Bill, *Commons Debates*, Fifth Series, Vol. 114, Col. 2775, 15 April 1919.
5. *Jewish Chronicle*, 7 March 1919, p. 6.
6. *Pall Mall Gazette*, 12 March 1919, pp. 5 and 6.
7. *Morning Post*, 20 March 1919, p. 6.
8. *Commons Debates*, Fifth Series, Vol. 114, Cols 2775–8, 15 April 1919.
9. Ibid., Cols 2275–2803.
10. Another Unionist, Sir Watson Rutherford, who represented Liverpool, Edge Hill, considered the attacks on immigrants unjust as the number of aliens in England was less than in other countries and furthermore there were more British subjects abroad than aliens in the country.
11. *Commons Debates*, Fifth Series, Vol. 120, Cols 57–90, 22 October 1919.
12. Ibid., Col. 103, Lieut. Wilfred Sugden who represented Royston division of Lancashire.
13. Ibid., Col. 104, Sir Clement Kinloch-Cooke, Plymouth, Devonport.
14. Ibid., Cols 108–9.
15. Both this and the Wild amendment were supported by the Jewish Unionist MP Arthur Samuel, who represented Farnham. This contrasts particularly with Major Lionel de Rothschild, who represented Aylesbury in the Unionist interest. He put down an amendment which would have relaxed the proposed entry criteria (it was withdrawn as a result of the Government undertaking to review the appeal procedure).
16. *Commons Debates*, Fifth Series, Vol. 120, Col. 238, 23 October 1919.
17. *The Times*, 25 October 1919, p. 12.
18. Aliens Restriction (Amendment) Act, 23 December 1919 (9 & 10 Geo. 5, Chapter 92).
19. John M. McEwen, 'Unionist and Conservative Members of Parliament 1914–1939', unpublished University of London PhD thesis (1959).
20. Alderman, *London Jewry*, pp. 55–68. Board of Deputies of British Jews, Archives ACC 3121/C13/3/9. The Board of Deputies were concerned with the policies of the Municipal Reform Party. In its meeting on 15 March 1925, the Board was referred to the Conservatives' eve of election memorandum: 'The original policy was to keep aliens out; now the policy appeared to be to harry those who were in the county. The LCC had already decided to grant no scholarships to the children of aliens and now they were attacking the adults.'
21. At the date of the Carlton Club vote there were six Jewish Conservative MPs. Brunel Cohen was absent from the meeting and of the other five only Arthur Samuel supported the motion to withdraw from the Coalition.
22. Bonar Law's Election Address cited in Craig, *Manifestos*, p. 37.
23. Twelve other members were returned to complete the number of 615 MPs.

24. *The Times*, 12 November 1922, p. 12.
25. *Commons Debates*, Fifth Series, Vol. 160, Col. 2083 *passim*, 28 February 1923.
26. This statement echoed Bridgeman's by-election address in July 1904 when he wrote that 'aliens have lowered the standard of living, and driven English hands from English work', see P. Williamson (ed.), *The Modernisation of Conservative Politics – The Diaries and Letters of William Bridgeman 1904–1935* (London, 1988) p. 16.
27. Stuart Ball (ed.), *Parliament and Politics in the Age of Baldwin and MacDonald – The Headlam Diaries 1923–1935* (London, 1992), p. 38.
28. The 'Zinoviev Letter', which was purportedly written by the President of the Communist International in Moscow to incite class warfare in Britain, probably played some role in furthering the view of the Labour Party as being under the control of socialist extremists.
29. Craig, *Manifestos*, p. 55.
30. Reported in the *Jewish Chronicle*, 24 October 1924, p. 25.
31. *The Times*, 25 October 1924, p. 8.
32. *Daily Telegraph*, 20 November 1924, p. 9.
33. *The Times*, 27 November 1924, p. 13.
34. Ibid., 15 December 1924, p. 15.
35. *Commons Debates*, 5th Series, Vol. 179, Col. 513–19, 12 December 1924.
36. *Daily Mail*, 20 December 1924, p. 9. This letter was reported elsewhere including *The Times*, 23 December 1924, p. 5 and the *Jewish Chronicle*, 26 December 1924, p. 5.
37. *The Times*, 21 January 1925, p. 8.
38. *Commons Debates*, Fifth Series, Vol. 180, Col. 285, 11 February 1925.
39. Ibid., Col. 314.
40. *The Times*, 7 February 1925, p. 7.
41. *Jewish Chronicle*, 13 February 1925, p. 7.
42. This view is forcefully expressed by David Cesarani, 'Joynson-Hicks and the Radical Right in England after the First World War', in Tony Kushner and Kenneth Lunn (eds), *Traditions of Intolerance* (Manchester, 1989). This view is opposed by W. D. Rubinstein, 'Recent Anglo-Jewish Historiography and the Myth of Jix's Anti-Semitism, Parts I & II', in *Australian Journal of Jewish Studies*, Vol. VII(1) (1993), pp. 41–70 and VII(2) (1993), pp. 24–45. His thesis has, however, been rebutted by Geoffrey Alderman, 'Recent Anglo-Jewish Historiography and the Myth of Jix's Anti-Semitism: A Response', *Australian Journal of Jewish Studies*, Vol. VIII(1) (1994), pp. 112–21.
43. H. A. Taylor, *Jix: Viscount Brentford* (London, 1933), pp. 63–4.
44. *Jewish Chronicle*, 24 April 1908, p. 10.
45. Taylor, p. 101. *Jewish Chronicle*, 22 May 1908, p. 17.
46. Taylor, p. 102.
47. *Commons Debates*, Fifth Series, Vol. 179, Col. 519, 12 December 1924.
48. *The Times*, 7 February 1925, p. 7.
49. *Jewish Chronicle*, 2 April 1926, p. 11.
50. *Commons Debates*, Fifth Series, Vol. 208, Col. 2392, 14 July 1927.
51. Joynson-Hicks and Zionism are examined in Chapter 7.
52. Baldwin Papers, 163/L2/94-5, J. C. C. Davidson to W. Joynson-Hicks 19 July 1928.
53. *Commons Debates*, Fifth Series, Vol. 188, Col. 229, 17 November 1925.
54. PRO HO 45/24765/432156/28, 13 February 1925.
55. *Commons Debates*, Fifth Series, Vol. 210, Col. 1100, 16 November 1927.
56. Joynson-Hicks fell out of favour with the Conservative leadership, according to Churchill, not least for his unauthorised promise of increasing the

franchise to include women over 21 years of age (*Sunday Pictorial*, 9 August 1931). He did not contest the 1929 General election but accepted a peerage as Viscount Brentford, and died in June 1932.

57. *Commons Debates*, Fifth Series, Vol. 220, Col. 2360, 2 August 1928.
58. Board of Deputies, Archives ACC 3121/B4/NA/18, Report of Aliens Committee, 10 April 1929.
59. Lt-Col. A. H. Lane, *The Alien Menace*, 3rd edn (London, 1932), pp. xiii and 1.

6: The Conservatives and the Palestine Mandate, 1920–29

1. *The Times*, 27 April 1920, p. 17.
2. Ibid., 16 June 1920, p. 17.
3. *Commons Debates*, Fifth Series, Vol. 128, Col. 1512, 29 April 1920.
4. Ibid., Vol. 128, Col. 1223, 28 April 1920.
5. Ibid., Vol. 128, Col. 1222, 28 April 1920; Vol. 128, Col. 1715, 3 May 1920; Vol. 130, Col. 628, 10 June 1920; Vol. 131 Col. 232, 29 June 1920.
6. Ibid., Vol. 1130, Col. 1430, 17 June 1920; Col. 1735, 21 June 1920; Vol. 131, Col. 442, 30 June 1920.
7. *The Times*, 22 April 1920, p. 16.
8. For an examination of the military administration see Bernard Wasserstein, *The British in Palestine – the Mandatory Government and the Arab Jewish Conflict, 1917–1921*, 2nd edn (Oxford, 1991), Chapters 1–3.
9. *Commons Debates*, Fifth Series, Vol. 131, Col. 2595, 15 July 1920.
10. Ibid., Vol. 135, Col. 1439, 2 December 1920; Col. 2405, 9 December 1920; Vol. 136, Col. 1514, 21 December 1920.
11. *Lords Debates*, Fifth Series, Vol. 40, Col. 1006, 29 June 1920.
12. Ibid., Col. 1013.
13. PRO FO/371–5199, 20 March 1920.
14. Bernard Wasserstein (ed.), *The Letters and Papers of Chaim Weizmann, Vol. X July 1920–December 1921* (Jerusalem, 1977), Weizmann to Balfour, 8 October 1920 and 11 October 1920, pp. 56–7; Weizmann to Lloyd George, 11 October 1920, p. 59; Weizmann to Curzon, 11 October 1920, p. 59; Weizmann to Ormsby-Gore, 23 November 1920, p. 94.
15. Davidson Papers, 119/726, Ormsby-Gore to Sir M. Hankey, 10 November 1920.
16. *The Times*, 25 October 1920, p. 11.
17. *Commons Debates*, Fifth Series, Vol. 143, Col. 1542, 14 July 1921.
18. Ibid., Col. 332
19. *Daily Mail*, 25 February 1921, p. 6; *Jewish Chronicle*, 27 February 1921, p. 21
20. This provoked a leader in defence of government policy in the *Jewish Chronicle*, 3 June 1921, p. 5.
21. *Jewish Chronicle*, 8 April 1921, p. 23.
22. Ibid., 25 March 1921, p. 17.
23. *The Times*, 16 November 1921, p. 12.
24. Ibid., 3 March 1922, p. 14.
25. Ibid., 5 May 1922, p. 9.
26. Norman and Helen Bentwich, *Mandate Memories 1918–1948* (London, 1965), p. 81.
27. *The Times*, 15 February 1922, p. 10.
28. Ibid., 11 April 1922, p. 15.
29. Ibid., 26 April 1922, p. 15.
30. Ibid., 23 June 1922, p. 17.
31. Ibid., 3 July 1922, p. 15, and 25 July 1922, p. 15.

32. Conservative member for the Springburn division of Glasgow, 1918–22, and thereafter for Argyll, 1924–40.
33. *Commons Debates*, Fifth Series, Vol. 151, Col. 1599, 9 March 1922.
34. Ibid., Col. 1947, 14 March 1922.
35. The Conservative Member of Parliament for Bath.
36. *Commons Debates*, Fifth Series, Vol. 151, Col. 1649, 26 June 1922.
37. Islington had sat in the Commons as a Unionist but had taken the Liberal whip in the Lords.
38. *Lords Debates*, Fifth Series, Vol. 50, Cols. 1003, 1006–1007, 21 June 1922.
39. Ibid., Cols 1022–3.
40. Ibid., Col. 1032.
41. *Commons Debates*, Fifth Series, Vol. 156, Cols 296 and 307, 4 July 1922.
42. Ibid., Col. 314.
43. Conservative MP for York, 1892–1906 and 1910–23.
44. *Commons Debates*, Fifth Series, Vol. 156, Col. 320.
45. *The Interim Report of The High Commissioner for Palestine*, Cmd Paper 1499 (1922).
46. *Commons Debates*, Fifth Series, Vol. 156, Col. 337, 4 July 1922.
47. Ibid., Col. 340.
48. Ibid., Col. 329, 4 July 1922.
49. However, Freemantle supported the government in the Supply vote despite his attendance at the luncheon.
50. *Correspondence with the Palestine Arab Delegation and the Zionist Organization*, Cmd 1700 (1922).
51. See David Cesarani, 'Anti-Zionist Politics and Political Antisemitism in Britain, 1920–24', in *Patterns of Prejudice*, Vol. 23, No. 1 (1989).
52. *Daily Express*, 28 October 1922, p. 1.
53. Ibid., 12 November 1922, p. 1, 16 November 1922, p. 1.
54. Ibid., 4 January 1923, p. 1
55. *Sunday Express*, 11 February 1923, p. 1.
56. J. M. N. Jeffries, *The Palestine Deception* (London, 1923), p. 9.
57. K. O. Morgan, *Consensus*, p. 237.
58. *Spectator*, 22 April 1922, p. 484.
59. Ibid., 15 April 1922, p. 450.
60. Ibid., 18 November 1922, p. 714.
61. *The Morning Post*, 2 November 1921, p. 6.
62. Ibid., 26 April 1922, p. 6.
63. Ibid., 18 July 1922, p. 6.
64. *Jewish Chronicle*, 9 December 1921, p. 9.
65. Conservative Manifesto cited in Craig, p. 36.
66. Bonar Law Papers, 107/2/78, undated letter, Beaverbrook to Bonar Law (?) 25 October 1922.
67. *Daily Express*, 26 October 1922, p. 6 and 27 October 1922, p. 6.
68. Central Zionist Archives, Z4/1878 I. The figure was reduced to 16 with the resignation of H. R. Cayzer.
69. *Daily Mail*, 23 October 1922, p. 8.
70. *The Times*, 6 November 1922, p. 9. Bonar Law's election meeting took place on Saturday, 4 November at the Majestic Cinema, Leeds.
71. *The Times*, 8 November 1922, p. 14. Meeting at the Old Kent Road Baths, 7 November 1922.
72. *Jewish Chronicle*, 10 November 1922, p. 11.
73. Bonar Law Papers, 108/2/21, E. Harmondsworth to Bonar Law, 27 November 1922; 108/9/27, Bonar Law to E. Harmondsworth, 28 November 1922.

74. Ibid., 111/12/38, Bonar Law to Curzon, 5 December 1922.
75. Ibid., 111/12/46, Curzon to Bonar Law, 14 December 1922.
76. Central Zionist Archives, Z4/1878 I.
77. PRO CAB/158.
78. PRO CAB/159.
79. PRO CO/733/54/454, Note by Sir John Shuckburgh, head of the Middle East Department of the Colonial Office.
80. PRO CAB/46/33(23)7.
81. PRO CAB/23/46/43(24)4.
82. Baldwin Papers, 93/E1/57, Frank Anderson to Stanley Baldwin, 24 July 1923.
83. Davidson Papers, 159/475, F. Sanderson to J. C. C. Davidson, 2 August 1923, with the list of Conservative signatories.
84. Viscount Curzon was a Junior Lord of the Treasury, November 1924–January 1929; Henry Page-Croft was under-secretary of state for war, May 1940–May 1945; Sir John Edmondson was a Junior Lord of the Treasury, April–November 1939, and H. M. Household Treasurer, March 1942; Archibald Skelton was under-secretary of state for Scotland, September 1931–November 1935; and Hugh O'Neill was under-secretary of state for India in September 1939.
85. PRO CAB/24/159(47).
86. PRO CO/733/54/454. Ormsby-Gore minuted on the draft report: 'This is very good – much better than I feared'.
87. *Jewish Chronicle*, 5 October 1923, p. 23.
88. Ibid., 19 October 1923, p. 28.
89. *The Times*, 15 October 1923, p. 13.
90. PRO CAB/24/162/332, 27 October 1923.
91. PRO CO/733/51/83, Devonshire to Samuel, 16 November 1923.
92. *Zionist Review*, Vol. VII, No. 9 (January 1924), p. 84. The party affiliations of the anti-Zionists are not identified but there can be little doubt that they were primarily Conservatives.
93. *New Judea*, Vol. I, No. 17 (8 May 1925), p. 279, and Vol. I, No. 24 (14 August 1924), p. 397.
94. *Amery Diaries*, 21 April 1925, p. 408.
95. *Zionist Review*, Vol. X, No. 8 (29 October 1926), p. 108.
96. Wilfred Hart Sugden, who sat for Hartlepools, and A. R. Jephcott, who represented Birmingham Yardley.
97. Sir Leslie Scott had served as Solicitor-General, March–October 1922; F. B. M. Merriman was to hold that post from March 1928–June 1929 and January 1932–September 1933; E. W. S. Cavendish, Marquis of Hartington, and later Duke of Devonshire, was under-secretary of state for the Dominions, March 1936–May 1940, parliamentary secretary at the India Office, May 1940–January 1943, and under-secretary of state at the Colonial Office, January 1943–July 1945; A. U. M. Hudson served as a Junior Lord of the Treasury, November 1931–April 1935, parliamentary secretary for transport, April 1935–July 1939, Civil Lord of the Admiralty, July 1939–May 1945, and parliamentary secretary for fuel and power, May 1945–July 1945; H. G. Williams was the parliamentary secretary at the Board of Trade, January 1928–June 1929; and W. J. Womersley served as a Junior Lord of the Treasury, November 1931–December 1935, assistant postmaster-general, December 1935–June 1939, and minister of pensions, June 1939–July 1945.
98. Lt-Commander Kenworthy, a Labour member, maintained in April 1929 that the Conservative Party remained hostile to the Balfour Declaration, *Commons Debates*, Fifth Series, Vol. 22,7 Col. 1467, 30 April 1929.

99. Amery, *Diaries I*, 4 April 1928, p. 541, and 20 June 1928, p. 546.
100. Beaverbrook Papers, C5, L. S. Amery to Lord Beaverbrook, 23 November 1928.
101. Amery, *Diaries I*, 26 July 1928, p. 558. Amery expounded these views to Col. Josiah Wedgwood, Labour Member for Newcastle-under-Lyme, at a dinner at the House. He had expressed these views to the South African Zionist Federation in a speech in Johannesburg on 11 September 1927. See *New Judaea*, Vol. IV, No. 1 (7 October 1927), p. 10.
102. *Commons Debates*, Fifth Series, Vol. 227, Cols 1477 and 1505, 30 April 1929.

7: The Conservatives, Anti-Semitism and Jewish Refugees, 1933–39

1. *The Times*, 31 March 1933, p. 16. Report of meeting held on 30 March attended by about 3,000 Jews at Kingsway Hall.
2. Ibid., 1 April 1933, p. 10.
3. Ibid., 9 April 1933, p. 19.
4. Churchill Papers, CHAR 1/398A/48-50, R. Boothby to W. Churchill, 22 January 1932.
5. *Jewish Chronicle*, 31 March 1933, p. 33.
6. *The Times*, 12 May 1933, p. 11. Meeting on 10th May 1933 at Hendon Town Hall.
7. *Jewish Chronicle*, 30 June 1933, p. 27. The Conservative peers were Earl Iddesleigh, Lord Jessell and Lord Rankeillour. The MPs present were: Brigadier-General John Nation (East Hull), Terence O'Connor (Luton), William O'Donovan (Mile End), Sir John Smedley Crooke (Deritend, Birmingham), David Reid (Down), Sir George Jones (Stoke Newington), Capt. George Elliston (Blackburn), Edward Salt (Yardley, Birmingham), Sir Nicholas Grattan-Doyle (Newcastle-upon-Tyne), Lt-Colonel Herbert Spender-Clay (Tonbridge), Gordon Touche (Reigate), James Guy (Edinburgh Central), Sir John Haslam (Bolton), Capt. Sidney Herbert (Abbey, Westminster), Major John Hills (Ripon, West Riding Yorkshire), Lt-Col. Thomas Moore (Ayr Burghs), Sir Gerald Hurst (Moss Side, Manchester), Sir Archibald Boyd-Carpenter (Chertsey, Surrey), Tom Howard (Islington South), Louis Gluckstein (Nottingham East), Thomas Levy (Elland, West Riding, Yorkshire), Walter Liddall (Lincoln), Sir Isadore Salmon (Harrow), Samuel Samuel (Putney), Mary Pickford (Hammersmith North), and Dudley Joel (Dudley).
8. Conservative Party Archives, 506/1/4/231, Executive Committee of the Junior Imperial League, 8 April 1935.
9. *The Times*, 8 April 1933, p. 14. Report of meeting on 7 April 1933. Neville Chamberlain was not present; the meeting was held on the eve of the Budget.
10. Amery, *Diaries*, p. 292, 7 April 1933.
11. *Commons Debates*, Fifth Series, Vol. 276, Col. 2782, 13 April 1933.
12. Ibid., Vol. 277, Col. 1030, 4 May 1933.
13. Ibid., Vol. 280 Col. 2604, 26 July 1933.
14. Ibid., Vol. 273, Col. 1239, 22 December 1932.
15. Ibid., Vol. 275, Col. 1355, 9 March 1933.
16. Ibid., Vol. 276 Col. 2359, 11 April 1933.
17. *Jewish Chronicle*, 12 May 1933, p. 33. Report of a meeting on 10 May of the Primrose League.
18. Ibid., 26 May 1933, p. 12.

19. Ibid., 25 August 1933, p. 23. Report of the meeting held at the Tottenham Palais de Dance on 21 August 1933.
20. Conservative Party Archives, B130/124/N7.
21. *Commons Debates*, Fifth Series, Vol. 275, Col. 1355, 9 March 1933.
22. PRO CAB/27/549, CP96/33. The undertaking was signed by representatives of the Board of Deputies, the Anglo-Jewish Association and the Jewish Refugee Committee. It appeared as an Appendix to the Memorandum by the Home Secretary, 'The Present Position in Regard to the Admission of Jewish Refugees from Germany to this Country', 5 April 1933.
23. PRO CAB/23/77/446, 27(33)8, 12 April 1933.
24. *Commons Debates*, Fifth Series, Vol. 276, Col. 2555, 12 April 1933.
25. PRO CAB/27/549 CP 96/33, Cabinet committee on aliens restrictions, Report, 7 April 1933.
26. Cecil of Chelwood Papers, Add. Mss 51082/198–205, Sir John Simon to Lord Cecil, 1 December 1933.
27. Figures quoted in Annex II to Report on Second Session of the Governing Body of the High Commission for Refugees coming from Germany, 4 May 1934, cited in A. J. Sherman, *Island Refuge – Britain and Refugees from the Third Reich 1933–1939*, 2nd edn (London, 1994), p. 47.
28. Amery, *Diaries*, 8 June 1934, p. 381.
29. *The Times*, 8 June 1934, p. 14.
30. Ibid., 12 June 1934, p. 15.
31. Although, as Thomas Linehan has pointed out, dissident Conservatives occupied pivotal administrative positions in the BUF in East London and south-west Essex; Thomas P. Linehan, *East London for Mosley: The British Union of Fascists in East London and South-West Essex 1933–40* (London, 1996) p. 138.
32. Robert Skidelsky, *Oswald Mosley*, 3rd edn (London, 1990), p. 417.
33. Nigel Nicolson (ed.), *Harold Nicolson: Diaries and Letters 1930–1939* (London, 1966), 24 November 1931, p. 97.
34. There had, however, been racialist rioting in Britain during the earlier part of the century, in South Wales in 1911 and during the First World War in both the East End of London and Leeds.
35. *Truth*, 31 March 1937, p. 497.
36. There were some Conservative MPs, most notoriously Captain Maule Ramsay (see below), who were pro-Nazi. In July 1939 Mosley hosted a dinner party. The guests of honour were reported to be Ramsay and two other Conservative MPs, Col. Moore-Brabazon and Sir Jocelyn Lucas, the latter being newly elected as the member for Portsmouth South; *Evening Standard* 27 July 1939. Moore-Brabazon had been involved in extensive discussions with Mosley about the future of the BUF since 1934. Lucas was a member of the Anglo-German Fellowship and the National Socialist League. PRO HO 144/20140/117 and HO 144/20140/283. Cited in Richard Griffiths, *Patriotism Perverted: Captain Ramsay, The Right Club and British Anti-Semitism 1939–1940* (London, 1998), pp. 113–14 and 324.
37. *The Times*, 24 March 1937, p. 8. The motion was proposed by L. Silver of the Mile End division, who reported to the meeting that there was fighting almost every day in the East End and that windows were smashed because the owners of the premises were Jews.
38. Ibid., 1 May 1937, p. 9.
39. *Commons Debates*, Fifth Series, Vol. 333, Col. 852, 2 March 1938.
40. Ibid., Vol. 333, Col. 991, 22 March 1938.
41. Ibid., Vol. 334, Col. 943, 12 April 1938.

42. *The Times*, 5 May 1938, p. 8.
43. *Commons Debates*, Fifth Series, Vol. 333, Col. 1984, 30 March 1938.
44. Ibid., Vol. 335, Col. 498, 2 May 1938 and Vol. 336, Col. 1399, 26 May 1938.
45. Ibid., Col. 1059, 5 May 1938.
46. *The Times*, 6 May 1938, p. 12.
47. Ibid., 19 July 1938, p. 10. The other signatories were Lord Lytton, William Elar, George Cicester, Violet Bonham-Carter, Dorothy Gladstone and Evelyn Jones. The Evian Conference increased proportionately asylum quotas for Jews and other refugees fleeing from the Greater German Reich; it notably included the United States of America, which was not part of the League of Nations.
48. *Commons Debates*, Fifth Series, Vol. 338, Cols 3567–71, 29 July 1938.
49. Ibid., Vol. 333, Col. 1642, 28 March 1938.
50. Ibid., Vol. 334, Col. 512, 7 April 1938.
51. Ibid., Vol. 335, Col. 530, 2 May 1938 and Col. 1249, 9 May 1938.
52. Ibid., Vol. 338, Col. 605, 7 July 1938.
53. Ibid., Col. 3577, 29 July 1938.
54. PRO CAB 23/93/11, Cabinet Conclusions 14(38)6, meeting on 16 March 1938.
55. *Commons Debates*, Fifth Series, Vol. 341, Col. 281, 10 November 1938.
56. Channon, *Diaries*, 15 and 21 November 1938, pp. 177–8.
57. Harold Macmillan, *Winds of Change 1914–1939* (London, 1966), p. 587.
58. *The Times*, 19 November 1938, p. 7.
59. However, a Commission was established to report on possible Jewish settlement in British Guiana. In May 1939 Chamberlain made a statement to the House in respect of their report, which recommended an experimental settlement. *Commons Debates*, Fifth Series, Vol. 347, Col. 862, 12 May 1939. However, no actual course of action was subsequently agreed.
60. PRO CAB/27/624 F P (36) Series, 32nd meeting of the cabinet committee on foreign policy, 14 November 1938.
61. This view contrasts that of Chamberlain the previous day when he met a Jewish delegation comprising, amongst others, Samuel and Weizmann. They requested that 1,500 children and 6,000 young men who had been incarcerated by the Nazis, but whose release could be secured, be allowed into Palestine. According to Amy Zahl Gottlieb, in her history of the Central British Fund for German Jewry, Chamberlain was not stirred by Weizmann's appeal and committed himself only to 'benevolent interest' in the matters before him. He asked the delegation to discuss the matter with officials of the Home, Foreign and Colonial Offices. Record of meeting by Prime Minister's Private Secretary, PRO FO 371/22536, 15037/104/98, 16 November 1938, cited in Amy Zahl Gottlieb, *Men of Vision: Anglo-Jewry's Aid to Victims of the Nazi Regime 1933–1945* (London, 1998), pp. 105 and 233.
62. PRO CAB/23/96/221, Cabinet Conclusions 55(38)5, 16 November 1938.
63. A study with Ramsay as the central character has recently been produced. See Richard Griffiths, *Patriotism Perverted*.
64. A. H. M. Ramsay, *The Nameless War* (London, 1952), pp. 103–4, cited in R. Griffiths, *Fellow Travellers of the Right* (London, 1980), pp. 354–5.
65. Ramsay, *The Nameless War*, pp. 103–4, cited in Griffiths, *Patriotism Perverted*, p. 122.
66. Thurlow, *Fascism in Britain*, p. 79.
67. *The Times*, 24 May 1940, p. 3.
68. *Commons Debates*, Fifth Series, Vol. 360, Col. 1379, 9 May 1940.
69. *Peebleshire and South Midlothian Advertiser*, 10 February 1939, p. 4.

70. *Jewish Chronicle*, 17 February 1939, p. 33.
71. *Peebleshire and South Midlothian Advertiser*, 17 February 1939, p. 4.
72. Ibid., 24 February 1939, p. 4.
73. Ibid., 17 March 1939, p. 5.
74. Neville Chamberlain Papers, NC/7/11/33/19, Joseph Ball to Neville Chamberlain, July 1940.
75. See Richard Cockett, *Twilight of Truth: Chamberlain, Appeasement and the Manipulation of the Press* (London, 1989), pp. 9–11; and 'The Party, Publicity, and the Media', in Seldon and Ball, *Conservative Century*, pp. 555–7.
76. *Truth*, 12 October 1938, p. 461, and 16 November 1938, p. 635.
77. Ibid., 9 June 1939.
78. Ibid., 11 May 1938, p. 622.
79. Ibid., 8 June 1938, p. 766.
80. Ibid., 18 May 1938, p. 658.
81. Ibid., 20 January 1939, p. 68, and 26 May 1939, p. 697.
82. Ibid., 23 June 1939, p. 830.
83. Ibid., 11 August 1939, p. 169.
84. Ibid., 24 November 1939, p. 566.
85. Neville Chamberlain Papers, NC18/1/1108, Neville Chamberlain to Ida Chamberlain, 23 July 1939.
86. A. J. P. Taylor (ed.), *Off the Record – Political Interviews 1933–1943: W. P. Crozier* (London, 1973), interview with Neville and Nathan Laski, 8 January 1940, p. 120.
87. Peake Papers, 19 February 1957, cited in Andrew Roberts, *The Holy Fox* (London, 1991), p. 128.
88. Channon, *Diaries*, 27 January 1935, p. 23, 29 January 1935, p. 24, and 27 April 1937, p. 120.
89. Ibid., 9 September 1938, p. 164, and 15 September 1938, p. 166.
90. Ibid., 11 May 1939, p. 198.
91. Ibid., 18 March 1935, p. 28.
92. Nicolson, *Diaries*, 25 February 1938, p. 327. The rebuke was levelled at Alan Graham, the Conservative MP for the Wirrall division of Cheshire, who was not Jewish.
93. Shinwell had defeated Ramsay MacDonald in the 1935 general election.
94. Channon, *Diaries*, 4 April 1938, p. 153.
95. Robert Rhodes James, *Bob Boothby* (London, 1992), p. 134. The author was later quite prominent in the Conservative Friends of Israel.
96. *Commons Debates*, Fifth Series, Vol. 341, Col. 1314, 21 November 1938.
97. See *House of Commons Papers*, Home Office (HO), Reports under the Aliens Order 1920, Statistics in Regard to Alien Passengers who Entered and Left the United Kingdom, 1932–38.
98. Hammersley had previously sat in the Conservative interest for Stockport from 1924 to 1935 and had been the parliamentary private secretary to Arthur Samuel from 1927 to 1929.
99. *Commons Debates*, Fifth Series, Vol. 341, Col. 1441, 21 November 1938.
100. Ibid., Col. 1458, 21 November 1938.
101. Shaw subsequently called for a White Paper to be published setting out the terms upon which refugee children would be admitted to Britain. This proposal was dismissed by Geoffrey Lloyd, the under-secretary of state at the Home Office. See *Commons Debates*, Fifth Series, Vol. 342, Col. 22, 28 November 1938.
102. Herbert Samuel recalled that when he introduced a joint deputation to the Home Secretary on 21 November 1938, and asked that the children might be

brought to England without the slow procedure of passports and visas, Hoare 'at once consented, in view of the extreme urgency of the case'. Samuel, *Memoirs*, p. 255.

103. *Commons Debates*, Fifth Series, Vol. 341, Col. 1463, *passim*, 21 November 1938.
104. Ibid., Vol. 342, Col. 578, 1 December 1938.
105. Ibid., Vol. 342, Col. 1346, 8 December 1938, and Col. 2172, 15 December 1938.
106. Ibid., Col. 1795, 13 December 1938.
107. Another Conservative MP member of the Right Club was Commander Peter Agnew, the member for Camborne from 1931, who had produced a series of questions and statements in relation to aliens in the early 1930s. Perhaps ironically, he was PPS to Sir Philip Sassoon from 1937–39. See Griffiths, *Patriotism Perverted*, pp.19, 145–6.
108. *Commons Debates*, Fifth Series, Vol. 343, Col. 21, 31 January 1939.
109. Ibid., Vol. 344, Col. 209, 21 February 1939.
110. Ibid., Vol. 348, Col. 1828, 19 June 1939.
111. *The Times*, 9 February 1939, p. 19, reporting a meeting held on 8 February.
112. *The Times*, 17 February 1939, p. 16, reporting a meeting held on 16 February.
113. Ibid., 27 April 1939, p. 10, reporting a meeting held on 26 April.
114. Amery, *Diaries*, 1 December 1938, p. 538.
115. *Jewish Chronicle*, 16 December 1938, p. 15. In addition to Cazalet and Salter, the other government supporters were L. Gluckstein, S. S. Hammersley, I. Hannah, G. Nicolson, and J. Henderson Stewart (Conservative), D. L. Lipson (Ind. Conservative), H. W. Butcher (Lib. National), and H. Nicolson (Nat. Labour).
116. *Daily Telegraph*, 6 July 1938, p. 16.
117. Harold Macmillan, *Winds of Change 1914–1939* (London, 1966) p. 587.
118. Reported in the *Jewish Chronicle*, 16 December 1938, p. 30.
119. *The Times*, 14 July 1939, p. 8.
120. Ibid., 28 September 1939, p. 10.
121. Ibid., 19 December 1938, p. 17.
122. Ibid., 11 January 1939, p. 11.
123. PRO CAB/23/100/175, Cabinet Conclusions 37(39)11. Meeting on 12 July 1939.
124. *The Times*, 18 July 1939, p. 16.
125. *Commons Debates*, Fifth Series, Vol. 350, Col. 406, 19 July 1939.
126. The *Daily Mail*, 20 July 1939, p. 8, was concerned that Britain had assumed enormous liabilities which were Germany's responsibility. The *Daily Express*, 21 July 1939, p. 8, argued that it was for the Jews not the British Exchequer to bear the cost.

8: The Conservatives and Palestine, 1930–39

1. *Report of Commission on Palestine Disturbances of August 1929*, Cmd 3530 (London, 1930).
2. PRO CAB 23/63, 2 April 1930.
3. *Palestine: Report on Immigration, Land Settlement and Development*, Cmd 3686 (London, 1930).
4. *Palestine: Statement of Policy*, Cmd 3692 (London, 1930).
5. Weizmann, *Trial and Error*, p. 413.
6. *The Times*, 23 October 1930, p. 13.
7. *Commons Debates*, Fifth Series, Vol. 244, Col. 18, 28 October 1930.
8. J. Barnes and D. Nicholson (eds), *The Empire at Bay: The Leo Amery Diaries 1929–1945* (London, 1988), 22 October 1930, p. 85.

9. Camillo Dresner (ed.), *The Letters and Papers of Chaim Weizmann, Vol. XV October 1930–June 1933* (Jerusalem, 1978), C. Weizmann to F. Warburg 24 October 1930, p. 3.
10. *The Times*, 24 October 1930, p. 13, and 4 November 1930, p. 13.
11. Ibid., 4 November 1930, p. 15.
12. *Commons Debates*, Fifth Series, Vol. 244, Col. 1655, *passim*, 12 November 1930.
13. Amery, *Diaries*, 16 November 1930, p. 89.
14. *Commons Debates*, Fifth Series, Vol. 245, Cols. 104–15, 17 November 1930.
15. Ibid., Cols 187–96.
16. Ibid., Vol. 245, Cols 138–44, 17 November 1930.
17. Amery, *Diaries*, 3 November 1930, p. 88.
18. *The Times*, 5 September 1929, p. 11, reporting on a speech made on 3 September.
19. Ibid., 5 October 1929, p. 12, reporting the speech to the Montreal Canadian Club on 2 October.
20. Ibid., 31 October 1929, p. 11.
21. *Commons Debates*, Fifth Series, Vol. 231, Col. 2023, 13 November 1929.
22. Ibid., Vol. 232, Col. 479, 20 November 1929.
23. Ibid., Col. 1401, 27 November 1929.
24. Ibid., Vol. 233, Col. 24, 9 December 1929.
25. Ibid., Vol. 235, Col. 1984, 24 February 1930.
26. Ibid., Col. 1987.
27. *Jewish Chronicle*, 28 February 1930, p. 5.
28. Ibid., 18 April 1930, p. 19.
29. *The Times*, 31 March 1930, p. 13.
30. N. A. Rose, *The Gentile Zionists* (London, 1973), pp. 5 and 30. Pro-Zionist MPs had constituted committees at various times during the 1920s and 1930s. In 1922 the Group had included Lord Robert Cecil, Brunel Cohen, Ormsby-Gore and, interestingly, Walter Guinness, who as Lord Moyne was to be assassinated by Jewish extremists as he was considered an anti-Zionist (see Chapter 10); Central Zionist Archives, Z4/1878 I.
31. *Jewish Chronicle*, 11 April 1930, p. 34.
32. Malcom Macdonald was elected the Labour MP for the Bassetlaw division of Nottingham in May 1929, re-elected to that seat as National Labour in October 1931. He was defeated in the November 1935 general election but won the by-election in the Ross and Cromarty division of Inverness in February 1936.
33. Archibald Sinclair was elected in November 1922 as the member for Caithness and Sutherland in the Liberal interest. Before entering Parliament he had served as an assistant secretary to Churchill in the Colonial Office in 1921–22.
34. *The Times*, 2 April 1930, p. 15.
35. *The Times*, 3 April 1930, p. 15.
36. Ibid., 10 April 1930, p. 12.
37. Reproduced in W. Lacqueur, *The Israel–Arab Reader* (London, 1969), pp. 73–9.
38. Conservative Party Archives, CCO 506/2/10, 9 May 1931.
39. Alderman, *Jewish Community*, p. 112 and N. A. Rose, *Gentile Zionists*, p. 37.
40. *Jewish Chronicle*, 28 November 1930, p. 16.
41. Ibid., p. 18.
42. *The Times*, 21 November 1930, and the *Jewish Chronicle*, 5 December 1930, p. 13.
43. The Communist candidate, Harry Pollitt, received 2,106 votes.
44. Thomas was to return to that office in November 1935.
45. PRO CAB 23/71/10, Cabinet meeting 6 April 1930.

46. PRO CAB 23/72/447, Cabinet meeting 20 April 1930.
47. Central Zionist Archives, Z4/10034.
48. B. Janner, 'The Parliamentary Palestine Committee', in I. Cohen (ed.), *The Rebirth of Israel* (London, 1952), p. 100.
49. These were: Winston Churchill, Leo Amery, Duchess of Atholl, John Buchan, Austen Chamberlain, Marquess of Hartington, Victor Cazalet, S. Hammersley and Lord Melchett.
50. *Jewish Chronicle*, 18 March 1932, p. 22.
51. *Commons Debates*, Fifth Series, Vol. 264, Cols 1816–18, 22 April 1932.
52. *The Times*, 3 March 1933, p. 17.
53. There were parliamentary private secretaries, such as Thomas Dugdale, who were present who, although members of the government, were not ministers of the Crown.
54. *The Times*, 17 November 1930, p. 19.
55. *Commons Debates*, Fifth Series, Vol. 281, Col. 343, 9 November 1933.
56. Ibid., Vol. 283, Col. 864, 29 November 1933.
57. PRO CAB 23/78/372, Cabinet meeting, 11 April 1934.
58. *Jewish Chronicle*, 8 August 1930, p. 18.
59. *The Times*, 30 June 1934, p. 11.
60. He was at that time a vice-president of the United Synagogue and, although he had been opposed to political Zionism, was active in promoting the economic development of Palestine. See Robert Henriques, *Sir Robert Waley Cohen 1877–1952* (London, 1966).
61. *The Times*, 21 August 1935, p. 6.
62. Cecil of Chelwood Papers, Add Mss 51157/249, Dugdale to Cecil, 17 February 1936.
63. Christopher Sykes, *Cross Roads to Israel* (London, 1965), p. 179.
64. See *The Proposed New Constitution for Palestine*, Cmd 5119 (London, 1936).
65. *The Times*, 10 January 1936, p. 8.
66. *Commons Debates*, Fifth Series, Vol. 310, Cols 1090–94, 24 March 1936.
67. Ibid., Cols 1123–4.
68. Ibid., Col. 1111.
69. Ibid., Cols 1112–16.
70. Ibid., Cols 1118–22.
71. Ibid., Cols 1129–34.
72. Ibid., Cols 1139–40.
73. Ibid., Cols 1147–50.
74. Amery, *Diaries*, 24 March 1936, p. 412.
75. Norman A. Rose (ed.), *The Diaries of Blanche Dugdale 1936–1947* (London, 1973), 24 March and 25 March 1936, p. 10.
76. PRO CAB 23/83/408, Cabinet meeting, 1 April 1936.
77. Sykes, *Cross Roads to Israel*, p. 183.
78. *Commons Debates*, Fifth Series, Vol. 313, Cols 1313–24, 19 June 1936.
79. Dugdale, *Diaries*, 6 July 1936, p. 24.
80. *Commons Debates*, Fifth Series, Vol. 313, Col. 1339, 19 June 1936.
81. Ibid., Col. 1360.
82. Amery, *Diaries*, 1 July 1936, p. 423.
83. The other members of the Commission were: Sir Horace Rumbold, a diplomat who had served as Ambassador to Germany, Sir Lucas Hammond, previously Governor of Assam, Sir William Carter, a former Chief Justice and Acting Governor in Colonial Africa, Sir Harold Morris who was Recorder in Folkestone, and Professor Reginald Coupland of All Souls, Oxford.
84. *The Times*, 30 July 1936, p. 15.

85. The other signatories were J. A. Herbert (Monmouth), Hon. Ralph Beaumont (Portsmouth), Kenneth Pickthorn (Cambridge University), Derrick Gunston (Thornby), William Spens (Ashford, Kent), Geoffrey Ellis (Ecclesall, Sheffield), Frank Heilgers (Bury St Edmunds), Annesley Somerville (Windsor), Charles Peat (Darlington), Bernard Cruddas (Wansbeck, Northumberland), Victor Raikes (Essex, South East) and the Independent National Austin Hopkinson.

86. *The Times*, 4 August 1936, p. 15.

87. PRO CAB 23/85/200-220, Cabinet meeting, 2 September 1936.

88. *Commons Debates*, Fifth Series, Vol. 317, Col. 251, 5 November 1936.

89. *Report of the Palestine Royal Commission*, Cmd 5479 (London, 1937).

90. Dugdale, *Diaries*, 20 July 1937, p. 53.

91. *Commons Debates*, Fifth Series, Vol. 326, Cols 2235–47, 21 July 1937.

92. Ibid., Cols. 2274–80.

93. *The Times*, 13 July 1937, p. 14. Report of the meeting held on 12 July by those MPs who had sent the pro-Arab letter to *The Times* the previous July.

94. *Commons Debates*, Fifth Series, Vol. 326, Col. 2292, 21 July 1937.

95. Ibid., Col. 2307.

96. Ibid., 2322–7.

97. He had been appointed Chancellor of the Duchy of Lancaster in May 1937.

98. *Commons Debates*, Fifth Series, Vol. 326, Col. 2354, 21 July 1937.

99. Ibid., Cols 2329–32.

100. According to Dugdale, Ormsby-Gore had told Melchett that in reality the government 'thought the [Peel] Report rotten in almost every respect'. Dugdale, *Diaries*, 13 July 1937, p. 52.

101. Amery, *Diaries*, 8 June 1937, p. 444.

102. Weizmann, supported by David Ben-Gurion, Moshe Shertock and Nachum Goldmann, received the support of the Twentieth Zionist Congress at Zurich in August 1937, by 299 votes to 160.

103. Amery, *Diaries*, 8 June 1937, p. 444. Dugdale, *Diaries*, 9 June 1937, p. 45.

104. *The Times*, 21 July 1937, p. 14. Report of a meeting on 20 July attended by MPs which was addressed by Jamal Husseini, the leader of the Arab Delegation.

105. *Jewish Chronicle*, 3 September 1937, p. 25.

106. *Evening Standard*, 23 July 1937, p. 7.

107. *The Times*, 15 September 1937, p. 11.

108. PRO CAB 24/273, CP 281(37), 19 November 1937.

109. Dugdale, *Diaries*, 23 November 1937, p. 66.

110. PRO CAB 24/273 CP 289(37), 1 December 1937.

111. Aaron Klieman, 'Bureaucratic Politics at Whitehall in the Partitioning of Palestine, 1937', in Uriel Dann (ed.), *The Great Powers in the Middle East 1919–1939* (London, 1988), pp. 128–53.

112. Dugdale's description of Ormsby-Gore, *Diaries*, 23 November 1937, p. 67.

113. See Weizmann, *Trial and Error*, pp. 411 and 482, Wasserstein, *The British in Palestine*, p. 11, and Norman Rose, *Chaim Weizmann* (1986), p. 279.

114. Dugdale, *Diaries*, 11 December 1937, p. 70.

115. Ibid., 8 December 1937, p. 69.

116. *Policy on Palestine, A Despatch of 23 December 1937 to the High Commissioner*, Cmd 5634 (London, 1938).

117. Earl of Avon, *The Eden Memoirs: Facing the Dictators* (London, 1962), p. 589.

118. *Commons Debates*, Fifth Series, Vol. 332, Col. 1769, 8 March 1938.

119. Ibid., Col. 1780.

120. Ibid., Col. 1773.

121. Ibid., Vol. 337, Col. 185, 14 June 1938.

122. *The Times*, 16 July 1938, p. 12.
123. *Commons Debates*, Fifth Series, Vol. 341, Cols 1989–95, 24 November 1938.
124. Ibid., Cols 2031–7. Weizmann had 'jumped' at this plan when it was put to him by Churchill in advance of the debate. See Amery, *Diaries*, 10 November 1938, p. 535.
125. *Commons Debates*, Fifth Series, Vol. 341, Cols 2074–85, 24 November 1938.
126. Ibid., Cols 2015–17.
127. Ibid., Cols 2020–72.
128. Ibid., Cols 2089–91.
129. Dugdale, *Diaries*, 19 September 1938, p. 99.
130. PRO CAB 23/96/256, Cabinet meeting, 22 November 1938.
131. PRO CAB 23/96/392, Cabinet meeting, 14 December 1938.
132. Dugdale, *Diaries*, 27 January 1939, p. 120.
133. PRO CAB 23/97/391-394, Cabinet meeting, 8 March 1939.
134. Cazalet was the other Conservative delegate; Wedgwood and Williams (Labour) and Denman (National Labour) were the other delegates.
135. *The Times*, 14 March 1939, p. 8.
136. *Jewish Chronicle*, 17 March 1939, p. 26.
137. PRO CAB 23/99/66, Cabinet Conclusions, 26 April 1939.
138. Central Zionist Archives, Z4/17309, Cazalet to Capt. H. D. Margesson, the Government Chief Whip, 21 March 1939.
139. PRO CAB 23/99/68, Cabinet Conclusions, 26 April 1939.
140. PRO CAB 23/99/167, Cabinet Conclusions, 10 May 1939.
141. PRO CAB 23/99/88 CP 100 (3a), Cabinet Conclusions, 1 May 1939.
142. *Palestine: A Statement of Policy*, Cmd 6019 (London, 1939).
143. *Commons Debates*, Fifth Series, Vol. 347, Cols 1938–54, 22 May 1939.
144. Ibid., Cols 1967–9.
145. Ibid., Cols 1991–2.
146. Ibid., Col. 2029.
147. Ibid., Cols 2145–7, 23 May 1939.
148. Dugdale, *Diaries*, 22 May 1939, p. 139.
149. *Commons Debates*, Fifth Series, Vol. 347, Cols 2002–16, 22 May 1939.
150. Ibid., Cols. 2158–62, 23 May 1939.
151. Ibid., Cols. 1169–2178.
152. Those Conservatives who voted against the government were: V. Adams, L. Amery, B. Bracken, J. R. H. Cartland, V. Cazalet, S. Hammersley, Sir J. Haslam, Sir G. Jones, R. Law, D. Lipson (Ind. Con.), O. Locker-Lampson, H. Macmillan, A. Moreing, J. Morris, and R. Pilkington. The other government supporters who voted against the motion were H. Holsworth (Lib. Nat.), H. Nicolson (Nat. Lab.), and J. Henderson Stewart (Lib. Nat.).
153. *Jewish Chronicle*, 12 November 1937, p. 14.
154. This should be compared with Elliot's participation in the Palestine Supply vote on 20 July 1939.
155. Amery, *Diaries*, 23 May 1939, p. 553.
156. Dugdale, *Diaries*, 23 May 1939, p. 139.
157. Rose, *Diaries of Blanche Dugdale*, p. 218.
158. *Commons Debates*, Fifth Series, Vol. 360, Cols 1361–6, 8 May 1940.
159. Norman A. Rose, *The Letters and Papers of Chaim Weizmann, Vol. XIX* (Jerusalem, 1979), Weizmann to W. E. Rappard, 26 June 1939, p. 133.
160. Harold Macmillan, *Tides of Fortune 1945–1955* (London, 1969), p. 142. Amery was to write to Churchill four years later that 'the White Paper was undoubtedly, as you and I both pointed out at the time, a direct repudiation of specific pledges to the Jews at large and to the League, as well as an act of

appeasement in the worst Munich tradition'. PRO PREM 4/52/1, Amery to Churchill, 29 April 1943.

161. *The Times*, 15 September 1936, p. 14, and 26 September 1936, p. 12.
162. PRO CAB 23/83/408, Cabinet Conclusions, 1 April 1936.
163. PRO CAB/23/84/145, Cabinet Conclusions, 13 May 1936, and PRO CAB 23/84/271, Cabinet Conclusions, 10 June 1936.
164. PRO CAB 23/85/205, Cabinet Conclusions, 2 September 1936.
165. PRO CAB 23/90/137, Cabinet Conclusions, 17 November 1937.
166. PRO CAB 23/90/250, Cabinet Conclusions, 8 December 1937.
167. PRO CAB 23/97/394, Cabinet Conclusions, 8 March 1939.
168. *The Times*, 3 February 1936, p. 11.
169. Ibid., 3 September 1936, p. 12.
170. Ibid., 15 October 1938, p. 11.
171. PRO CAB 23/97/391, Cabinet Conclusions, 8 March 1939, and PRO CAB 23/98/104, Cabinet Conclusions, 22 March 1938.
172. PRO CAB 23/99/66, Cabinet Conclusions, 26 April 1939.
173. Cited in John H. Davis, *The Kennedy Clan: Dynasty and Disaster 1848–1984* (London, 1985), p. 81.
174. PRO CAB 23/99/167, Cabinet Conclusions, 10 May 1939.
175. Kennedy was anti-British as well as anti-Semitic. He advised Roosevelt, after the outbreak of hostilities in September 1939, to stay out of the war, telling him 'the real fact is that England is fighting for her possessions and her place in the sun'. Cited in John H. Davis, p. 82.
176. Headlam, *Diaries*, 14 September 1931, p. 216.
177. Crozier, *Interviews*, meeting between Nall and W. P. Crozier, 14 February 1935, p. 34.
178. Nicolson, *Diaries*, 18 October 1935, p. 219.
179. G. R. Searle, *Country Before Party: Coalition and the Idea of 'National Government' in Modern Britain, 1885–1987* (London, 1995), Chapter 8.
180. Nicolson, *Diaries*, 24 February 1936, p. 245.
181. *The Times*, 29 May 1930, p. 17.
182. Ibid., 25 March 1936, p. 17.
183. Ibid., 5 May 1936, p. 17.
184. *Daily Express*, 9 July 1937, p. 9.
185. *The Times*, 9 March 1938, p. 15.
186. Ibid., 24 May 1939, p. 17.

9: The Conservatives and the Jews during the Second World War

1. John Ramsden, *The Age of Balfour and Baldwin, 1902–1940* (London, 1978), pp. 370–1.
2. See J. M. Lee, *The Churchill Coalition 1940–1945* (London, 1980); Paul Addison, *The Road to 1945*, 2nd edn (London, 1994), and John Ramsden, 'Winston Churchill and the Leadership of the Conservative Party 1940–51', *Contemporary Record*, Vol. 9, No. 1 (Summer 1995).
3. Channon, *Diaries*, 17 December 1942, p. 347.
4. *Commons Debates*, Fifth Series, Vol. 385, Cols 2082–7, 17 December 1942.
5. Lloyd George later said to Eden: 'I cannot recall a scene like that in all my years in Parliament', Earl of Avon, *The Eden Memoirs: The Reckoning* (London, 1965), p. 358.
6. PRO CO 733/446/13 (76021/45), Note dated 1st July 1943.
7. Nigel Nicolson (ed.), *Harold Nicolson Diaries and Letters 1939–1945* (London, 1967), 11 January 1944, p. 344.

8. *Commons Debates*, Fifth Series, Vol. 389, Col. 1120, 19 May 1943. This statement contradicts the published report of the Inter-Allied Information committee which issued a leaflet, published by His Majesty's Stationary Office, which stated that 'the German objective is nothing less than the utter destruction of Jewish life' and that the number of those who have been deported or who have perished since 1939 'now reaches the appalling figure of two million and that five million are in danger of extermination'. *Conditions in Occupied Territories 6: Persecution of the Jews* (London, 1942), p. 3.
9. *Commons Debates*, Fifth Series, Vol. 389, Col. 1121.
10. Ward represented North-West Hull during 1918–45. He was a parliamentary private secretary in 1923–24, 1924–26 and 1928–29. He was thereafter a Lord Commissioner of the Treasury, 1931-35 and member of H.M. Household, 1935-37.
11. *Commons Debates*, Fifth Series, Vol. 389, Col. 1146, 19 May 1943.
12. On 3 March 1943, 173 people were killed in a panic at the entrance to the Bethnal Green tube shelter. In fact, there were relatively few Jews who used that shelter, in part owing to anti-Semitic attitudes which had been experienced there and partly because that part of the East End had a relatively small percentage of Jewish inhabitants. Although the rumour that the disaster was caused by 'Jewish panic' spread across London and the rest of the country, in Bethnal Green, according to Home Intelligence, 'there was full knowledge that any such statement is untrue'. See Kushner, *Persistence of Prejudice*, pp. 60–1 and 125–6.
13. *Commons Debates*, Fifth Series, Vol. 389, Col. 1169, 19 May 1943.
14. Ibid., Cols 1190–1.
15. Ibid., Cols 1197–8.
16. Note of conversation by Harry Hopkins, 27 March 1943, *Foreign Relations of the United States 1943*, Vol. III, pp. 38–9, cited in Wasserstein, *Britain and the Jews of Europe*, p. 188.
17. Richard Breitman, *Official Secrets: What the Nazis Planned, What the British and Americans Knew* (London, 1999), pp. 207 and 303, cites the literature on the technical debate including: James H. Kitchens III, 'The Bombing of Auschwitz Revisited', *Journal of Military History* (1994), pp. 233–66, and Richard Levy 'The Bombing of Auschwitz Revisited: A Critical Analysis', *Holocaust and Genocide Studies*, 10 (1996), pp. 267–98.
18. Wasserstein, *Britain and the Jews of Europe*, p. 316.
19. Ibid., Col. 1160.
20. Neville Chamberlain Papers, NC/8/32/1, note of interview between Leslie Hore-Belisha and Lord Camrose, 5 January 1940.
21. Neville Chamberlain Papers, NC18/1/1137, Neville Chamberlain to Ida Chamberlain, 7 January 1940.
22. R. J. Minney, *The Private Papers of Hore-Belisha* (London, 1960), pp. 266–86.
23. Cockett, *Twilight of Truth*, p. 168.
24. Crozier, *Interviews*, 20 January 1940, p. 132.
25. Ibid., 8 January 1940, p. 120.
26. Fleming had represented Withington since 1931.
27. *Commons Debates*, Fifth Series, Vol. 402, Col. 1008, 28 July 1944.
28. PRO PREM 4/51/8/443, Hertz to Churchill, 8 May 1944.
29. PRO CAB 65/42/121, Cabinet Conclusions, 12 June 1944.
30. Churchill to Eden, 11 July 1944, cited in Winston Churchill, *The Second World War, Vol. VI: Triumph and Tragedy* (London, 1985), p. 597.
31. Martin Gilbert, *The Holocaust* (London, 1986), p. 701.
32. Wasserstein, *Britain and the Jews of Europe*, p. 262.

33. PRO CAB 95/15/198, Eden to Cabinet Committee on Refugees, 3 August 1944.
34. PRO CAB 65/43/95, Cabinet Conclusions, 16 August 1944.
35. Churchill to Lord Lloyd, 23 May 1940, cited in Winston Churchill, *The Second World War, Vol. II: Their Finest Hour* (London, 1985 edn), p. 559.
36. Ibid., 28 June 1940, p. 154.
37. Ibid., p. 373.
38. Eden to Churchill, 24 September 1940, cited in Avon, *The Reckoning*, p. 565. The reference to Churchill's memorandum is at p. 139.
39. PRO CAB 65/9/126, Cabinet Conclusions, 10 October 1940.
40. Michael J. Cohen (ed.), *The Letters and Papers of Chaim Weizmann, Vol. XX: July 1940–January 1943* (Jerusalem, 1979), Weizmann to Moyne 1 December 1941, pp. 232–3.
41. See, for example, Weizmann, *Letters and Papers*, Weizmann to Halifax, 1 July 1942, p. 321.
42. PRO CAB 65/19/21, Cabinet Conclusions, 13 October 1941.
43. PRO CAB 65/43/82, Cabinet Conclusions, 9 August 1944.
44. Churchill to Sir James Grigg, 26 July 1944, cited in Winston Churchill, *The Second World War, Vol. VI: Triumph and Tragedy*, p. 601.
45. PRO CAB 65/10/112, Cabinet Conclusions, 27 November 1940.
46. Dugdale, *Diaries*, 3 October 1941, p. 187.
47. PRO CAB 65/19/190, Cabinet Conclusions, 2 October 1941.
48. PRO FO/371/ 32661/22a, 11 February and 12 February 1942.
49. Dugdale, *Diaries*, 25 February 1942, p. 193.
50. PRO CAB 65/25/119, Cabinet Conclusions, 5 March 1942.
51. *Commons Debates*, Fifth Series, Vol. 378, Cols 1048–9, 11 March 1942.
52. PRO CAB 65/26/83, Cabinet Conclusions, 18 May 1942.
53. Dugdale, *Diaries*, 22 May 1942, p. 195.
54. Wasserstein, *Britain and the Jews of Europe*, p. 161.
55. Stanley had replaced Cranborne as colonial secretary in November 1942.
56. PRO CAB 65/39/5, Cabinet Conclusions, Confidential Annex, 7 July 1943.
57. Dugdale, *Diaries*, 21 July 1943, p. 206.
58. PRO PREM 4/52/1/200, 14 July 1943.
59. PRO PREM 4/52/1/202, Churchill to Eden, 11 July 1943.
60. Amery, *Diaries*, 2 July 1943, pp. 896–7.
61. PRO CAB 65/39/6, Cabinet Conclusions, 2 July 1943.
62. PRO PREM 4/52/1/201, Eden to Churchill, 12 July 1943. The other members were Herbert Morrison (chairman), Cranborne, Stanley, Archibald Sinclair (Liberal leader and a pro-Zionist), and subsequently Moyne.
63. PRO CAB 65/4/46, Cabinet Conclusions, 25 January 1944.
64. PRO CAB 66/44/102, Report of Palestine Committee, 20 December 1943. Law submitted a minority report proposing even less territory for the Jews.
65. PRO PREM 4/52/1/177, Amery to Churchill, 22 January 1944.
66. Eden set out his views in a memorandum entitled 'The Case Against Partition', in which he argued that the Zionists would fill up the Jewish State beyond its capacity and would continue to hope for a larger state covering the whole of Palestine and Transjordan, resulting in continual bloodshed and disorders. However, the nub of his argument was that British interests in the Middle East depended upon good relations with the Arabs and that Britain could not afford to alienate them. PRO CAB 95/14 Eden, 'The Case Against Partition', 15 September 1944.
67. PRO PREM 4/52/1/79, Churchill, 'Palestine – Summary of Present Position', 3 November 1944.
68. Moshe Pearlman, *Ben Gurion Looks Back: In Talks with Moshe Pearlman*

(London, 1965), p. 95.
69. Dugdale, *Diaries*, 5 November 1944, pp. 217–18.
70. Churchill to Cranborne, 17 November 1944. Cited in Churchill, *Second World War, Vol. VI*, p. 612.
71. *Commons Debates*, Fifth Series, Vol. 404, Col. 2242, 17 November 1944.
72. *Daily Express*, 18 December 1942, p. 2.
73. *Daily Mail*, 19 December 1942, p. 2.
74. *The Times*, 12 December 1942, p. 5.
75. *Daily Telegraph*, 18 December 1942, p. 4.
76. *Daily Mail*, 7 November 1944, p. 1.
77. Ibid., 9 November 1944, p. 2.
78. *Daily Telegraph*, 8 November 1944, p. 4.
79. *The Times*, 10 November 1944, p. 5.
80. See Wasserstein, *Britain and the Jews*, p. 337, Nicholas Bethell, *The Palestine Triangle: The Struggle between the British, the Jews and the Arabs 1935–49* (London, 1979), p. 186, and Norman Rose 'Churchill and Zionism', in Robert Blake and W. Roger Louis (eds), *Churchill* (Oxford, 1993), p. 164.
81. PRO FO 371/35033/28, Churchill to Cranborne, 18 April 1943.
82. Weizmann, p. 536. See also Central Zionist Archives, Z4/302/27. Churchill had told Weizmann at an earlier meeting that, according to the latter's report to the meeting of the Zionist Executive on 25 October 1943, after 'they had crushed Hitler they would have to establish the Jews in the position where they belong. He had an inheritance left to him by Lord Balfour and he was not going to change.'
83. PRO PREM 4/51/1/3, 16 May 1945.
84. Amery, *Diaries*, 11 June 1945, pp. 1046–7.
85. PRO CAB 65/19/190, Cabinet Conclusions, 2 October 1941.
86. PRO CAB 65/25/119, Cabinet Conclusions, 5 March 1942.
87. PRO CAB 65/39/6, Cabinet Conclusions, 2 July 1943.

10: The Conservatives and Palestine, 1945–48

1. *Commons Debates*, Fifth Series, Vol. 426, Col. 1251, 1 August 1946.
2. *The Times*, 7 October 1946, p. 2. Report of Churchill's address of the previous day to the Conservative Party Conference at Blackpool.
3. For a detailed account of the workings of the Committee see Richard Crossman, *Palestine Mission* (London, 1947).
4. See Bethell, *The Palestine Triangle*, Chapters 8–10, Martin Gilbert, *Exile and Return: The Struggle for a Jewish Homeland* (London, 1978), Chapter 21 and Epilogue, and for the riots in Britain see Tony Kushner, 'Anti-Semitism and Austerity: The August 1947 Riots in Britain', in Panikas Panayi (ed.), *Racial Violence in Britain 1840–1950* (Leicester, 1993).
5. *Commons Debates*, Fifth Series, Vol. 419, Cols 1419 and 1423, 21 February 1946.
6. Ibid., Vol. 424, Col. 1880, 1 July 1946.
7. Ibid., Vol. 426, Cols 977–8, 31 July 1946.
8. Ibid., Cols 981–2, 985–7.
9. Macmillan, *Tides of Fortune 1945–1955* (London, 1969), pp. 144–5.
10. *Commons Debates*, Fifth Series, Vol. 424, Cols 1247–8, 1251–4, 1 August 1946.
11. Central Zionist Archives, F13/292. Report of a deputation to Capt. John Crowder, the Conservative MP for Finchley, 19 July 1946, when Crowder related his discussion with Churchill on the issue of Palestine .
12. *Commons Debates*, Fifth Series, Vol. 432, Cols 1306, 1309–10, 31 January 1947.
13. Ibid., Cols 1347–9.

14. Ibid., Vol. 434, Col. 36, 3 March 1947.
15. *The Times*, 24 April 1947, p. 2. Report of Churchill's meeting the previous evening in Wanstead.
16. *Commons Debates*, Fifth Series, Vol. 445, Cols 1220–2, 11 December 1947.
17. Ibid., Vol. 448, Col. 1274, 10 March 1948.
18. *The Times*, 28 April 1948, p. 4.
19. During the wartime period Pickthorn was chairman of the Palestine Arab Committee; Glyn was treasurer and Beaumont was its secretary. See PRO CO 733/444/5/75872. Pickthorn also apparently proposed to help in an organisation for those detained under Regulation 18B, PRO HO 45/25728/33. Cited in Griffiths, *Patriotism Perverted*, pp. 270 and 337.
20. *Commons Debates*, Fifth Series, Vol. 424, Col. 1887, 1 July 1946.
21. Ibid., Vol. 426, Col. 1271, 1 August 1946.
22. Ibid., Col. 1278.
23. Ibid., Vol. 448, Col. 1284, 10 March 1948.
24. Ibid., Vol. 419, Cols 1399–400, 21 February 1946.
25. Ibid., Vol. 448, Col. 1328, 10 March 1948.
26. Cited in Bethell, *Palestine Triangle*, p. 267.
27. *Commons Debates*, Fifth Series, Vol. 426, Col. 1002, 31 July 1946.
28. Ibid., Col. 1067.
29. Ibid., Col. 975.
30. Macdonald had only served in government for a short period when he was the parliamentary private secretary to the President of the Board of Trade from June 1928 until June 1929.
31. *Commons Debates*, Fifth Series, Vol. 432, Cols 1317 and 1320–1, 31 January 1947.
32. Ibid., Vol. 448, Col. 1293–4, 10 March 1948.
33. Manningham-Buller was elected in 1943 and had served as the parliamentary secretary at the Ministry of Works from May to July 1945.
34. *Commons Debates*, Fifth Series, Vol. 432, Col. 1328, 31 January 1947.
35. Ibid., Vol. 445, Cols 1269–70, 11 December 1947.
36. Smithers had been the member for Chislehurst from 1924 until 1945 and for Orpington since July 1945.
37. *Commons Debates*, Fifth Series, Vol. 445, Cols 1356–7, 12 December 1947.
38. Dodds-Parker was elected as the member for Banbury in July 1945.
39. *Commons Debates*, Fifth Series, Vol. 445, Col. 1362, 12 December 1947.
40. Cooper-Key represented Hastings and was elected in July 1945. He was married to the daughter of Viscount Rothermere and he was a director of Associated Newspapers Ltd.
41. *Commons Debates*, Fifth Series, Vol. 445, Cols 1402–3, 12 December 1947. The likely figure for the total Jewish population was in the region of 14 million, see *Jewish Year Book* (1949), pp. 298–300.
42. Amery, however, gave evidence to the Anglo-American Committee of Enquiry at the request of Weizmann. See Joseph Heller (ed.), *The Letters and Papers of Chaim Weizmann, Vol. XXII May 1945–July 1947* (Jerusalem, 1979), Weizmann to Amery, 22 January 1946, p. 92.
43. Channon, *Diaries*, 5 July 1943, p. 370.
44. Teeling was the member for Brighton and had represented it since 1944.
45. *Commons Debates*, Fifth Series, Vol. 419, Cols 1386–9, 21 February 1946.
46. Ibid., Vol. 426, Cols. 1047–8, 31 July 1946.
47. Cited in Bethell, *The Palestine Triangle*, p. 44.
48. Pearlman, *Ben Gurion Looks Back*, p. 106.
49. Amery, *Diaries*, 12 September 1941, pp. 714–15.
50. Michael J. Cohen (ed.), *The Letters & Papers of Chaim Weizmann, Vol. XXI*

January 1943–May 1945 (Jerusalem, 1979), Weizmann to Churchill, 2 April 1943, p. 19, to which there was no reply; Weizmann to Churchill, 18 May 1943, p. 32, requested a meeting but it did not take place nor did the proposed meeting with him which was referred to in a letter from Weizmann to Jan Smuts, 6 April 1945, p. 297.

51. Dugdale, *Diaries*, 26 July 1945, p. 223.
52. Lord Boothby, *My Yesterday, Your Tomorrow* (London, 1962), p. 211.
53. When Weizmann in a letter to Churchill appealed to him 'in extremis' for help in respect of the Anglo-American Commission of Enquiry, Churchill replied that he had passed his letter to Attlee and wrote: 'Apart from this there is nothing that I personally can do in the matter' but did add that it 'continues to be of profound interest to me'. See Weizmann, *Letters and Papers*, Weizmann to Churchill, 14 April 1946 and Note 9, p. 120.
54. Cited in Aaron Klieman (ed.), *The Letters and Papers of Chaim Weizmann, Vol. XXIII August 1947–June 1952*, Note 1 to letter no. 241, p. 196.
55. *Daily Express*, 14 November 1945, p. 2, and *The Times*, 14 November 1945, p. 5.
56. *Daily Mail*, 24 July 1946, p. 2.
57. *Daily Telegraph*, 23 July 1946, p. 4.
58. *Daily Mail*, 24 July 1946, p. 2, and *The Times*, 23 July 1946, p. 5.
59. *Daily Mail*, 1 August 1947, p. 1, and *The Times*, 1 August 1947, p. 5.
60. *Daily Express*, 1 August 1947, p. 2.
61. *Daily Telegraph*, 1 August 1947, p. 4.
62. Ibid., 1 December 1947, p. 4
63. *The Times*, 22 November and 28 November 1947, p. 5, and *Daily Express* 2 December 1947, p. 2.
64. *The Times*, 15 May 1948, p. 5.
65. *Daily Telegraph*, 15 May 1948, p. 4
66. *Daily Express*, 15 May 1948, p. 2.
67. Nigel Nicolson (ed.), *Harold Nicolson: Diaries and Letters 1945–62* (London, 1968), 25 May 1948, p. 140.

11: Conclusion

1. *National Review*, Vol. LX, December 1912, pp. 552*–5*. See also Chapter 1, pp. 4–5, in this volume.
2. Lord Curzon, in the course of a speech delivered in Leeds, said: 'Do not imagine that the Russian Government is a body of Russians who represent, at any rate, some section of their country. That is not the case. They are a small gang, only a few hundred in number, few of them Russians by birth, and most of them Jews in origin, who are preying like vultures on the bodies of that unhappy people.' Board of Deputies Annual Report, 24 December 1925, p. 32.
3. Leon Poliakov, *The History of Anti-Semitism, Vol. IV* (Oxford, 1985), p. 218.
4. It was perhaps ironic that imperialists such as Amery saw the role of the Jews as promoting 'the English idea' in the Middle East. However, in view of Amery's own Jewish forebears, perhaps he believed that non-assimilated Jews would share his views. See Amery, *Diaries*, 26 July 1928, p. 559.
5. Neville Chamberlain Papers, NC18/1/1076, Neville Chamberlain to Ida Chamberlain, 10 November 1938.
6. Louise London, 'Jewish Refugees, Anglo-Jewry and British Government Policy, 1930–1940', in David Cesarani (ed.), *The Making of Modern Anglo-Jewry* (Oxford, 1990), p. 163.
7. Tony Kushner, 'The Impact of British Anti-Semitism 1918–1945', in David

Cesarani (ed.), *The Making of Modern Anglo-Jewry*, p. 165, and 'Beyond the Pale? British Reactions to Nazi Anti-Semitism 1933-39', in Tony Kushner and Kenneth Lunn (eds), *The Politics of Marginality – Race, the Radical Right and Minorities in Twentieth Century Britain* (London, 1990), p. 154.

8. Sherman, *Island Refuge*, p. 267.
9. Ibid., p. 7.
10. Ibid., p. 265.
11. Louise London, 'British Immigration Control Procedures and Jewish Refugees 1933–1942', University of London PhD thesis (1992), p. 469. See also Louise London, 'British Reactions to the Jewish Flight from Europe', in P. Catterall and C. J. Morris (eds), *Britain and the Threat to Stability in Europe* (Leicester, 1993), p. 65.
12. Viscount Templewood (Sir Samuel Hoare), *Nine Troubled Years* (London, 1954), p. 239.
13. Central Zionist Archives, Z4/6017. Duff Cooper's address to the United Palestine Appeal meeting in Washington, 7 January 1940.
14. John Charmley, *Lord Lloyd and the Decline of the British Empire* (London, 1987), p. 251.
15. Channon, *Diaries*, 2 June 1948, p. 426.
16. PRO FO 371/35033, Cranborne to Eden, May 1943, cited in Bethell, *The Palestine Triangle*, p. 146.
17. Eden to Harvey, 7 September 1941, Harvey Papers Add. Manuscript 56399, cited in Wasserstein, *Britain and the Jews*, p. 34.
18. Macmillan, *Tides*, pp. 141 and 149.
19. *Jewish Chronicle*, 10 October 1947, pp. 1 and 5.
20. Stanley Baldwin Papers, 170/L2/83-4, Pat Gower to Geoffrey Lloyd, 5 April 1935.
21. Neville Chamberlain Papers, NC/7/11/30/25, Lord Mancroft to Neville Chamberlain, 6 July 1937.
22. See Harry Defries, 'The Attitudes of the Conservative Party towards the Jews c.1900–c.1948', University of London PhD thesis (1998), Chapter XI. The definition of Jewish for this purpose is those who, according to Jewish religious law, are Jews; namely, those born of a Jewish mother. Hence, Alfred Mond, the Liberal MP (who defected to the Conservatives in 1926 but is not among the 28 as he was never elected as a Conservative), who is discussed in relation to his ministerial appointment, is defined as a Jew, but his son Henry, who was elected as the Conservative MP for East Toxteth in 1929, is not, as his mother was not Jewish. Henry would, however, have been included as being Jewish, as he converted to Judaism – but by then he had succeeded his father as the second Baron Melchett and was no longer an MP.
23. See Finburgh's role in the protests against Joynson-Hick's immigration policies in Chapter 6.
24. *Jewish Chronicle*, 22 July 1921, p. 6, bemoaned the lack of identity amongst Jewish MPs (not only Conservatives).
25. Channon, *Diaries*, 29 January 1935, p. 24.
26. Ibid., 3 June 1939, p. 202.
27. Headlam, *Diaries*, 2 November 1927, p. 130, 2 May 1928, p. 146, and 30 April 1929, p. 171.
28. Channon, *Diaries*, 2 January–17 January 1940, pp. 227–31, and Minney, *Private Papers of Hore-Belisha*, pp. 266–86.
29. John Ramsden (ed.), *Real Old Tory Politics: The Political Diaries of Sir Robert Sanders, Lord Bayford, 1910–35* (London, 1984), 19 June 1921, p. 157.
30. *Jewish Chronicle*, 17 August 1945, p. 16.

31. McEwen, *Unionist and Conservative MPs*, p. 424.
32. See Peter Catterall, 'The Party and Religion', in Seldon and Ball (eds), *Conservative Century*, pp. 637–70.
33. Lipson is not included in the 28 Jewish Conservative MPs, as this figure is for those who were elected as the Party's official candidates.
34. Cheltenham Conservative Association committee minute book and notebook.
35. *Gloucestershire Echo*, 28 May 1937, p. 1, and 24 June 1937, p. 1.
36. Austen Chamberlain Papers, AC/40/4/14, Austen Chamberlain to E. H. Canning, 25 April 1933.
37. R. C. Self (ed.), *The Austen Chamberlain Diary Letters*, AC5/1/166, Austen Chamberlain to Hilda Chamberlain, 27 June 1920, p. 136.

Bibliography

The bibliography lists sources consulted, though not necessarily cited, and found useful in preparing the work. Unless otherwise stated, all books cited were published in London.

PRIMARY SOURCES

Manuscript Sources

Public Record Office, Kew (PRO)
Cabinet Office Papers (CAB)
Foreign Office Papers (FO)
Colonial Office Papers (CO)
Prime Minister's Papers (PREM)
Home Office Papers (HO)

Central Zionist Archives, Jerusalem
The Zionist Organisation – Central Office London Papers (Z4)
English Zionist Federation Papers (F13)

Other Institutional Records
Board of Deputies of British Jews Archives (Greater London Record Office)
Conservative Party Archives (Bodleian Library, Oxford)
Cheltenham Conservative Association Archives (Cheltenham Conservative Association Offices)

Private Papers

Ashley Papers (Southampton University Library)
Baldwin Papers (Cambridge University Library)
Balfour Papers (British Library)

Beaverbrook Papers (House of Lords Record Office)
Bonar Law Papers (House of Lords Record Office)
Cecil of Chelwood Papers (British Library)
Austen Chamberlain Papers (Birmingham University Library)
Joseph Chamberlain Papers (Birmingham University Library)
Neville Chamberlain Papers (Birmingham University Library)
Churchill Papers (Churchill Archives, Churchill College Cambridge)
Davidson Papers (House of Lords Record Office)
Lloyd George Papers (House of Lords Record Office)
Milner Papers (Bodleian Library, Oxford)
Samuel Papers (House of Lords Record Office)

Parliamentary and Government Sources

Parliamentary Debates
Commons Debates, Fourth and Fifth Series (Hansard)
Lords Debates, Fifth Series (Hansard)

Command Papers
Report of the Royal Commission on Alien Immigration, Cmd 1742 (1903)
Regulations made by the Home Secretary under the Aliens Act, Cmd 2879 (1906)
The Interim Report of The High Commissioner for Palestine, Cmd 1499 (1922)
Correspondence with the Palestine Arab Delegation and the Zionist Organization, Cmd 1700 (1922)
Report of Commission on Palestine Disturbances of August 1929, Cmd 3530 (1930)
Palestine: Report on Immigration, Land Settlement and Development, Cmd 3686 (1930)
Palestine: A Statement of Policy, Cmd 3692 (1930)
The Proposed New Constitution for Palestine, Cmd 5119 (1936)
Report of the Palestine Royal Commission, Cmd 5479 (1937)
Policy on Palestine, A Dispatch of 23rd December 1937 to the High Commissioner, Cmd 5634 (1938)
Palestine: A Statement of Policy, Cmd 6019 (1939)

Other Papers
Conditions in Occupied Territories 6: Persecution of the Jews (1942)

Diaries and Letters

S. Ball (ed.), *Parliament and Politics in the Age of Baldwin and MacDonald – The Headlam Diaries 1923–1935* (1992).

John Barnes and David Nicholson (eds), *The Leo Amery Diaries: Vol. I, 1896–1929* (1980).

John Barnes and David Nicholson (eds), *The Empire at Bay: The Leo Amery Diaries, Vol. II, 1929–1945* (1988).

Dvorah Barzilay and Barnet Litvinoff (eds), *The Letters and Papers of Chaim Weizmann: Vol. VIII, November 1917–October 1918* (Jerusalem, 1977).

Michael J. Cohen (ed.), *The Letters and Papers of Chaim Weizmann: Vol. XX, July 1940–January 1943* (Jerusalem, 1979).

Michael J. Cohen (ed.), *The Letters and Papers of Chaim Weizmann: Vol. XXI, January 1943–May 1945* (Jerusalem, 1979).

Artemis Cooper (ed.), *A Durable Fire: The Letters of Duff Cooper and Diana Cooper 1913–1950* (1983).

Camillo Dresner (ed.), *The Letters and Papers of Chaim Weizmann: Vol. XIV, July 1929–October 1930* (Jerusalem, 1978).

Camillo Dresner (ed.), *The Letters and Papers of Chaim Weizmann: Vol. XV, October 1930–June 1933* (Jerusalem, 1978).

Joshua Freundlich (ed.), *The Letters and Papers of Chaim Weizmann: Vol. XII, August 1923–March 1926* (Jerusalem, 1977).

Martin Gilbert, *Winston S. Churchill, Vol. IV Companion, Part 3: Documents, April 1921–November 1922* (1977).

Martin Gilbert, *Winston S. Churchill, Vol. V Companion, Part 3: Documents, The Coming of War 1936–1939* (1982).

C. Headlam (ed.), *The Milner Papers, Vol. II* (1933).

Joseph Heller (ed.), *The Letters and Papers of Chaim Weizmann: Vol. XXII, May 1945–July 1947* (Jerusalem, 1979).

Aaron Klieman (ed.), *The Letters and Papers of Chaim Weizmann: Vol. XVIII, January 1937–December 1938* (Jerusalem, 1979).

Aaron Klieman (ed.), *The Letters and Papers of Chaim Weizmann: Vol. XXIII, August 1947–June 1952* (Jerusalem, 1980).

Marvin Lowenthal (ed.), *Theodor Herzl Diaries* (New York, 1956)

R. Meinertzhagen, *Middle East Diary 1917–1956* (1959).

Nigel Nicolson (ed.), *Harold Nicolson Diaries and Letters 1930–1939* (1966).

Nigel Nicolson (ed.), *Harold Nicolson Diaries and Letters 1939–1945* (1967).

Nigel Nicolson (ed.), *Harold Nicolson Diaries and Letters 1945–62* (1968)

Pinhas Ofer (ed.), *The Letters and Papers of Chaim Weizmann: Vol. XIII, March 1926–July 1929* (Jerusalem, 1978).

John Ramsden (ed.), *Real Old Tory Politics: The Political Diaries of Sir Robert Sanders, Lord Bayford, 1910–35* (1984).

Jehuda Reinharz (ed.), *The Letters and Papers of Chaim Weizmann: Vol. IX, October 1918–July 1920* (Jerusalem, 1977).

Robert Rhodes James (ed.), *'Chips', The Diaries of Sir Henry Channon* (2nd edition, 1993).

Robert Rhodes James (ed.), *Memoirs of a Conservative: J. C. C. Davidson's Memoirs and Papers 1910–1937* (1969).

Jane Ridley and Clayre Percy (eds), *The Letters of Arthur Balfour and Lady Elcho, 1885–1917* (1992).

Norman A. Rose (ed.), *Baffy: The Diaries of Blanche Dugdale 1936–1947* (1973).

Norman A. Rose (ed.), *The Letters and Papers of Chaim Weizmann: Vol. XIX, January 1939–June 1940* (Jerusalem, 1979).

Yemima Rosenthal (ed.), *The Letters and Papers of Chaim Weizmann: Vol. XVII, August 1935–December 1936* (Jerusalem 1979).

R. C. Self (ed.), *The Austen Chamberlain Diary Letters* (Cambridge, 1995).

Gabriel Sheffer (ed.), *The Letters and Papers of Chaim Weizmann: Vol. XVI, June 1933–August 1935* (Jerusalem. 1978).

Leonard Stein (ed.), *The Letters and Papers of Chaim Weizmann: Vol. VII, August 1914–November 1917* (1975).

A. J. P. Taylor (ed.), *W. P. Crozier: Off the Record-Political Interviews, 1933–1943* (1973).

John Vincent (ed.), *The Crawford Papers: The Journals of David Lindsay, twenty-seventh Earl of Crawford and tenth Earl of Balcarres, 1871–1940, during the years 1892 to 1940* (1984).

Bernard Wasserstein (ed.), *The Letters and Papers of Chaim Weizmann: Vol. X, July 1920–December 1921* (Jerusalem, 1977).

Bernard Wasserstein (ed.), *The Letters and Papers of Chaim Weizmann: Vol. XI, January 1922–July 1923* (New Brunswick, 1977).

P. Williamson (ed.), *The Modernisation of Conservative Politics: The Diaries and Letters of William Bridgeman 1904–1935* (1988).

Keith Wilson (ed.), *The Rasp Of War: The Letters of H. A. Gwynne to The Countess of Bathurst, 1914–1918* (1988).

Trevor Wilson (ed.), *The Political Diaries of C. P. Scott 1911–1928* (1970).

Memoirs

L. S. Amery, *My Political Life, Vol. 1: England Before The Storm, 1896–1914* (1953)

L. S. Amery, *My Political Life, Vol. 2: War and Peace, 1914–1929* (1953).

Earl of Avon, *The Eden Memoirs: Facing the Dictators* (1962).

Earl of Avon, *The Eden Memoirs: The Reckoning* (1965).

Norman and Helen Bentwich, *Mandate Memories, 1918–1948* (1965).

Lord Boothby, *My Yesterday, Your Tomorrow* (1962).

Viscount Cecil of Chelwood, *All The Way* (1949).

Austen Chamberlain, *Down The Years* (1935).

Sir Brunel Cohen, *Count Your Blessings* (1956).

Winston Churchill, *The Second World War, Vol. II: Their Finest Hour* (1949).

Winston Churchill, *The Second World, War Vol. VI: Triumph and Tragedy* (1951).

Tom Clarke, *My Northcliffe Diary* (1931).

Duff Cooper, *Old Men Forget* (1953).

David Lloyd George, *War Memoirs, Vol. I* (1938).

David Lloyd George, *Memoirs of the Peace Conference, Vol. II* (New Haven, CT, 1939).

Harold Macmillan, *Winds of Change, 1914–1939* (1966).

Harold Macmillan, *Tides of Fortune, 1945–1955* (1969).

James Margach, *The Abuse of Power: The War between Downing Street and the Media from Lloyd George to Callaghan* (1978).

Earl of Oxford and Asquith, *Memories and Reflections, 1852–1927, Vol. 2* (1928).

Viscount Samuel, *Memoirs* (1945).

Ronald Storrs, *Orientations*, definitive edition (2) (1945).

Earl of Swindon, *Sixty Years of Power* (1966).

Viscount Templewood (Sir Samuel Hoare), *Nine Troubled Years* (1954).

Chaim Weizmann, *Trial and Error* (1949).

Henry Wickham Steed, *Through Thirty Years, 1892–1922: A Personal Narrative* (in two volumes, 1924).

Newspapers and Journals

Daily Express
Daily Mail
Daily Telegraph
Contemporary Review
East London Observer
Evening Standard
Gloucestershire Echo
Illustrated Sunday Herald
Jewish Chronicle
Morning Post
National Review

New Judea
Observer
Pall Mall Gazette
Peebles and South Midlothian Advertiser
Popular View
Spectator
Sunday Express
Sunday Pictorial
The Times
Truth
Zionist Review

Other Contemporary Published Material

Stanley Baldwin, *Our Inheritance* (1928).
John Buchan, *A Lodge in the Wilderness* (1906).
John Buchan, *The Thirty-Nine Steps* (1915).
Lord Hugh Cecil, *Conservatism* (1912).
Richard Crossman, *Palestine Mission* (1947).
William Evans-Gordon, *The Alien Immigrant* (1903).
Isidore Harris (ed.), *Jewish Year Book* (1901).
Quintin Hogg, *The Case for Conservatism* (1947).
Albert M. Hyamson (ed.), *Jewish Year Book* (1947).
Albert M. Hyamson (ed.), *Jewish Year Book* (1949).
J. M. N. Jeffries, *The Palestine Deception* (1923).
Lt-Col. A. H. Lane, *The Alien Menace* (3rd edn, 1932).
C. Russell and H. S. Lewis, *The Jew in London: A Study of Racial Character and Present-Day Conditions* (1900).
Nahum Sokolow, *History of Zionism: 1600–1918* (in two volumes, 1919).
Israel Zangwill, *The War For The World* (1916).

SECONDARY SOURCES

Reference Works

F. W. S. Craig, *British General Election Manifestos 1900–1974* (1975).
Dod's Parliamentary Companion.
David Butler and Gareth Butler, *British Political Facts 1900–1985* (6th edn, 1986).
David Englander (ed.), *A Documentary History of Jewish Immigrants in Britain, 1840–1920* (1994).
Encyclopaedia Judaica (Jerusalem, 1972).

Michael Stenton and Stephen Lees, *Who's Who of British Members of Parliament, Vol. II: 1886–1918* (Sussex, 1978) and *Vol. III: 1919–1945* (Sussex, 1979).

Biographies

Roger Adelson, *Mark Sykes* (1975).
Julian Amery, *The Life of Joseph Chamberlain, Vol. IV* (1951).
A. W. Baldwin, *My Father: The True Story [Stanley Baldwin]* (1955).
Alex Bein, *Theodor Herzl* (2nd edn, Philadelphia, 1962).
Earl of Birkenhead, *'F. E.', The Life of F. E. Smith, First Earl of Birkenhead* (1959).
Hector Bolitho, *Alfred Mond* (1933).
John Bowle, *Viscount Samuel: A Biography* (1957).
John Charmley, *Duff Cooper: The Authorized Biography* (1986).
John Charmley, *Lord Lloyd and the Decline of the British Empire* (1987).
Viscount Chilston, *Chief Whip: The Political Life and Times of Aretas Akers-Douglas, 1st Viscount Douglas* (1961).
Randolph S. Churchill, *Lord Derby: 'King of Lancashire'* (1959).
Blanche E. C. Dugdale, *Arthur James Balfour* (two volumes, 1936).
David Dutton, *Austen Chamberlain: Gentleman in Politics* (Bolton, 1985).
David Dutton, *Simon: A Political Biography of Sir John Simon* (1992).
Max Egremont, *Balfour: A Life of Arthur James Balfour* (1980).
Keith Feiling, *The Life of Neville Chamberlain* (1946).
Martin Gilbert, *Winston S. Churchill, Vol. IV: 1916–1922* (1975).
Martin Gilbert, *Winston S, Churchill, Vol. V: 1922–1939* (1976).
David Gilmour, *Curzon* (1994).
Robert Henriques, *Sir Robert Waley Cohen 1877–1952* (1966).
Alistair Horne, *Macmillan, Vol. I: 1894–1956* (1988).
Denis Judd, *Radical Joe: A Life of Joseph Chamberlain* (1977).
Denis Judd, *Lord Reading: Rufus Isaacs, First Marquis of Reading, Lord Chief Justice and Viceroy of India, 1860–1935* (1982).
Shane Leslie, *Mark Sykes: His Life and Letters* (1923).
Naomi B. Levine, *Politics, Religion and Love: The Story of H. H. Asquith, Venetia Stanley and Edwin Montagu, Based on the Life and Letters of Edwin Samuel Montagu* (1991).
Ruddock F. Mackay, *Balfour: Intellectual Statesman* (Oxford, 1985).
Iain Macleod, *Neville Chamberlain* (1961).
John Marlowe, *Milner: The Apostle of Empire* (1976).
Keith Middlemas and John Barnes, *Baldwin: A Biography* (1969).
R. J. Minney, *The Private Papers of Hore-Belisha* (1960).

H. Montgomery Hyde, *Lord Reading: The Life of Rufus Isaacs, First Marquis of Reading* (1967).

Moshe Pearlman, *Ben-Gurion Looks Back: In Talks with Moshe Pearlman* (1965).

Sir Charles Petrie, *The Chamberlain Tradition* (1938).

Reginald Pound and Geoffrey Harmsworth, *Northcliffe* (1959).

Lord Reading, *Rufus Isaacs: First Marquess of Reading, Vol. I* (1942).

Lord Reading, *Rufus Isaacs: First Marquess of Reading, Vol. II* (1945).

Jehuda Reinharz, *Chaim Weizmann: The Making of a Zionist Leader* (Oxford, 1985).

Jehuda Reinharz, *Chaim Weizmann: The Making of a Statesman* (Oxford, 1993).

Robert Rhodes James, *Bob Boothby* (1992 edn).

Robert Rhodes James, *Churchill: A Study in Failure, 1900–1939* (1970).

Andrew Roberts, *The Holy Fox* (Edward, Lord Halifax) (1991).

Earl of Ronaldshay, *The Life of Lord Curzon, Being the Authorized Biography of George Nathaniel Marquis Curzon of Kedleston, K. G., Vol. 3* (1928).

Kenneth Rose, *The Later Cecils* (1975).

Norman Rose, *Chaim Weizmann* (1986).

Norman Rose, 'Churchill and Zionism', in Robert Blake and Wm. Roger Louis (eds), *Churchill* (Oxford, 1993).

Stanley Salvidge, *Salvidge of Liverpool: Behind the Political Scene, 1890–1928* (1934).

Robert Skidelsky, *Oswald Mosley* (3rd edn, 1990).

H. A. Taylor, *Jix: Viscount Brentford* (1933).

John Turner, *Macmillan* (1994).

S. D. Waley, *Edwin Montagu: A Memoir and an Account of his Visits to India* (1964).

Bernard Wasserstein, *Herbert Samuel – A Political Life* (Oxford, 1992).

General Works

C. Abramsky, *War, Revolution and the Jewish Dilemma* (1975).

Paul Addison, *The Road to 1945* (2nd edn, 1994).

Geoffrey Alderman, 'The Political Impact of Zionism in the East End before 1940: Some Thoughts Prompted by the Experience of Whitechapel', in Aubrey Newman (ed.), *The Jewish East End 1840–1939* (1981).

Geoffrey Alderman, *The Jewish Community in British Politics* (Oxford, 1983).

Geoffrey Alderman, *London Jewry and London Politics* (1989).

Geoffrey Alderman, *Modern British Jewry* (Oxford, 1992).

Geoffrey Alderman, 'Recent Anglo-Jewish Historiography and the Myth of Jix's Anti-Semitism: A Response', *Australian Journal of Jewish Studies*, Vol. VIII, No. 1 (1994).

Anthony Alfry, *Edward VII and his Jewish Court* (1992).

Stuart Ball, *Baldwin and the Conservative Party: The Crisis of 1929–1931* (1988).

Stuart Ball, 'Local Conservatism and Party Organization', in Anthony Seldon and Stuart Ball (eds), *Conservative Century: The Conservative Party Since 1900* (Oxford, 1994).

Stuart Ball, *The Conservative Party and British Politics, 1902–1951* (1995).

Steven Bayne, 'Jewish Leadership and Anti-Semitism in Britain, 1898–1918', University of Columbia PhD thesis (1977).

Max Beloff, *The Intellectual in Politics and Other Essays* (1970).

Chaim Bermant, *The Cousinhood* (1971).

Nicholas Bethell, *The Palestine Triangle: The Struggle between the British, the Jews and the Arabs, 1935–49* (1979).

Eugene C. Black, *The Social Politics of Anglo-Jewry, 1880–1920* (Oxford, 1988).

Robert Blake, *The Conservative Party from Peel to Thatcher* (1985).

Neal Blewett, *The Peers, the Parties and the People: The General Election of 1910* (1972).

Ronald Blythe, *The Age of Illusion: England in the Twenties and Thirties, 1919–1940* (1963).

Richard Bolchover, *British Jewry and the Holocaust* (Cambridge, 1993).

John Bradley, *Allied Intervention in Russia* (1968).

Richard Breitman, *Official Secrets: What the Nazis Planned, What the British and Americans Knew* (1999).

Michael Burns, *Dreyfus: A Family Affair, 1789–1945* (1992).

Julia Bush, *Behind the Lines: East London Labour, 1914–1919* (1984)

Lord Butler (ed.), *The Conservatives: A History from their Origins to 1965* (1977).

Peter Catterall, 'The Party and Religion', in Anthony Seldon and Stuart Ball (eds), *Conservative Century: The Conservative Party Since 1900* (Oxford 1994).

David Cesarani, 'Zionism in England, 1917–1939', University of Oxford, DPhil thesis (1986).

David Cesarani, 'Anti-Zionist Politics and Political Antisemitism in Britain, 1920–24', *Patterns of Prejudice*, Vol. 23, No. 1 (1989).

David Cesarani, 'Joynson-Hicks and the Radical Right in England after the First World War', in Tony Kushner and Kenneth Lunn (eds), *Traditions of Intolerance – Historical Perspectives on Fascism and Race Discourse in Britain* (Manchester, 1989).

David Cesarani, 'Communal Authority in Anglo-Jewry 1914–1940', in David Cesarani (ed.), *The Making of Modern Anglo-Jewry* (Oxford, 1990).

John Charmley, *A History of Conservative Politics 1900–1996* (1996).

Bryan Cheyette, 'Jewish Stereotyping and English Literature 1875–1920: Towards a Political Analysis', in Tony Kushner and Kenneth Lunn (eds), *Traditions of Intolerance – Historical Perspectives on Fascism and Race Discourse in Britain* (Manchester, 1989).

Alan Clark, *The Tories: Conservatives and the Nation State, 1922–1997* (1998).

Richard Cockett, *Twilight of Truth: Chamberlain, Appeasement and the Manipulation of the Press* (1989).

Richard Cockett, 'The Party, Publicity, and the Media', in Anthony Seldon and Stuart Ball (eds), *Conservative Century: The Conservative Party Since 1900* (Oxford 1994).

Frans Coetzee, *For Party or Country: Nationalism and the Dilemmas of Popular Conservatism in Edwardian England* (Oxford, 1990).

Michael J. Cohen, *Churchill and the Jews* (1985).

Norman Cohn, *Warrant for Genocide* (Pelican edn, 1970).

Maurice Cowling, *The Impact of Labour 1920–1924: The Beginning of Modern British Politics* (Cambridge, 1971).

Maurice Cowling, *The Impact of Hitler: British Politics and British Policy, 1933–1940* (Cambridge, 1975).

Byron Criddle, 'Members of Parliament', in Anthony Seldon and Stuart Ball (eds), *Conservative Century: The Conservative Party Since 1900* (Oxford, 1994).

Nicholas J. Crowson, 'Facing the Fuhrer: The Conservative Party's Attitudes and Responses to Germany 1937–1940', University of Southampton PhD thesis (1994).

Hugh Cunningham, 'The Conservative Party and Patriotism', in Robert Colls and Philip Dodd (eds), *Englishness: Politics and Culture, 1880–1920* (1986).

A. J. Davies, *We, the Nation: The Conservative Party and the Pursuit of Power* (1995).

John H. Davis, *The Kennedy Clan: Dynasty and Disaster, 1848–1984* (1985).

Harry Defries, 'The Attitudes of the Conservative Party towards the Jews c.1900–c.1948', University of London PhD thesis (1998).

Frances Donaldson, *The Marconi Affair* (1962).

David Dutton, *'His Majesty's Loyal Opposition': The Unionist Party in Opposition, 1905–1915* (Liverpool, 1992).

David Feldman, *Englishmen and Jews: Social Relations and Political Culture, 1840–1914* (1994).

Mathew Fforde, *Conservatism and Collectivism, 1886–1914* (Edinburgh, 1990).

Israel Finestein, 'Jewish Immigration in British Party Politics in the 1890s', in Aubrey Newman (ed.), *Migration and Settlement* (1971).

Israel Finestein, *Jewish Society in Victorian England* (1993).

William J. Fishman, *East End Jewish Radicals 1875–1914* (1975).

William J. Fishman, 'Jewish Immigrant Anarchists in East London 1870–1914', in Aubrey Newman (ed.), *The Jewish East End 1840–1939* (1981).

Martin Francis and Ina Zweiniger-Bargielowska (eds), *The Conservatives and British Society, 1880–1990* (1996).

Isaiah Friedman, *The Question of Palestine, 1914–1918: British–Jewish–Arab Relations* (1973).

David Fromkin, *A Peace to End All Peace: The Fall of the Ottoman Empire and the Creation of the Modern Middle East* (New York, 1989).

Bernard Gainer, *The Alien Invasion* (New York, 1972).

John A. Garrard, *The English and Immigration 1880–1910* (1971).

Lloyd Gartner, *The Jewish Immigrant in England 1870–1914* (2nd edn, 1973).

Martin Gilbert, *The Roots of Appeasement* (1966).

Martin Gilbert, *Exile and Return: The Struggle for a Jewish Homeland* (1978).

Martin Gilbert, *The Holocaust* (1986).

Peter and Leni Gillman, *Collar the Lot: How Britain Interned And Expelled Its Wartime Refugees* (1980).

Alfred Gollin, *Balfour's Burden: Arthur Balfour and Imperial Preference* (1965).

Amy Zahl Gottlieb, *Men of Vision: Anglo-Jewry's Aid to Victims of the Nazi Regime, 1933–1945* (1998).

E. H. H. Green, *The Crisis of Conservatism: The Politics, Economics and Ideology of the British Conservative Party, 1880–1914* (1995).

Richard Griffiths, *Fellow Travellers of the Right* (1980).

Richard Griffiths, *Patriotism Perverted: Captain Ramsay, The Right Club and British Anti-Semitism, 1939–1940* (1998).

Jose Harris, *Private Lives, Public Spirit: A Social History of Britain, 1870–1914* (Oxford, 1993).

J. D. Hoffman, *The Conservative Party in Opposition, 1945–1951* (1964).

Colin Holmes, *Anti-Semitism in British Society 1876–1939* (1979).

Michael Howard, 'Empire, Race and War in pre-1914 Britain', in H. Lloyd-Jones *et al.* (eds), *History and Imagination: Essays in Honour of H. R. Trevor-Roper* (1981).

Michael Howard, *The Continental Commitment* (1989 edn).

Albert M. Hyamson, *The Sephardim of England* (1951).

Samuel Hynes, *The Edwardian Turn of Mind* (1968).

Doreen Ingrams (ed.), *Palestine Papers, 1917–1922: Seeds of Conflict* (1972).

B. Janner, 'The Parliamentary Palestine Committee', in J. Cohen (ed.), *The Rebirth of Israel* (1952).

Sharman Kadish, *Bolsheviks and British Jews* (1992).

Elie Kedourie, *The Chatham House Version and other Middle-Eastern Studies* (1970).

Elie Kedourie, *Arabic Political Memoirs and Other Studies* (1974).

Paul Kennedy, *The Rise and Fall of the Great Powers* (1988).

Aaron Klieman, 'Bureaucratic politics at Whitehall in the Partitioning of Palestine, 1937', in Uriel Dann (ed.), *The Great Powers in the Middle East, 1919–1939* (1988).

Stephen Koss, *The Rise and Fall of The Political Press in Britain: Vol. 2, The Twentieth Century* (1984).

Tony Kushner, *The Persistence of Prejudice: Antisemitism in British Society during the Second World War* (Manchester, 1989).

Tony Kushner, 'The Impact of British Anti-Semitism 1918–1945', in David Cesarani (ed.), *The Making of Modern Anglo-Jewry* (Oxford, 1990).

Tony Kushner, 'Beyond the Pale? British Reactions to Nazi Anti-Semitism, 1933–39', in Tony Kushner and Kenneth Lunn (eds), *The Politics of Marginality: Race, the Radical Right and Minorities in Twentieth Century Britain* (1990).

Tony Kushner, 'Anti-Semitism and Austerity: The August 1947 Riots in Britain', in Panikos Panayi (ed.), *Racial Violence in Britain 1840–1950* (Leicester, 1993).

W. Laqueur, *The Israel–Arab Reader* (1969).

J. M. Lee, *The Churchill Coalition, 1940–1945* (1980).

Elkan D. Levy, 'Antisemitism in England at War, 1914–1916', in *Patterns of Prejudice*, Vol. 4, No. 5 (1970).

Mark Levene, *War, Jews, and the New Europe: The Diplomacy of Lucien Wolf, 1914–1919* (Oxford, 1992).

Mark Levene, 'The Balfour Declaration: A Case of Mistaken Identity', *English Historical Review*, Vol. CVII (January 1992).

Bruce Lincoln, *Red Victory: A History of the Russian Civil War* (Cardinal edn, 1990).

T. F. Lindsay and Michael Harrington, *The Conservative Party 1918–1979* (1979).

Thomas P. Linehan, *East London for Mosley: The British Union of Fascists in East London and South-West Essex, 1933–40* (1996).

V. D. Lipman, *Social History of the Jews in England, 1850–1950* (1954).

V. D. Lipman, *History of the Jews in Britain since 1858* (1990).

V. D. Lipman, *A Century of Social Service 1859–1959: The Jewish Board of Guardians* (1959).

Louise London, 'British Government Policy and Jewish Refugees 1933–45', in *Patterns of Prejudice*, Vol. 23, No. 4 (1989).

Louise London, 'Jewish Refugees, Anglo-Jewry and British Government Policy, 1930–1940', in David Cesarani (ed.), *The Making of Modern Anglo-Jewry* (Oxford, 1990).

Louise London, 'British Immigration Control Procedures and Jewish Refugees 1933–1942', University of London PhD thesis (1992).

Louise London, 'British Reactions to the Jewish Flight from Europe', in P. Catterall and C. Morris (eds), *Britain and the Threat to Stability in Europe* (Leicester, 1993).

Kenneth Lunn, 'The Marconi Scandal and Related Aspects of British Anti-Semitism 1911–1914', University of Sheffield PhD thesis (1978).

Kenneth Lunn, 'Political Anti-Semitism before 1914: Fascism's Heritage?', in Kenneth Lunn and Richard C. Thurlow (eds), *British Fascism* (1980).

R. B. McCallum and Alison Readman, *The British General Election of 1945* (1947).

John M. McEwen, 'Unionist and Conservative Members of Parliament 1914–1939', PhD thesis, London University (1959).

George Monger, *The End of Isolation* (1963).

Elizabeth Monroe, *Britain's Moment in the Middle East 1914–1956* (1963)

Kenneth O. Morgan, *Consensus and Disunity: The Lloyd George Coalition Government 1918–1922* (Oxford, 1979).

A. J. A. Morris, *The Scaremongers: The Advocacy of War and Rearmament, 1896–1914* (1984).

Rudolf Muhs, 'Jews of German Background in British Politics', in Werner E. Mosse (ed.), *Second Chance: Two Centuries of German-speaking Jews in the United Kingdom* (Tübingen, 1991).

Panikos Panayi, 'An Intolerant Act by an Intolerant Society: The Internment of Germans in Britain During the First World War', in David Cesarani and Tony Kushner (eds), *The Internment of Aliens in Twentieth Century Britain* (1993).

Gillian Peele and Chris Cook (eds), *The Politics of Reappraisal, 1918–1939* (1975).

Henry Pelling, *Social Geography of British Elections, 1885–1910* (1967).

Gregory D. Phillips, *The Diehards: Aristocratic Society and Politics in Edwardian England* (1979).

Michael Pinto-Duschinsky, *British Political Finance, 1830–1980* (Washington, 1981).

Leon Poliakov, *The History of Anti-Semitism, Vol. IV* (Oxford, 1985).

Harold Pollins, *Economic History of the Jews in England* (1982).

Martin Pugh, *The Tories and the People 1880–1935* (Oxford, 1985).

John Ramsden, *The Age of Balfour and Baldwin, 1902–1940* (1978).

John Ramsden, *The Age of Churchill and Eden* (1995).

John Ramsden, *An Appetite for Power: A History of the Conservative Party since 1830* (1998).

John Ramsden, 'Winston Churchill and the Leadership of the Conservative Party 1940–51', *Contemporary Record*, Vol. 9, No. 1 (Summer 1995).

John Raymond (ed.), *The Baldwin Age* (1960).

Richard A. Rempel, *Unionists Divided: Arthur Balfour, Joseph Chamberlain and the Unionist Free Traders* (1972).

T. W. E. Roche, *The Key in the Lock: A History of Immigration Control in England from 1066 to the Present Day* (1969).

N. A. Rose, *The Gentile Zionists* (1973).

Cecil Roth, *The Magnificent Rothschilds* (1939).

W. D. Rubinstein, 'Jews Among Top British Wealth Holders', *Jewish Social Studies*, Vol. XXIV, No. 1 (1972).

W. D. Rubinstein, 'Recent Anglo-Jewish Historiography and the Myth of Jix's Anti-Semitism', Parts I and II, *Australian Journal of Jewish Studies*, Vol. VII, Nos 1 and 2 (1993).

W. D. Rubinstein, *A History of the Jews in the English Speaking World: Great Britain* (1996).

W. D. Rubinstein, 'The Secret of Leopold Amery', *History Today*, Vol. 49, No. 2 (February 1999).

A. K. Russell, *Liberal Landslide: The General Election of 1906* (Newton Abbot, 1973).

Ronald Sanders, *The High Walls of Jerusalem* (New York, 1984).

G. R. Searle, *Country Before Party: Coalition and the Idea of 'National Government' in Modern Britain, 1885–1987* (1995).

G. R. Searle, *Corruption in British Politics, 1895–1930* (Oxford, 1987).

G. R. Searle, *The Quest For National Efficiency* (Oxford, 1971).

Anthony Seldon (ed.), *How Tory Governments Fail: The Tory Party in Power Since 1783* (1996).

Anthony Seldon and Stuart Ball (eds), *Conservative Century: The Conservative Party Since 1900* (Oxford, 1994).

Robert Self, *Tories and Tariffs: The Conservative Party and the Politics of Tariff Reform, 1922–1932* (1986).

Milton Shain, *The Roots of Anti-Semitism in South Africa* (Charlottesville, VA, 1994).

A. J. Sherman, *Island Refuge: Britain and Refugees from the Third Reich, 1933–1939* (2nd edn, 1994).

Elaine R. Smith, 'Jews and Politics in the East End of London, 1918–1939', in David Cesarani (ed.), *The Making of Modern Anglo-Jewry* (Oxford, 1990).

Donald Southgate (ed.), *The Conservative Leadership, 1832–1932* (1974).

Henry Felix Srebrnik, *London Jews and British Communism, 1935–1945* (1995).

Leonard Stein, *The Balfour Declaration* (1961).

Keith Surridge, '"All You Soldiers Are What We Call Pro-Boer": The Military Critique of the South African War, 1899–1902', *History* (1997).

Alan Sykes, *Tariff Reform in British Politics 1903–1913* (Oxford, 1979).

Christopher Sykes, *Cross Roads to Israel* (1965).

A. J. P. Taylor, *Essays in English History* (1977).

J. A. Thompson and Arthur Mejia (eds), *Edwardian Conservatism: Five Studies in Adaptation* (1988).

Neville Thompson, *The Anti-Appeasers: Conservative Opposition to Appeasement in the 1930s* (Oxford, 1971).

The Office of The Times, *The History of the Times: The 150th Anniversary and Beyond, 1912–1948* (in two parts, 1952).

Richard Thurlow, *Fascism in Britain* (1987).

Barbara Tuchman, *Bible and Sword* (1957).

John Turner, 'The Higher Direction of War', in Kathleen Burk (ed.), *War and the State* (1982).

John Turner (ed.), *Britain and the First World War* (1988).

John Turner, *British Politics and the Great War: Coalition and Conflict 1915–1918* (1992).

Richard H. Ullman, *Britain and the Russian Civil War* (1968).

Mayir Vereté, 'The Balfour Declaration and its Makers', *Middle Eastern Studies*, Vol. 6 (1970).

David Vital, *Zionism: The Crucial Phase* (Oxford, 1987).

Bernard Wasserstein, *Britain and the Jews of Europe, 1939–1945* (2nd edn, Oxford, 1988).

Bernard Wasserstein, *The British in Palestine: The Mandatory*

Government and the Arab Jewish Conflict, 1917–1921 (2nd edn, Oxford, 1991).

G. C. Webber, *The Ideology of the British Right 1918–1939* (1986).

Robert G. Weisbord, *African Zion* (Philadelphia, PA, 1968).

Keith M. Wilson, *A Study in the History and Politics of the Morning Post, 1905–1926* (1990).

Trevor Wilson, *The Myriad Faces of War* (Oxford, 1986).

Robert S. Wistrich, *Revolutionary Jews from Marx to Trotsky* (1976).

Robert S. Wistrich (ed.), *The Left Against Zion: Communism, Israel and the Middle East* (1979).

Robert S. Wistrich, *Between Redemption and Perdition* (1990).

Index

Lightning Source UK Ltd.
Milton Keynes UK
27 January 2011

166508UK00001B/24/P